CHRIST CRUCIFIED

CHRIST CRUCIFIED

But we preach Christ crucified, unto the Jews a
stumblingblock, and unto the Greeks foolishness
I CORINTHIANS 1:23

THE APOSTOLIC FOUNDATION
OF THE
CHRISTIAN CHURCH

Volume Five

JOHN METCALFE

THE PUBLISHING TRUST
Church Road, Tylers Green, Penn, Buckinghamshire.

Printed and Published by
John Metcalfe Publishing Trust
Church Road, Tylers Green
Penn, Buckinghamshire

—

First Published 1987

—

ISBN 1 870039 08 4

—

CONTENTS

PART ONE
THE CRUCIFIXION

CHRIST CRUCIFIED

PART ONE
THE CRUCIFIXION

I

Matthew

E VENTS follow swiftly one after the other in the closing chapters of Matthew. The twenty-sixth chapter is the beginning of the end. The rulers of the people take counsel together to put Jesus to death. But it is the determinate counsel and foreknowledge of God that conspire to bring to pass by their wicked hands all that was before ordained concerning Israel's Messiah, the King of the Jews.

1

These chapters are not so much teaching, as the re-cording of unfolding events. Before the end, but leading directly to it, we see two valuations of Jesus. One was reckoned in the house of a leper, by a dubious woman, and amounted to a great sum, coming as it did from 'The house of the poor'. The other was that of 'one of the twelve', together with the chief priests of Jewry, and consisted of thirty pieces of silver.

Then there are the events of the first day of unleavened bread, the fourteenth of the first month, in the evening of which the passover lamb, kept for four days, was slain and eaten with bitter herbs. Jesus, called 'Christ our passover sacrificed for us', is he whom that lamb typified. Jesus: rejected by the Jews, condemned by the rulers, forsaken by his disciples, denied by Peter, and betrayed by an apostle: 'with bitter herbs shall ye eat of it'.

On the night in which he was betrayed Jesus partook of the last supper with his disciples. There is no question of the supper being regarded as an ordinance of remembrance in Matthew. Here it is a single historical event, descriptive of his death and of their receiving the benefits of it. This is followed by the agony in the garden of Gethsemane, a secret insight into what passed, and must pass, between the Father and the Son.

Jesus, having been betrayed, is forsaken, arrested, ar-raigned, and condemned by the Jews through their highest religious assembly, and by the rulers of all the people. Meanwhile, Peter denies him thrice, and the cock crows.

The chief priests and elders, having agreed in assembly together to put Jesus to death, hasten forward the event. Judas repents, returns to them with remorse, but is dismissed. He casts down the thirty pieces of silver in the temple, goes out, and hangs himself.

The Crucifixion

Jesus, brought before the governor and asked if he were the King of the Jews, replies, Thou sayest. To the accusations of the chief priests and elders he answers nothing. Pilate marvels greatly. Now, because it was the custom at that feast for the governor to release a prisoner to the people, whom they would, Pilate offers either Barabbas, a robber, or Jesus, which is called Christ. Ascending to the judgment seat, Pilate is warned by his wife of her troubled dream concerning Jesus: Have thou nothing to do with that just man.

But the chief priests and elders had persuaded the people, and when Pilate asks, 'Whom will ye that I release unto you?', expecting it to be Jesus, they cry, 'Barabbas'. But, Pilate appeals, 'What shall I do then with Jesus which is called Christ?' The people cry out, and cry out the more, 'Let him be crucified'. Pilate washes his hands. All the people accept the guilt of his blood, upon them and their posterity, even upon their seed to all generations.

Jesus is scourged, derided, assaulted, mocked, and led away to be crucified. Another is compelled to bear his cross. Coming to Golgotha, the place of a skull, they give him vinegar to drink mingled with gall, but he would not take of it. They crucify him. Parting his garments, they cast lots for his vesture. And sitting down they watch him there. His accusation, set up over his head, reads, THIS IS JESUS THE KING OF THE JEWS.

This is he who was taken from prison and from judgment. Who shall declare his generation? For he was cut off out of the land of the living. He was numbered with the transgressors, condemned as a malefactor and crucified between two thieves, yet he had done no violence, neither was any deceit found in his mouth. He was the one who was without sin, who did no sin, who knew no sin. Notwithstanding, he was hung upon the tree, naked and accursed, to die in shame, as it is written, 'Cursed is every one that hangeth on a tree.'

3

For three hours he hung under the sun, from nine in the morning until twelve noon: three hours of light.

What did they see, those who watched him there?

They saw what could be seen, that is, what was outward and visible. They saw that it was Jesus himself hanging there: they could read his name in the superscription. All who passed by recognised that it was Jesus of Nazareth. In the mouth of two or three witnesses, it is written, every matter is established. The three hours of daylight clearly establish the fact that Jesus was crucified at Golgotha. It is a matter of fact. And three classes of witnesses testify to that fact. Although men may date time from Jesus' birth, nonetheless it is clear that everything for man begins and ends at the cross: 'Now is the judgment of this world.' But, like the witnesses of the crucifixion, despite the light, mankind entirely misses the significance of the cross. Consider these witnesses.

First, the fickle multitude, the crowds that lately came to him for healing, deliverance, teaching and blessing, that cried out as he entered Jerusalem, 'Hosanna to the Son of David: Blessed is he that cometh in the name of the Lord; Hosanna in the highest.' Where are they now? Now they pass by, reviling him, wagging their heads, and saying, 'Thou that destroyest the temple, and buildest it in three days, save thyself. If thou be the Son of God, come down from the cross.' Is this witness in the light?

Likewise also came the chief priests mocking him, with the scribes and elders, declaring, 'He saved others; himself he cannot save. If he be the King of Israel, let him now come down from the cross, and we will believe him. He trusted in God; let him deliver him now, if he will have him: for he said, I am the Son of God.' For all their priestly and ministerial attainments, all their biblical learning, all their wisdom and prudence in the law, they could not see that, to bring God's salvation to others, Jesus must lose his life, not save it. Then where is the light in their witness?

Lastly, the thieves also, crucified with him, cast the same in his teeth. About to depart this life, their heart clave to the one slender prospect of remaining in it: that Jesus should save himself, and them, by a miraculous deliverance from the cross. To the thieves salvation lay in preserving the life that now is, not in looking for the life to come. That Jesus would not exert his power to this end was the cause of bitter railing, through the mists of pain, on the part of those crucified with him. This is all that the first gospel reveals of the thieves. The Saviour could deliver them, but he would not, and they revile him in the hour of their death, because all that their heart desired lay under the light of the sun.

Now from the sixth hour there was darkness over all the land unto the ninth hour. That is, three hours of darkness, from high noon until three o'clock, following after the three hours of light.

Ordained of God, this darkness was supernatural, providing divine testimony to the truth that man was altogether in ignorance of what was happening on the cross. The light by which the world lived had proved—in the preceding three hours—to be entirely inadequate to enable men to perceive the mysteries of the cross.

The threefold witness of men in that light showed their minds to be blinded, their hearts to be darkened, and their understanding to be void of spiritual enlightenment.

According to the ancient prophecy, 'Behold, a day of darkness and of gloominess', he who formed the light and created darkness caused darkness to cover the earth and gross darkness the people, declaring, 'The sun shall be turned into darkness'. And the sun was turned into darkness, yea,

5

Psalm 105:28, 'He sent darkness, and made it dark', as that came to pass which was written, 'I will cause the sun to go down at noon.' Why? That God might demonstrate, as it pertains to the meaning of the cross, the covering cast over all people, and the veil that is spread over all nations: which covering and veil, with their consequent darkness and blindness, are interior and spiritual.

This inward darkness of the whole world to the truth of the cross is signified by the outward darkness spread for three hours over all the earth at the crucifixion. The same token is given in order that by it God might make known his power in shrouding from the eye of man the mystery of God and of the Father, and of Christ. This evidently demonstrates that, according to his will, he hides holy and divine things from the curious and uncomprehending gaze of the flesh.

As Matthew relates it, for three hours there was a silent darkness. This was terminated about the ninth hour, the silence being rent by the loud cry, 'Eli, Eli, lama sabachthani'. It was this cry that brought in the light.

Man misunderstood everything. Some supposed, from the name Eli, that Jesus called for Elias. But why suppose such an absurdity? In their superstition others cast about to see whether Elias would come. It is hardly likely that he who forbids us to call upon saints and intermediaries would do so himself. Man's superstition at the cross, adulterating the word of Christ, set the precedent for this malpractice. But the Son of man called upon none other than his God: 'My God, my God, why hast thou forsaken me?'

The understanding of these words, in the power of the Holy Ghost, dispels the darkness of the mind, and brings light and illumination to the heart. Then what is the meaning of this cry out of the darkness, a cry exclusive to the record of Matthew and Mark, a cry which broke the long silence by the word of the Lord, and which caused the light to shine abroad with a brightness that conquered and overcame the realm and power of darkness?

To understand the cry in the dark, it is necessary first to enquire, Why the darkness?

The mystery of the darkness is a witness to the truth that no natural eye can see what took place on the cross between Jesus and his God, between the Father and the Son. No natural mind can understand the mystery of what lay outside the comprehension of the senses, beyond what was visible, in the realm of the divine and supernatural. Of this the apostle testifies, quoting the ancient prophet, and saying, 'Eye hath not seen, nor ear heard, neither have entered into the heart of man, the things which God hath prepared for them that love him. But God hath revealed them unto us by his Spirit: for the Spirit searcheth all things, yea, the deep things of God.' 'But the natural man receiveth not the things of the Spirit of God: for they are foolishness unto him: neither can he know them, because they are spiritually discerned.' Of this truth the darkness bears witness: man can see nothing that is spiritual, except it be given him of God.

One might object, the words quoted, I Cor. 2:9-10, and 14, do not apply to the cross in particular, but spiritual things in general. On the contrary, these words do apply to the cross in particular, the occasion of their utterance being the two verses immediately preceding, namely, vv. 7-8, 'But we speak the wisdom of God in a mystery, even the hidden wisdom, which God ordained before the world unto our glory: Which none of the princes of this world knew: for had they known it, they would not have crucified the Lord of glory.'

The darkness indicates the supernatural mystery of what took place on the cross between the Father and the Son. The fact that man was covered with confusion due to his inability to see anything spiritually, shows that this mystery is all darkness to mankind. But if darkness shrouds the mystery, the cry from the cross brings light. Therefore it behoves men to enquire with great earnestness, Why did God forsake him? With the divine answer, light pulses within by the Holy Ghost and brings illumination upon the mystery of God, and of the Father, and of Christ.

During those hours on the cross, in an inward spiritual way that never could and never shall be seen by natural vision, or understood by the natural mind, the Son of man was submerged beneath the seas of God's wrath. All God's waves and billows tossed over his head. The waters had come in to his soul, he sank into deep mire, where there was no standing; the roaring of the great deep assailed him, yea, the proud waters had gone over his soul.

In that darkness, if a stone could have been dropped into the well of his silent sufferings, neither in time nor in eternity would ever be heard the sound of its striking bottom. Here are infinite sufferings, whilst about him raged the powers of darkness in their hour. All the strength of Satan in his fury, principalities, powers, might, dominion, all spiritual wickedness in the heavenlies, the prince of the power of the air, the prince of demons, and the rulers of the darkness of this world, all combined together to vent their implacable enmity against the silent figure on the cross, shrouded with darkness, outcast of men, and forsaken of God.

'My God, my God, why hast thou forsaken me?' The sorrows of death compassed him, the sorrows of hell compassed him about: the snares of death prevented him. He felt the pangs of death and hell. He sensed the great, the outer darkness. He experienced the burning wrath that is to come. He anguished alone, rejected of men, and forsaken of God.

Eternity was in a mystery compressed into the hours on the cross. The endless reaches of infinity bowed themselves

together, converging upon the man on the tree. An incalculable multitude, as the stars in the sky, the sand on the sea
shore innumerable, was joined to the soul of the suffering
Saviour, so that their sin became his sin, their iniquities, his
iniquities, in a mystical union so intimate that he could cry
in spirit, 'Mine iniquities are gone over mine head'. So
intimate, this divinely wrought union, that he should bear
their sins in, yes, in his own body on the tree.

Thereupon the great deep of the vengeance, indignation
and wrath of Almighty God broke up, issued forth, and
drained through the agonising sufferer on the cross. And
with what effect? 'Eli, Eli, lama sabachthani?'

'My God', saith he, 'My God'. God is smiting him as his
people, for his people, in the place of his people. 'For the
transgression of my people was he stricken.' 'It pleased the
LORD to bruise him; he hath put him to grief.' How can men
be so blind to this? In such darkness? O, earth, earth, earth,
enquire, Why was he, The Messiah, forsaken of God? Why
did it please the LORD to bruise him? If this is not love beyond
compare, immense, immeasurable, passing all understanding,
what is?

Darkness came over all the land until the ninth hour. As
the Son of man suffered, unknown, unwanted and unanswered; suffered for the sin of the world amidst the darkness that
covered the earth, there sounded the cry from the cross, 'My
God, my God, why hast thou forsaken me?' But why this cry
from the cross? Listen to the cry! What is it that brings forth
such anguish? After—according to Matthew; that is, relative
to the messianic doctrine which he emphasises—six hours of
silence. Denied, betrayed, forsaken by his own, rejected by
the Jews, yes, but it was these hours, all these hours, forsaken
of God, it was what took place in these hours, that called
forth the cry from the darkness of Golgotha.

Here is the cry of manhood: of man to his God. Not the cry of the Son to the Father. It is of man, for men, the cry of humanity. Behold the man! It is the Christ, the anointed, not with oil, but by the Holy Ghost, that divine, heavenly, spiritual anointing which declares him to be the seed of Abraham, the son of David, the King of Israel. It is the Messiah, the prophet that should come into the world, the priest after the order of Melchisedek, he whose unique humanity was conceived of the Holy Ghost in the womb of the virgin Mary: that manhood. It is Jesus Christ come in the flesh.

The Christ, the sinless One, made sin. God's perfect One, Jehovah's fellow. He who said, 'I come to do thy will, O God' before ever he had entered into the world or assumed humanity. God said, Do my work. He said, 'My meat is to do the will of him that sent me, and to finish his work.'

Again he said, 'The cup which my Father hath given me, shall I not drink it?' This was said on the night before the crucifixion. Then, What a cup! A cup of trembling; the cup of the unmixed wine of the fury and indignation, tribulation and anguish, of the fierceness of the wrath of Almighty God.

Yet no complaint escaped his lips, no bitterness. Though there was never sorrow like unto his sorrow, though reproach had broken his heart. Though, full of heaviness, he looked for some to take pity, but found none, and looked for comforters, but there were not any. He suffered alone; he suffered in silence; he suffered without complaint. Until that great vehement cry of love, 'My God, my God'!

This is the cry of the forsaken man to his God, the cry taken from the opening of the twenty-second psalm, the cry of persecution and rejection. It is the cry of the sinless One made sin, of the spotless One bearing iniquity, of the Substitute in the place of judgment. It is the cry of the Man, the Saviour, the sacrificial Lamb of God in the place of his people.

Why cried he thus to God? Because he was glorifying God in the place of judgment: at the price, the incalculable, inconceivable, immeasurable price, the price of bearing sin. Because for this cause came he into the world. Because he lived and breathed to do God's will and please him. Because this was his life, his breath, his being, who set his face as a flint to go to Jerusalem. And now he was cut off, forsaken, even at the altar of God. Truly Psalm twenty-two was his language: but his experience, no psalmist, no, nor any creature formed, ever knew or could ever tell, world without end.

Yet at Gethsemane, all had been anticipated. Anticipated, yes, but in the event, beyond anticipation: 'My God, my God, why hast thou forsaken me?' In the event the bearing of sin was so dreadful; the receiving of sins in his body so terrible; the experience of God's wrath so unendurable, that, in the intensity of his love for God, his lips broke silence at last, and he cried out in anguish 'Why hast thou forsaken me?'

In the depths of his perfect Sonship, doubtless, he knew why. Yet in the perfection of his spotless humanity, made sin, bearing transgressions, under wrath, and beneath the curse, he could not but cry, 'Why hast thou forsaken me?' Hence the heart-broken cry to God, and thus the fulfilment of the twenty-second psalm, in a way beyond the psalmist's remotest conception.

Why forsaken? Because in the place of the sinner under judgment, he was forsaken. God had forsaken him, in that he had put him to grief, bruised him, stricken him: the LORD had laid upon him the iniquity of us all. In no other way could sin be covered, atonement made, or God be just in forgiving sinners. For this to happen, God must be glorified in the place of sin, and if so, in righteous judgment upon the sin-bearer of his people. Then, he is both 'Just and the justifier of him which believeth in Jesus.'

Having been made sin, that is, inbred sin common to all the posterity of Adam, that which came down on the race in consequence of the fall, it followed likewise that he must bear the sins of his people. This divine and mysterious transference of sin and guilt, encompassing God's elect from the beginning of the world to the end of it, took place as the crucified Son of man, by that tremendous work of God, was identified with all his people in their condemned, sinful state, as if on the day of judgment. He bore their sins in his own body, and with him they died. This total identification, this fusion by divinely wrought union at the cross, under the Almighty power and absolute foreknowledge of God, was what brought in full atonement, real deliverance, and divine salvation for a people now seen as without sin, having no offence, and entirely justified.

It was not—nor could it be—the bearing of guilt alone. The iniquity itself was borne: that was what was laid upon him. He bore our sins, not only our guilt. That was how he bore our guilt. Because he is a real Saviour, a total Substitute, verily the sin-bearer on behalf of the people given to him before the foundation of the world. Well, once, in the end of the world, he made atonement for their sins. He bore their sins, and took on himself their guilt. Then how just must be that judgment which fell upon him.

The flail of God's wrath was laid across his soul, and, in him, across that innumerable company with which he was identified, and whose transgressions were the cause of the wrath. The flail fell, and fell again. 'With his stripes we are healed.' He was 'stricken, smitten of God, and afflicted.'

He was the smitten rock. Moses' rod smote the rock indeed, and that Rock was Christ. He was accursed of the law. All the curses of the law were roared out against him, not from mount Ebal, but from the heights of heaven, till the last measure of vengeance from the last curse of the law against the last one of his people, was exacted from the Surety. 'Christ hath redeemed us from the curse of the law, being made a curse for us: for it is written, Cursed is every one that hangeth on a tree.' Every last one of the debts of all his people he paid in suffering, discharged in blood, and cleared before the great Creditor of heaven.

Through his sufferings and death he delivered his people from sin, by really taking that sin as his own, who knew no sin, and who did no sin. Only he could, but he did, free his people from their sins for ever. In his humiliation he was taken from prison and from judgment. In his suffering he was ground between the upper and nether millstone of the judgment and justice of God, that he might deliver the guilty from the wrath to come.

How iniquitous sin is made to appear in such a light. How evil it is, that it should require such an atonement, from such a substitute. How holy God is seen to be, who 'Spared not his own Son, but delivered him up for us all.' Surely the revelation of God is love, when the darkness is dispelled, and the cry from the cross brings light: God is love.

O what depravity was discovered in mankind, when the whole burnt offering of Christ was consumed and reduced to ashes by the avenging flames of the justice of God! The whole offering was consumed because the entire man was abominably offensive. This reveals total, absolute spiritual depravity. But the gospel declares a total Saviour, an absolute Substitute. He was put to death, the just for the unjust, that he might bring us to God. Then, what a full satisfaction in righteousness has been wrought on behalf of the ungodly, whom God freely justifies by grace! Once in the end of the world hath he appeared to put away sin by the sacrifice of himself: 'For by one offering he hath perfected for ever them that are sanctified.'

What is seen at the cross, and heard in the cry, in the Gospel according to Matthew, is the divinely appointed equivalent of everlasting punishment, meted out to the Saviour, against all the sins of an innumerable company, as they would have appeared at the day of judgment. This peerless sacrifice of love brings in the righteousness of God to the account of all them that believe, to the praise of the glory of God's grace, and the everlasting acclaim of the Messiah, the redeemer of all that seed given to him before the foundation of the world.

'O the depth of the riches both of the wisdom and knowledge of God! how unsearchable are his judgments, and his ways past finding out! For who hath known the mind of the Lord? or who hath been his counsellor? Or who hath first given to him, and it shall be recompensed unto him again? For of him, and through him, and to him, are all things: to whom be glory for ever. Amen.'

II

Mark

THE first gospel, the Gospel according to Matthew, proclaims Jesus to be the son of David, the son of Abraham, the heir to the promises, and the promised seed. The birth, life, deeds, words, death and resurrection of Jesus Christ are ordered and set forth to the one end of proclaiming the Anointed of God, the Kingdom of Heaven. The detail which Matthew includes, that which he excludes, the order in which he presents events, all these things are subservient to the grand design of his doctrine: the setting forth of Christ, the Messiah, the King of Israel.

The evangelist Mark, on the other hand, proclaims the Servant and Service of God. Whatever the Gospel according to Mark admits, or whatever that Evangel omits, from the sum of the service, works, ministry, travels, crucifixion, burial, rising again and ascension of the Lord Jesus, all is made to serve this single purpose. The order of Mark, the narrative of events, everything is subject to one end: to declare who is the Servant, the true Servant, and what is the Service, the divine Service, acceptable to God and the Father.

Because the distinct offices of Jesus Christ set forth by Matthew and Mark respectively are very close, that is, the Messiah and the Servant, the Kingdom of Heaven and the Service of God, it follows, there is a similarity in the first two evangelists, not to be found in any other of the gospels.

15

Notwithstanding this similarity, there are, however, considerable differences. Noticeably, a genealogy is given by Matthew, but none exists in Mark. The birth of Jesus Christ is spoken of in the first gospel, but not in the second. Matthew opens with Christ, Mark with John the Baptist. In one case there is the ascension, in the other not.

Then there are more subtle differences. For example, of arrangement, as with the parables of the kingdom; or of wording, as in the case of the healing of the man sick of the palsy. Notice that this healing took place, in the first evangelist, 'In his own city', Mt. 9:1; and in the second, 'In the house', Mk. 2:1. The spiritual will soon perceive the relation between the city and the Kingdom on the one hand, and the house and the Service on the other.

In the account of the crucifixion, the rejection of Messiah, and the spurning of the Servant, call for much the same emphasis. Whether the Kingdom be rejected, or the Service refused, the Spirit of God brings out to prominence, or reduces to background all that is required to set forth the doctrine from the vast mass of words and deeds that make up the full account of the crucifixion. Everything serves to emphasise this tremendous, momentous verity: they crucified the Messiah, they hung up the Servant on a tree. Such narrative demands stark, clear-cut reality; a reduction of the terrible things that took place to the sharpest possible focus, a focus of remarkable similarity in view of the merging in death of the distinction between the rejected Messiah and the suffering Servant.

Because the record of the crucifixion in the Gospel according to Mark is substantially the same as that found in Matthew, it would be superfluous to repeat what has already been said. It remains to observe what was omitted from the first account, and to draw attention to the few essential differences between the two narratives.

Two days before the feast of the passover, and of un-leavened bread, the chief priests and scribes sought by craft to put Jesus to death. That was their intention. What was in God's counsel was that they by wicked hands should crucify and slay the Just One, the Prince of life. The occasion was provided by the covetous treachery of Judas, whom Satan filled, in order that what was written should be brought to pass.

In Bethany, the house of the poor, at the house of one Simon, a leper, Jesus' disciples were outraged at the extrava-gance of the woman who entered, and, breaking an alabaster box, poured out the precious ointment of spikenard upon Jesus' head. Waste? To them it was the waste of three hun-dred pence. To the woman, it was the measure of her love for the Saviour. This should be preached in the gospel, through-out the world, to the end of the age, for a memorial of her.

Straightway Judas Iscariot went to the chief priests, to betray him unto them. When they heard it, they were glad, and promised to give him money. Thereupon Judas sought how he might conveniently betray him.

The Gospel according to Mark emphasises the next inci-dent, concerning which Matthew records but little. It is that of the finding of the upper room, by those sent of the Lord Jesus.

Two were to go into the city, and, in a mystery, there should meet them a man bearing a pitcher of water, whom they were to follow with unquestioning obedience. He would go into a certain house. This concluded his remarkable service. The goodman of the house, however, would answer their enquiry, 'The Master saith, Where is the guestchamber, where I shall eat the passover with my disciples?' He would show them to a large upper room furnished and prepared. Here they were to make ready.

One wonders what the advocates of the fictional source 'Q' would make of this passage? Could they tell us the meaning? Could they say why these details are excluded from Matthew? No, they can tell us neither what it means, nor why Matthew omits the detail. These scholars know not the way to the city. Neither would so spiritual a figure as the man with the pitcher of water ever appear to them at the gates, who make void the word of God by their traditions.

Hence to them it is not given to discover the mysteries of God's kingdom, or of his house. How then shall they, with all their imaginary sources, documents, and scraps (which they say lie behind the four gospels), of which the four evangelists neither heard, nor wrote, nor dreamed, how shall they, I say, tell us of such spiritual matters? They will never find out the city, nor its gates, nor the man, nor yet the pitcher of water. Much less shall they discover how to follow what is spiritual. How can they know the way, the door, the goodman, the ascent, or the upper room? How shall they tell us why the room is large, wherein its aspect is high, or with what, and by whom, it is furnished? Can they tell us? Of course not. To them, he that hath the key of both the city and the house shutteth. And no man openeth.

But to Jesus' disciples, who found even as he had said unto them, he that is holy, he that is true, he that hath the key of David, openeth, and no man shutteth.

Following upon this incident, in succession, the passover is kept, the betrayal foretold, and the last supper, much as in Matthew, is taken by Jesus and his disciples.

Next, Jesus prophesies of his death, as the shepherd of the sheep, at the hand of God, the sheep being scattered. Likewise he foretells of Peter's denying him thrice, before the cock crew twice. But Simon Peter refutes Jesus' words vehemently, and so said they all.

In the garden of Gethsemane Jesus began to be sore amazed, and to be very heavy. He declared to Peter, James and John, whom he had taken apart, 'My soul is exceeding sorrowful unto death: tarry ye here, and watch.' And he went, and fell on the ground, and prayed that the cup might be taken from him, only, 'Not what I will, but what thou wilt.' He came and found them sleeping, and admonished them. All this is repeated. And he comes the third time, but does not admonish them. Now they may sleep on and take their rest, because the hour is come.

How important to the perception of the Servant and the Service of God is the difference between the record of Gethsemane in Mark, and that in the first evangelist. Let the devout and discerning reader observe and ponder.

Now, straightway, Judas comes with a multitude to arrest him, betraying him with a kiss, and the words, 'Master, master.' 'And they all forsook him, and fled.'

Jesus is brought before the high priest, with whom were assembled all the chief priests, elders and the scribes. The chief priests and all the council sought for witnesses. It was not that there were any. They sought for them. And precisely, for those witnesses whose testimony would put him to death. Then 'many bare false witness against him', doubtless to gain favour with the authorities. But their witness agreed not together. Throughout these proceedings, Jesus held his peace.

At last, exasperated, the high priest rose up and asked him, 'Art thou the Christ, the Son of the Blessed?' And Jesus said, 'I am.' For this confession of truth he was condemned to death by the entire unlawful assembly, in the darkness of the night.

Meanwhile, the prophecy concerning Peter came to pass, and the cock crew twice.

In the morning the chief priests held a consultation with the elders and scribes and the whole council, after which they bound Jesus and delivered him to Pilate.

All this was lawless. His arrest the night before was contrary to the law. The council at night was unlawful. The false witnesses were lawless. All that had been lawful, was that to which they were at last reduced: the truth of his person. Who was he? It was for his answering this question that the rulers of the people condemned him to death. He was taken from prison and from judgment for this. For existing. 'Art thou the Christ?' said they. 'I am.' 'He is worthy of death.'

To justify the condemnation passed by their assembly, they meet again by day, ratifying the deed done in the night. However, it was the prerogative of the Roman authority to put him to death.

Having delivered up Jesus to Pilate in bonds, necessarily the Jews must bring some serious accusation against him before the governor. To be credible this must be other than that of their prisoner's existence, for which they themselves had condemned him. Without a thought for what was legal these custodians of the law change the accusation to suit the occasion. That he was the Christ, the Son of the Blessed, meant nothing to Pilate, nor to his jurisdiction. Hence, arbitrarily, they alter the charge: He claims to be the King of the Jews.

This accusation was aimed at Pilate's office and responsibility. A king of the Jews was a threat to Caesar's dominion. 'Art thou the King of the Jews?' 'Thou sayest.' And the chief priests accused him of many things. But Jesus answered nothing at all.

Pilate felt their malice. He sensed that there was some deeper reason for their animosity towards Jesus. But though

Pilate knew of the fact, he could not discover the cause. Could he, he would have been helpless, for the Jews had trapped him into doing their will against his, Pilate's, sense of justice, by implying that Jesus was a king contrary to the authority and appointment of Caesar.

However, he perceived that it was for envy that the Jews had delivered Jesus up to him. Wishing to frustrate them, Pilate attempted the subterfuge of offering to free one of two prisoners, either Jesus or Barabbas. Believing Jesus to be popular with the people, he appealed to the populace over the heads of the Jewish council.

But the chief priests moved the people. Raised to a tumult, they demanded pardon for the guilty but condemnation for the innocent. Pilate, willing to content the people, released unto them Barabbas. He delivered Jesus, when he had scourged him, to be crucified.

The soldiers took Jesus away, and, having mocked him, led him out to be crucified.

They compelled Simon, a Cyrenian, to carry Jesus' cross, he himself being weakened by the scourging and cruelty. Jesus is taken to Golgotha to be crucified. He refuses the wine and myrrh. When they had crucified him, they parted his garments, casting lots upon them, what every man should take.

The hour of crucifixion was the third hour, 9.00 a.m.

Over his head was written his accusation. It was not that for which the Jews had condemned him, but—and it was equally the truth—the charge which they had contrived before Pilate: The King of the Jews.

Two thieves hung, crucified, on either side of Jesus, fulfilling the scripture which said, And he was numbered with the transgressors.

For three hours Jesus endured reviling. First, from those that passed by: 'Ah, thou that destroyest the temple, and buildest it in three days, save thyself, and come down from the cross.' Next, from the chief priests, mocking, and saying among themselves with the scribes, 'He saved others; himself he cannot save. Let Christ the King of Israel descend now from the cross, that we may see and believe.' Finally, they that were crucified with him reviled him.

This continued from nine until twelve noon.

When the sixth hour—that is, high noon—was come, there was darkness over all the land until the ninth hour, 3.00 p.m. The darkness was dispelled by the cry at the ninth hour, 'Eloi, Eloi, lama sabachthani?'

These words, according to Mark, are the Servant's last words in this life. They were completely misunderstood by those standing by, who confused the word Eloi with the name Elias, presuming, in their gross superstition, that Jesus was calling upon the saints.

The cry from the cross recorded in Mark is taken from the twenty-second psalm. This psalm indicates not so much what the Servant accomplished, as how much he suffered. The opening words differ from the form of address in Matthew, where it is 'Eli, Eli', as opposed to Mark's 'Eloi, Eloi'.

Matthew is particularly careful in transliterating the correct form of the Hebrew text taken from Psalm twenty-two, whereas the second gospel renders the pronunciation of the spoken word. Matthew gives the quotation from the original wording: Mark, the more common form of speech and the accent in which it was spoken. Well, what did they expect from a Galilaean? Scholarship? 'Is not this the carpenter?' 'How knoweth this man letters, having never learned?' With these words human learning had dismissed divine inspiration. At the cross the unscholarly Galilaean accents confirm the dismissal. Tradesman. Servant.

With the cry, light returns, after darkness over all the land for three hours.

The words, 'My God, my God, why hast thou forsaken me?' are those with which the first verse of the twenty-second psalm opens. But in fact the inscription above that verse is the true commencement of the psalm, and the words 'To the chief Musician upon Aijeleth Shahar, A Psalm of David', provide the inspiration and illumination which govern the entire text. It was with this in prospect, as indeed for the joy that was set before him, that the suffering described in the psalm was endured by the Servant.

But what was before David? In the spirit of Christ, David, prophesying, dedicates the psalm to 'Him that is over'. For so the word translated—or rather, interpolated—'chief Musician', means literally. This teaches that David's faith was fixed upon 'Him who is over', 'pre-eminent', or 'over all'. Who is this? None other than the God of peace, that raised up again Jesus our Lord from the dead: it is he that is over all.

David, in the spirit of prophecy, adds the phrase 'upon Aijeleth Shahar'. These Hebrew words mean literally 'The hind of the morning', a spiritual expression that is unique. Evidently, this indicates that to which the suffering Servant looked, beyond all the shame, rejection, and affliction that he must bear, yes, and past even the waters of death through which he must wade, or ever he could be heard from the horns of the unicorns. This is the vision that was set before him, a vision of love, illuminated by an expression of allegory.

23

The hind is feminine, and the morning indicates the break of day.

With the dawning of the day, the night of darkness forgotten, the young hind bounds forth with newness of life, set free, a hind let loose, to greet the sun in his risen glory. This inspired David's thoughts, as, in the spirit of Christ, he contemplates the suffering of death, and descent into the grave. But God would not suffer his Holy One to see corruption, no, nor leave his soul in hell. He should rise again after the darkness, as the ascending sun in his glory, and not alone, for a bride, an help-meet, should be taken out of his side during the deep sleep of death, to appear with him in a mystery of divinity upon his awakening.

Then shall she cry to him, this chaste virgin, this redeemed bride: 'The voice of my beloved! behold, he cometh leaping upon the mountains, skipping upon the hills. My beloved is like a roe or a young hart.' Yes, and to him, she to whom he dedicates his sufferings is like the hind of the morning, bounding forth in newness of life in that glorious resurrection day that declares his triumph, her deliverance, and their union.

That the suffering Servant had the church in view is clear from the text, just as the title reveals that the bride inspires his heavenly vision. For, in spirit having accomplished his sufferings, Psalm 22:1-21, he then says, verse 22, 'I will declare thy name unto my brethren.' But who are these brethren? Those joined with him in one, his bride, because 'Both he that sanctifieth and they who are sanctified are all of one: for which cause he is not ashamed to call them brethren.' Heb. 2:11.

And again David says, Psalm 22:22, 'In the midst of the congregation will I praise thee.' By the word 'congregation' we are to understand the church. On whose authority? That of the writer of the Epistle to the Hebrews, quoting this selfsame passage from Psalm 22:22 but substituting the word 'church' for 'congregation', 'In the midst of the church will I sing praise unto thee', Heb. 2:12. And, if so, it is the church viewed as the bride of him who is risen from the dead in the glory of the resurrection morning, for, Psalm 110:3 'From the womb of the morning: thou hast the dew of thy youth.' This answers to 'Aijeleth Shahar'.

All that is to live before God must come out of the death of Christ. A death marked by his being forsaken of God. A death in which he cried both in the daytime and in the night season, but was not heard. A death unique in Israel: the fathers cried, they were heard; 'But I am a worm, and no man; a reproach of men, and despised of the people.' That is it, the Servant's death: refused by Israel, forsaken of God, unheard by day and by night, cast out, rejected of men, and despised by the people. Then what love filled and moved the Servant, for God, for his people, for 'The hind of the morning', to endure such a death?

Seven persecutors roar and rage round about him. Firstly, the bulls of Bashan beset him around, they gape upon him with their mouths, they are like a ravening, roaring lion. He hangs suspended, he is poured out like water, all his bones are out of joint: his heart is like wax, it is melted in the midst of his bowels. His strength is dried up, his tongue cleaves to his jaws: he is brought to the dust of death.

Secondly, dogs have compassed him about. Beware of dogs, Phil. 3:2. Give not that which is holy unto the dogs, for they will turn again and rend the giver as surely as they rent the crucified. They go about the city, these dogs: and if so, outside the camp, Psalm 59:6, where they compass about the poor, suffering, and lonely Servant, agonising on the tree, Psalm 22:16.

Thirdly, the assembly of the wicked. That is, the con-gregation of the fleshly, outward, formal, letterish, cere-monial and legal in religion. Particularly the leaders, the chief priests, elders, scribes, and their whole council. These, in the name of the Lord, compassed Jesus about and inclosed him: 'They pierced my hands and my feet', Psalm 22:16.

'They parted my garments among them, and cast lots upon my vesture', Psalm 22:18. These things were written well over nine hundred years before the event: then, if this be not 'the end of the world', what is? In the day of judgment, all time, every generation, the ends of the earth shall bend down upon that day when the sun was turned into darkness, and the suf-fering Servant of God was crucified in weakness.

Now, fourthly, David refers to the sword, the flaming sword, the sword of justice, the sword that turned every way to keep the way to the tree of life, the sword of Jehovah, even the sword that is bathed in blood. This is the sword from which, viewing the resurrection, Psalm 22:20, the Servant cried for lawful and just deliverance for himself and for his people, that he might be vindicated and justified in his sufferings and death, by the righteous judgment of God.

Again, he cries to be saved from the power of the dog, Psalm 22:20. Here, the dog is singular, as opposed to the dogs, plural, that compassed him about, Psalm 22:16. The dog referred to in verse 20 is distinct. It is not the assembly of the wicked, as dogs, inclosing the psalmist. It is a threat to his soul from another source altogether, but one possessed of similar, dog-like characteristics to those seen in the religious assembly.

The dog that threatened Jesus was the son of perdition, the worst kind of the religious, numbered with us, yet a dog who turned again to his own vomit, and sold his Master for thirty pieces of silver. So it was ordained, and this was his power.

But the Servant cried for, and obtained, deliverance by the resurrection from the dead, all having been predestinated by the determinate counsel and foreknowledge of God.

Sixthly, the psalmist cries for salvation from the lion's mouth. The lion, also singular, refers to the devil, who, as a roaring lion, goeth about seeking whom he may devour. Surely principalities and powers were, under the prince of darkness, arrayed against the suffering Servant. 'This is your hour, and the power of darkness.' 'The prince of this world cometh.'

Paul prayed to be delivered 'Out of the mouth of the lion.' Christ was more than delivered. More than saved. His prayer was more than answered. He spoiled principalities and powers at the cross, triumphing over them openly in it. There he destroyed the devil and all his works, crushing the head of the prince of darkness beneath his foot. But his heel was bruised. Nevertheless, he was saved from the very mouth of the lion, out of the jaws of death, and from the power of the grave, by the resurrection from the dead.

The seventh and last power to which the psalmist refers is that of 'The horns of the unicorns', Psalm 22:21. Impaled upon these horns, the Servant cried out to God, and, 'Thou hast heard me from the horns of the unicorns.' It is a place of utmost extremity, beyond earthly help, past hope of deliverance from man, outside of what is natural or visible. The unicorn is a figure, like the serpent, behemoth, or leviathan,—the 'great red dragon' and 'the beasts'—which denotes those powers whose strength and aggression is concentrated in the great and terrible 'horn' which they thrust against the elect. Here, he whose cry had not been heard, beyond natural hope, transfixed, speaks with the voice of faith, and affirms, 'Thou hast heard me from the horns of the unicorns.' And so it was. All these powers were utterly destroyed and vanquished in the death of the suffering Servant.

Seven 'enemies'. Perfect opposition. Yet wholly overcome by the prayer of faith. Although the first few enemies are worldly and upon the earth, the last are invisible and in the heavens, being illustrated by figures of the true. Here was the suffering Servant. Here were the hosts of enemies, seen and unseen, carnal and spiritual, earthly and heavenly, through which he must pass, even through the realms of darkness, or ever he should break the bands of death, and rise victorious over the grave. 'Aijeleth Shahar, A Psalm of David.' Yes, but a prophecy of the Servant, the son of David, who enquired 'Eloi, Eloi, lama sabachthani?'

Finally, the Gospel according to Mark records that Jesus cried with a loud voice, and gave up the ghost.

'And the veil of the temple was rent in twain from the top to the bottom.'

This thorough and irrevocable rending of the veil 'from the top to the bottom', indicated that the way into the holiest had been made manifest. The old legal system had passed away. The first covenant had run its course. The pattern of things in the heavenlies had concluded its usefulness. The New Testament, of righteousness and life, grace and glory, was ushered in, and all that was heavenly, divine, spiritual and everlasting took the place of that which was earthly, human, legal and temporal.

The Servant appears on the threshold of that wonderful New Testament ministry and administration of righteousness, justification and everlasting redemption wrought for all his people in death, even the death of the cross. This death set free the predestinated adoption, by it many sons are brought to glory, and from the glory it is ministered.

By the resurrection from the dead, by lawful discharge from the curse of the law, by redemption from the law itself, by the ascension into the heavens, by the dawning of the glory, and by the hind of the morning, we see Jesus crowned with glory and honour. From the heights of heaven, spiritually, the Servant of God begins to administer, and will assuredly bring to a conclusion, all that Service of God grounded upon the work of righteousness wrought in death at the crucifixion in the place called Golgotha.

This is the very foundation of the world to come, it is that upon which the city of God is established, and it is the sure ground upon which the house of God shall be built up. Here is seen the basis upon which the mercy that endureth for ever meets with the justice which can never pass away to form the habitation of peace throughout the everlasting ages of glory, world without end. Amen.

III

Luke

WHEN the multitude came to arrest Jesus on the mount of Olives, Judas, one of the twelve, went before them, and drew near to Jesus to embrace him. Thus he betrayed the Son of man with a kiss. But Jesus suffered no violence, saying to the chief priests, and captains of the temple, and elders, which were come to him, 'Be ye come out, as against a thief, with swords and staves? When I was daily with you in the temple, ye stretched forth no hands against me: but this is your hour, and the power of darkness.'

It is the account of that hour, and the power of darkness, that occupies the closing chapters of Luke up to and including the crucifixion.

They took Jesus, and led him, and brought him into the high priest's house. And the men that held Jesus mocked him, and smote him. And when they had blindfolded him, they struck him on the face, and asked him, saying, 'Prophesy, who is it that smote thee?' And many other things blasphemously spake they against him.

And as soon as it was day, the elders of the people and the chief priests and the scribes came together, and led him into their council, saying, 'Art thou the Christ? tell us'. And he said unto them, 'If I tell you, ye will not believe: and if I also ask you, ye will not answer me, nor let me go. Hereafter shall the Son of man sit on the right hand of the power of God.'

That is, he whom men rejected in ignominy and shame on earth, should be received up into heaven at the right hand of God in glory.

Then said they all, 'Art thou the Son of God?' And he said unto them, 'Ye say that I am.' They themselves had said that he was the Son of God. But what they required was for him to say so, that they might crucify him, condemning him for blasphemy.

When was it that they had said that he was the Son of God? When the Father said, 'I will send my beloved son: it may be they will reverence him.' And they reasoned among themselves, saying, 'This is the heir: come, let us kill him, that the inheritance may be ours', Lk. 20:13-14. In the parable they confessed and acted on the knowledge that the heir was the Son. It followed, 'They perceived that he had spoken this parable against them', Lk. 20:19.

Then they said, 'What need we any further witness? for we ourselves have heard of his own mouth.'

And the whole multitude of them arose, and led him to Pilate.

Before Pilate, who had no love for their manipulations, they began to accuse him of things not mentioned when they themselves condemned him, such as, 'We found this fellow perverting the nation, and forbidding to give tribute to Caesar, saying that he himself is Christ a King.'

But Pilate perceived that in the eyes of the Jews he was not there to try the accused, or to give justice. Pilate was not there even to condemn Jesus. What the governor was there for, in the intention of the Jews, was to execute Jesus, further to their condemnation. The accusation before Pilate was immaterial to them, hence they varied it to suit the sentence put in the mouth of their executioner.

31

Pilate discerned, and detested the hypocritical Jews for manoeuvring him, and Roman justice, into becoming the assassins at the murder they had contrived.

He did his utmost, but, like Peter, he found the flesh, and all its labours, powerless before the great spiritual issues of heaven and earth, time and eternity, then reaching their climax. This was their hour, and the power of darkness.

He found no fault with him. Finding he was a Galilaean, and belonging to another jurisdiction, he sent him to Herod. Likewise went the chief priests and scribes, and, standing, vehemently accused him. Jesus answered nothing. Herod mocked him, and sent him back to Pilate.

Pilate called together the chief priests and rulers of the people, and said unto them, 'Ye have brought this man unto me, as one that perverteth the people: and, behold, I, having examined him before you, have found no fault in this man touching those things whereof ye accuse him: no, nor yet Herod: for I sent you to him; and, lo, nothing worthy of death is done unto him.'

Pilate did his utmost, but he was powerless.

Seeking to present Jesus to the people as the prisoner traditionally released to them at the feast, he found himself frustrated, for they cried out all at once, saying, 'Away with this man, and release unto us Barabbas.' Barabbas was one who, for a certain sedition made in the city, and for murder, had been cast into prison. Pilate therefore, willing to release Jesus, pleaded again with them. But they cried, saying, 'Crucify him, crucify him.'

Powerless. But he tried the third time, saying, 'Why, what evil hath he done? I have found no cause of death in him: I will therefore chastise him, and let him go.' And they were instant with loud voices, requiring that he might be crucified. And the voices of them and of the chief priests prevailed. They condemned Jesus, the Son of God, in whom no fault was found, and required to be released unto them Barabbas, son of the father, guilty of sedition and murder.

And Pilate gave sentence that it should be as they required.

They could stand the son of their father the devil, who was a liar and a murderer. What they could not stand was the Son of the Father in heaven. Thus they wove for eternity, and spun for the day of judgment, a web of contradictions, ironies, and apparent coincidences, that will for ever appear without parallel in the annals of those who are condemned out of their own mouths, and judged by the works of their own hands.

Jesus, being delivered up, was led away. And as they went, they laid hold upon one Simon, a Cyrenian, coming out of the country, and on him they laid the cross, that he might bear it after Jesus.

And there followed him a great company of people, and of women, which also bewailed and lamented him. To them Jesus turned, and said, 'Daughters of Jerusalem, weep not for me, but weep for yourselves, and for your children.' They wept for Jesus on that day. But, thereafter, Jerusalem's daughters should see days coming in which barrenness and dry breasts would be counted blessed. In those days they should cry to the mountains, 'Fall on us', and to the hills, 'Cover us', so terrible would be the present, and so awful the future prospect.

For if they do these things in a green tree, what shall be done in the dry?

And there were also two other, malefactors, led with him to be put to death.

And when they were come to the place, which is called
(Calvary) The place of a skull*, there they crucified him, and
the malefactors, one on the right hand, and the other on the
left.

Thereupon Jesus uttered his first words from the cross,
preceding the parting of and casting lots for his raiment. The
words occur only in Luke: 'Father, forgive them; for they
know not what they do.'

This is a prayer. Not a cry of anguish as in Matthew and
Mark, from the man to his God. But a prayer of intercession
from the Son to the Father. This is a prayer that was answered
forthwith, and one that lingers still over the remnant of Israel
according to the election of grace. In a sense, it lingers over
the Gentiles also, and must do so, until the day in which the
Son comes again.

Until that day, in view of man's blindness, Israel's veiled
heart, the Gentiles' interior darkness, Satan's deceiving the
whole world, of his carrying mankind headlong into destruction, of mankind being filled with perverse madness: 'Father,
forgive them; for they know not what they do.'

This, from one who had prayed in an agony, sweating as it
were great drops of blood. Who had, all night, been abused,
maligned, buffeted, falsely accused, mocked, scourged, denied,
betrayed, forsaken and rejected. Too weak for the task,
another must carry his cross. At the last, he had been impaled, and hung up to die upon the tree.

*Note: Very correctly Young comments, 'This name occurs only in
Luke 23:33, and is not a proper name, but arises from the translators
having literally adopted the word Calvaria (i.e. 'a bare skull'), from the
Latin by which the Greek is rendered in the (Roman Catholic) Vulgate.'
Neither is there any sanction for the expression 'Mount Calvary'. There is
no Mount. It is a 'place'. Golgotha is the 'place' of a skull.

What should his language be, having received such treatment? After such an entrance into the world? After such a heralding of his ministry? After such unprecedented years of blessing and wondrous grace? To be treated so by his disciples; by the twelve; by one of the twelve; by the first of the twelve; by the chief priests; by the elders of the people; by the Jews; by the Gentiles: by a world which with one accord thrust him from them in rejection. What shall his language be? Whatever shall he say?

He shall say: 'Father, forgive them; for they know not what they do.' He shall say this, because his name is called Jesus, because he is the Christ, the Saviour, the Son of the Father, the light and brightness of God's glory, the expression of the grace of God in a lost, dark, and fallen world.

They took what they could. It was little enough. They parted his raiment, and cast lots. That was all they cared for his prayer. And all they cared for eternity. They grasped his clothes in time.

Three classes of persons are spoken of in their reactions to the crucifixion.

First, the people stood beholding. That was all, according to Luke. They had come for blessing, healing, to hear him gladly, in times past. No longer. They had cried, Crucify him, crucify him, being moved to vehemence by their priests. No more. Now they were passive, inert, even apathetic. They stood beholding.

Next the rulers. They stood with the people, but, unlike them, their feelings of enmity were unabated. They derided him. 'He saved others; let him save himself, if he be the Christ, the chosen of God.' But the rulers, of all people, should have known that that for which they held him in derision, was the sober truth. He was saving others, because he was the Christ. This was the way in which the chosen of God, the Saviour, should by the grace of God taste death for every man, and bring in divine salvation.

Of necessity it was by vicarious sacrifice.

He had saved others, as they meant it, from temporal or bodily afflictions. From worldly torments. Or from being possessed by demons in this life. Even from death itself, by bringing the dead back to life. But that life to which those raised from the dead were brought back, was the remainder of their days in the present world. After that, they died again. Such a salvation was all that the priests, the religious, could see. What was outward, earthly, visible, pertaining to this present life, in the world that now is. Hence they said, 'He saved others, himself he cannot save.'

In the true meaning of salvation, that is, according to the doctrine of the gospel, he had saved none. Because salvation pertained to the work which he should accomplish on the cross. That is how he would save others. That is, save them from sin; save them from the wrath to come; save them from the works of the devil; and save them from the curse of the law.

He was saving others. All the previous temporal, bodily relief, shown forth in his earthly ministry, was not saving others. But it was a divine sign, both of salvation and of that Saviour whom God should send into the world to deliver his people.

How blind were the rulers! And how much more their followers with whom they stood, watching him there. This is the blind leading the blind with a witness.

Lastly, the soldiers also mocked him, coming to him, and offering him vinegar, and saying, 'If thou be the King of the

Jews, save thyself.' For it had been written over him in a super-scription with letters of Greek, and Latin, and Hebrew, THIS IS THE KING OF THE JEWS.

The soldiers, men of war, mocked him: King? where were his armies then? Call them: save thyself! Soldiers and super-scription deriding his kingdom as an idle dream, mocking what they supposed to be the emptiness of his claim.

He was crucified in weakness.

Then one of the malefactors, as if to seal Jesus' isolation, added his voice to the rest. In his dying hours, he railed upon him, cursing what he supposed to be the slipping by of the last vestige of hope: 'If thou be Christ, save thyself and us!'

The malefactor, with the people, the rulers, and the soldiers, conceived of salvation under the sun, in the present world, for the life that now is. Everything for time, nothing for eternity. All for material ends and earthly gains.

That was what the malefactor wanted, it was the motive for his railing. To him it was the only reason for a Saviour, the sole cause of that salvation for which he cried out in such desperation. A reprieve, life, a space to breathe, time.

None saw through time. Not one saw beyond this present world. No man looked for the resurrection of the dead. Relig-ious or irreligious, none saw through the veil of time and sense to things unseen and invisible, things approaching with absolute and inexorable certainty. The whole world was blind to the day of judgment, and the wrath to come. But Christ saw things invisible, and saw them afar off. For this cause he came into the world, and because of this vision he hung, suffering and dying, upon the cross.

But was it nothing to them that passed by? Was there none to see that there was no sorrow like unto his sorrow?

Whilst one of the malefactors crucified with Jesus railed upon him, the other raised his voice to rebuke his fellow: 'But the other, answering, rebuked him.' One voice was raised. Yet who can tell what that one voice conveyed to the rejected and suffering Saviour? One voice.

And if none other, so enduring is the mercy of God, so stupendous his grace, so vast the love of Father, Son, and Holy Ghost, in the cry for salvation of one sinner, it would have been enough. But there were many others. Countless myriads, from the beginning of time to the end of it, from the creation of the world to its dissolution, who, together with that lone malefactor, were being redeemed in the substitutionary body of the Saviour on the tree.

From such a great number, the dying thief possessed this distinction. When every voice was raised against Jesus, from all classes and conditions: when he was alone, forsaken and rejected: when he knew that the worst was yet to come: then it was that the thief brought consolation. For in that hour grace taught the condemned man to rebuke his fellow, and to plead for salvation from the dying Saviour. Surely the God of all comfort comforted Jesus by this singular token. He died neither alone nor in vain. By such a consolatory sign, it was made manifest that when Jesus died, he carried not only one malefactor, but countless malefactors, from death to life, from cursing to blessing, from condemnation to justification, and from judgment to victory.

Here was the closing comfort of God, the ultimate support of the Spirit, the crowning consolation of the Father. Though all the world appeared blind, insensitive and indifferent towards Jesus, the dying malefactor demonstrated that where sin abounded, grace did much more abound. Grace, by Jesus Christ, would bring a countless multitude to glory. And one solitary voice was raised aforetime as a testimony, and raised according to God's purpose of grace.

'Dost not thou fear God, seeing thou art in the same condemnation? And we indeed justly; for we receive the due
reward of our deeds: but this man hath done nothing amiss.'
What a rebuke, from the wicked, to the wicked. What light is
here, to the blind soldiers, to the darkened rulers, and to the
unseeing crowd.

Sentenced by the law, owning its justice, self-condemned,
the dying malefactor rebukes his railing fellow, judging himself with the other. And not only vindicating the authorities,
but submitting to the fear of God. Can this be, without saving
faith? Can the law work this? No. Grace works it, and faith
confesses it, as it is written, 'I believed, therefore I spake.'

'Lord, remember me when thou comest into thy kingdom.'
Here is the language of faith: 'Lord!'

Of course some esteemed scholars, those who have
wrought such devastation with their academically honoured
censorship of divine revelation, omit 'Lord'. But then, whenever were they constrained to say it?

The malefactor said it with an inward witness from the
Holy Spirit, who wrought the faith by which he spake, that
his confession was from the heart to the Lord Jesus. The eye
of faith, through the veil of pain, beheld the dissolution of all
things. The heavens and the earth in a flame of fire; the
resurrection of the dead; the great day of judgment; the
coming of the LORD; the raising of the saints; the bringing in
of the Holy City, New Jerusalem; and the coming in of the
kingdom. Yes, and the only way of salvation from the destruction of the one, to the glory of the other: that is, by the Spirit
to call Jesus 'LORD!'

When so-called scholars, today's scribes, lawyers and
doctors, can by the same Spirit of faith confess that, then we
shall have less difficulty in ignoring their mutilations of the

Textus Receptus, the text used of God to bring countless men and women from many generations to say, 'LORD', since the times of the Reformation. And what has their 'work' done? It has done nothing, and it has been used for nothing. But it has undone much.

'Remember me when thou comest into thy kingdom.'

It is not, Give me a seat. Much less the chief seat. No, too unworthy in his own eyes to ask for so much as a place, this greatly humbled, self-abased malefactor yet brings himself to ask in faith for a memory. But could this be, for a common criminal, receiving the just reward of his deeds? 'And Jesus said unto him, Verily I say unto thee, Today shalt thou be with me in paradise.' Grace had wrought in the malefactor, and so evidently did this interior work shine forth in the confession of faith, that grace, the grace of God, poured forth from the Saviour's lips in response to one that had heard and learned of the Father to come to him.

As to the word Paradise, about which there is much debate from those who are had in honour for learning, this word was not spoken in a study: the Saviour and the malefactor were in the dreadful throes of crucifixion. They were undergoing mortal agony. Mists of pain rose in waves to obscure the mind, to overwhelm all rational thought. Fires of anguish kindled every nerve, engulfing all feeling in a flame of torment. Not long: not for long. Said Jesus, 'Today'. The same day. Paradise. And yet the physical anguish the malefactor felt and Jesus shared was as nothing compared with the vicarious sufferings, answering to the wrath to come, to which the Saviour alone would be subjected, and through which he must pass, before the end could come.

Nevertheless, Jesus addresses himself to comforting the malefactor in his dying hours: 'Today'. That brought in hope. 'In paradise.' Despite the obscuring mists of pain, the penetrating words entered, giving light and bringing consolation. 'Thou shalt be with me.' Beyond a vision dimmed by torment, past senses numbed with anguish, the sight of the Saviour, the sound of salvation, the answer to faith, went home, carrying the agonising man through death to glory. 'This is my comfort in my affliction: for thy word hath quickened me.'

Thus the ultimate sufferings of the substitutionary Saviour commenced, for it was the sixth hour, and there was a darkness over all the land until the ninth hour. It is in these hours of darkness, and it is by the cries from the cross in the self-same hours, that we are pointed to the sin-bearing of the Son of man, and to his taking away the immeasurable wrath of God on behalf of all those for whom he died.

This darkness indicates that the reality of what took place on the cross was impenetrable to the natural sight of men. No more can the written account of it in the gospels be comprehended by the natural mind. For if the events themselves were shrouded to the perception, how much more the account of them? The reading of scripture itself, of sermons, books, commentaries, the comparing of texts, none of these things can take away the darkness. It is reading in the dark. Hence the darkness, sent of God at the cross, became an outward visible sign of an interior invisible reality. The darkness is within.

It is the work of God to dispel the interior darkness of the soul. That was the witness of the early church. 'For God, who commanded the light to shine out of darkness, hath shined in our hearts', II Cor. 4:6: God gave a specific command from heaven concerning the interior darkness of those whom he had chosen, and it brought forth an inward shining, 'in our hearts'. Of necessity, there must be a spirit of wisdom and revelation in the knowledge of him, that is, of Jesus Christ, who is the light of God's glory. The description of

that interior light by which others came to see Christ crucified, may serve to stimulate, but it cannot serve to illuminate.
It may inform the mind, but it cannot enlighten the heart.
That illumination and enlightenment is—and must be—the
direct work of God.

The interior darkness reigning over the mind and in the
heart of man, ruled by Satan, applies to everything spiritual.
But it is at its thickest and most dense, when it comes to the
person of the Son upon the cross at the place of a skull.

Yet that is the very place where the darkness was dispelled
in the beginning. When, and where, it is most palpable, then,
and there, God commands the light to shine. Faith is brought
to cry for light in the very place where the thickest darkness
lies: concerning the cross and within the heart. That cry
issues forth in the prayer that by revelation one might see
Christ crucified for oneself, and that such a saving sight
might be applied by the work of God to the inner man.

Because the cross is a mystery, however perfectly recorded
in scripture, faith owns that nothing can take away the veil,
open blind eyes, illuminate the mind, or give light to the
heart, but the revelation of the mystery. This is a divine
prerogative, and is called, 'Opening their understanding, that
they might understand the scriptures', Luke 24:45, and it is
achieved by 'a spirit of wisdom and revelation in the knowledge of him', Eph. 1:17.

Hence faith, which is from the heart, and answers to the
light, clamours from deep within the poor, blind, and lost
sinner, and cries long and loud over the crucified Redeemer,
'Lord, that I might receive my sight!' Such is the grace of God
that the answer to the cry of faith can never be in question.
He can no more fail to answer the cry of faith, than the cry of
faith can fail to reach the hearing of the Father of mercies.

This is the heart of the Christian religion: mystery and revelation. The mystery stands in what passed between the Father and the Son, and passed in a way that was invisible, divine, and spiritual; for God is a spirit.

The darkness shows that natural light could never provide the needed illumination to benighted faculties within a darkened interior. For darkness, spiritual darkness, hath covered the earth, and gross darkness the people. But faith, directed by the preaching of the gospel to a crucified Saviour, cries out for light, uncreated light, the light of Christ which God commands, to see the mystery in the darkness.

Hence it is that faith entreats God for those beams which shine from the glorious face of the Saviour, to give the light of the knowledge of the glory of God in the hidden and inward man of the heart, Psalm 51:6. This is called, revelation. And upon this, Christianity properly so called proceeds. 'Blessed art thou, Simon Bar-jona: for flesh and blood hath not revealed it unto thee, but my Father which is in heaven.' On this rock the church is built.

This revelation is of the Holy Ghost from heaven. He glorifies Christ, taking of his things and showing them unto us, thereby conforming us to his image, and revealing Christ in us as the hope of glory. It was this that Paul confessed, saying, 'It pleased God to reveal his Son in me.' The Holy Ghost takes the glory of Christ and reveals it in the believer. He dispels the darkness, and works within the hidden man of the heart to create a new spiritual vision: this is called, opening the eyes of the blind. Withal the Spirit bathes the inner man with uncreated light from heaven, and gives a clear, strong, sure view of Christ crucified in place of the believing, seeing, and illuminated soul.

But what was the mystery hidden by the darkness, concerning which man stands in such need of revelation?

Not the exterior sight of the crucified Son. For that sight had been seen for three hours by all classes and conditions, with no saving effect whatever; indeed with the opposite effect.

What appeared from the exterior sight of the cross was the blindness, enmity, and apathy of men on the one hand, and, on the other, a total inability to see the work of God in the death of the Son of man.

The mystery that divine illumination reveals, however, is the spiritual mystery of the sufferings of Christ. By nothing other than revelation can the soul see with a saving interest that there, in those hours, the transgression was finished, an end was made of sins, reconciliation was wrought for iniquity, and everlasting righteousness was brought in. As to the nature of that righteousness, it is called the righteousness of God by faith of Jesus Christ, unto all and upon all them that believe.

This mystery stands in the divine and supernatural work of God in Christ, a work far surpassing all creation. This was the work wrought upon the Son of man, offered up in his spotless, impeccable humanity as the sin-bearer of his people, and as the Lamb that should bear away the sin of the world.

The faith of Jesus Christ was that which carried him to the place of atonement. And it was that by which, with perfect submission, he yielded himself up to God for the fulfilment of that mysterious and divine work which was needful if ever God, consistent with his justice, was to justify a people.

In this work the Son was passive. It was God that was active. God 'made' him—the verb is $\pi o\iota \acute{\epsilon} \omega$—to be sin. It was not something that he who knew no sin did to himself. Or something that he did for God. It was something that God did to him who knew no sin. He made him to be sin.

The text, II Cor. 5:21, does not say that God imputed sin to him. That specious but highly damaging error—the result of the flesh attempting to shield Christ from that without which God could not be glorified nor man forgiven—is yet another blunder, and an immense blunder, of uninspired theological schoolmen. Immense, because it renders the atonement null and void in principle. Nowhere does the scripture say, or the Spirit teach, that sin was 'imputed' to the one who was without sin. He was 'made' sin: it was not merely imputed to him as an extrinsic calculation.

God made him to be sin, and made him to be sin so that sin might be punished, judged, and put away by the offering up of himself. And so it was.

Once in the end of the world hath he appeared to put away sin by the offering up of himself. First, in his being made sin; next in his bearing sin; third, in taking the judgment of sin upon himself; last, in vindicating God's judgment so that neither sin, nor wrath against it, remained any longer before God or man, in heaven or earth, time or eternity. 'Knowing this, that our old man is crucified with him, that the body of sin might be destroyed.'

Dead, unenlightened, 'orthodox' theology, begotten in the pride of life by that which is highly esteemed among men, patched together by unregenerate academics without a spark of revelation, is sure to lead into the congregation of the dead. These blind leaders of the blind teach a threefold error concerning imputation, or bare, exterior reckoning.

First, that Adam's sin was imputed to his posterity. It was not. Sin—and death by sin—was imparted, communicated, 'passed' from Adam to his posterity. Men were born in sin. It was not merely reckoned to them. Next, that the elect's sin was imputed to Christ. It was not. Christ was made sin. He bore it, itself, not a calculation of it. Lastly, that Christ's

righteousness was imputed to believers. It was not. The righteousness of God by faith of Jesus Christ was imputed to them.
The apostle did not say, 'The righteousness of Christ' but
'the righteousness of God' was that by which believers were
justified. Read Rom. 3:21-26.

These clergy are as wrong as can be, consistent with deceitful
language. Be sure, whoso meddles with this complex weaving
of man's intellect, rejecting the word of God in favour of the
tradition of man, will have hard labour or ever he shall come
out of the net.

The truth is in the word. Yes, but none shall find his way
into that truth by biblical studies, by 'divinity', by the
institutions of religious learning, by worldly degrees, or by
'systematic theology'. They may heap up scripture, but it is all
darkening counsel without knowledge. Only the Spirit can
lead into all truth, and those whom he leads are 'babes', and
none other. God has put out the eyes of the wise and prudent,
and quite hidden these things from them. The entirety of
their system is nothing but the tree of the knowledge of good
and evil. The tree of life is rooted in the truth that the Son of
man upon the cross really bore our iniquities.

Who laid them upon him, that he bore them? God laid them
upon him, and, being spiritual, upon him within, that is,
upon his soul. This was the work of God: the Son was passive. It does not say, and it could not say, that iniquities were
imputed. They were not imputed. They were borne, an entirely different thing. He 'bare our sins in his own body on
the tree', I Peter 2:24, and, again, 'The LORD hath laid on
him' —mark that, 'laid on him'—'the iniquity of us all.' Isaiah
53:6.

There is never a word, in any place at all, of 'imputing' to
Jesus at the cross. There could not be: it is an atonement, not
a gesture. And, if an atonement, sins must be borne 'in' the

body of the Saviour; iniquity must be 'laid upon' the soul of the Substitute. That takes it away, with a witness. It is what is called, making reconciliation for iniquity. Because these blind theologians were never taught of God, only by each other, both they and their sightless students, clamouring for the qualifications and honours which they dispense, and the doors to pulpit opportunities and religious careers which such dispensations open, stumble generation by generation, and fall one after the other into the ditch. Moreover they heap the poor, wretched sinners whom God has chosen and saved, who dare to challenge them, heap them, I say, with abuse and defamation, seeing they cannot answer them one among a thousand against the truth of real and experimental Christianity.

As the Son of man hung on the tree, God worked creatively upon his manhood so that he became united to and iden- tified with the real condition of all that people whom he would save. By the mysterious and supernatural work of God, a vast weight of divers and innumerable sins was laid upon him, whilst, withal, God wrought in his humanity—in and of itself spotless, without sin, and impeccable—so that he was made to be sin, offered up instead of his people in the place of judgment. This mighty work of God brought to pass every prophetic utterance of David in the Psalms, in which he spoke by the spirit of Christ of his sufferings beforehand. All was fulfilled when his people's sins became his own, their transgressions became his, and when he took upon himself the sin of the world.

This thorough exchange of places is what is called reconcili- ation. There was no other way of atonement. The burnt offering, the meat offering, the sin offering, the trespass offering, the peace offering, all these might imperfectly set forth substitutionary atonement in an outward figure, but the reality, no mere shadow could ever possibly depict. Totally and experimentally identified with the elect, Jesus entered into thick darkness, into sufferings beyond description, into torment defying imagination, into that which none could begin to share, no, not with the utmost perception and sympathy, world without end.

None of these things was seen by the eye of man. All that God wrought lay hidden behind the blackness of darkness. No mortal vision beheld the transaction between the Father and the Son, for the salvation of his people. But the Son of man believed God in the place of judgment, and in those dreadful hours in which his sore ran by night, and ceased not, his faith was not disappointed. As, passive, he hung there, God, active, wrought all that the Saviour looked for in faith.

Whilst Jesus hung there in the dark, 'God spared not his own Son, but delivered him up for us all.' All our uncleanness, defilement, corruption, iniquity, and sinfulness, broke in waves over his blameless soul, yea, the waters came in unto his soul. Upon him was laid a multitude of transgressions, sins innumerable, and errors past number, answering to all that the omniscient and Almighty God saw from Adam, from birth, throughout life, in death, at the very judgment, on the part and behalf of every last one of his people.

That this should be laid upon the Son of man, the suffering Saviour, entailed the divine and mysterious creative work of the stupendous love of God.

At last came the cause of his bearing iniquity: to bear it away. Not now its being laid upon him, but, being laid, its being punished in his soul and body. To this end he received the wrath of God against all that and all those with which and with whom he was identified. Worse than the flood, the terrible waters of wrath roared down upon the vicarious sacrifice of his humanity. Worse than the yawning pit, the dark depths gaped beneath the suffering soul of the Substitute.

Worse than the searing fire and brimstone that rained upon Sodom and Gomorrah, the wrathful vengeance of the indignation and fury of Almighty God issued as a deluge from heaven. He passed through fire and flood, poured out in judgment to engulf the lonely sin-bearer, hung in the midst of time at the end of the world.

But this was nothing to men. They saw nothing. It was all darkness to them. Though the pangs of hell gat hold of him, though the sorrows of death compassed him about, though an equivalent of unquenchable fire, of the undying worm, and of endless torment seized upon his unique humanity, supported and borne up upon the arms of his everlasting deity, as he bore the just punishment, the equal wrath, due to his people, men were completely uncomprehending and indifferent about what was taking place.

In a mystery, the heavenly vials of the wrath and vengeance of Almighty God were emptied and exhausted upon him in those hours on the cross. All the while, ringing in his ears with a continual roar that crashed and reverberated about the vaults of heaven, the thunders, lightnings, and voices of the curses of the law sounded with outraged indignation and unabated strength. But men heard not a sound. It was all silence to them.

And yet it was for men that he bore the dreadful penalty, that he was charged with so vast a number of transgressions, so great a multitude of trespasses, against the holy commandments. But at the last, with the uttermost execration exhausted, the last bolt of retributive justice shot, and the final sentence of vindictive judgment met, when the law could say no more, and the curse could find no further cause of vengeance, when the sounding trumpet had ceased to utter, and when nothing but satisfaction remained to the legal rule, there was a great calm.

Justice passed over with omniscient vision. Nothing was seen to offend. The Almighty viewed, he looked down from heaven, but there was no offence, nothing. Not one spot, not a blemish. Not in all those countless and innumerable souls united with the sin-bearer hanging dead upon the tree. There was nothing against them: nothing in time, nothing in eternity, nothing in heaven, nothing on earth. Nothing at all.

The sacrifice was consumed in the flames of the wrath of God, and in the fires of everlasting justice. The sin offering was burned to ashes without the camp, and with it, all that had been laid thereon. Nothing but ashes. He had finished the work which God gave him to do, and finished it to perfection.

'And the veil of the temple was rent in the midst.' Nothing remained between God and his people. The law could find no fault. The law could demand no more. Grace drew the justified into the presence of God, and God drew nigh in grace to the justified. What veil? 'The veil of the temple was rent in the midst.'

And when Jesus had cried with a loud voice, he said, 'Father, into thy hands I commend my spirit.' And having said thus, he gave up the ghost. Now when the centurion saw what was done, he glorified God, saying, 'Certainly this was a righteous man.' And all the people that came together to that sight, beholding the things which were done, smote their breasts, and returned. And all his acquaintance, and the women that followed him from Galilee, stood afar off, beholding these things.

But by the grace of God, not long after these things, the walls of Jerusalem rang and rang again with the words, 'And now, brethren, I wot that through ignorance ye did it, as did also your rulers: but those things, which God before had showed by the mouth of all his prophets, that Christ should suffer, he hath so fulfilled. Repent ye therefore, and be converted, that your sins may be blotted out.'

'Your sins may be blotted out'? Their sins? Those sins? That sin? Could guilty sinners find mercy for that sin? For such a sin? Yes, they could, and they did. And the Lord added to the church daily such as should be saved. Amen.

IV

John

IN the Gospel according to John, the events leading to the crucifixion begin in the garden into which Jesus entered with his disciples, on the other side of the brook Cedron. Judas, the traitor, having received a band of men and of officers from the chief priests and Pharisees, came thither with lanterns, and torches and weapons.

Jesus therefore, knowing all things that should come upon him, went forth, and said unto them, 'Whom seek ye?' They answered him, 'Jesus of Nazareth.' Jesus saith unto them, 'I am he.' And Judas also, which betrayed him, stood with them.

As soon as Jesus had said unto them, 'I am he', they went backward, and fell to the ground. Then asked he them again, 'Whom seek ye?' They said, 'Jesus of Nazareth.' Jesus answered, 'I have told you that I am he: if therefore ye seek me, let these go their way.' Thus was fulfilled the saying which he spake, Of them which thou gavest me have I lost none.

Jesus suffered none to offer resistance, either to succour or deliver him: 'The cup which my Father hath given me, shall I not drink it?'

Then the band and the captain and officers of the Jews took Jesus, and bound him, and led him away to Annas first; for he was father in law to Caiaphas, which was the high priest that same year. Having determined that it was he, the older man thereupon sent him bound unto Caiaphas.

The high priest began to ask Jesus of his disciples, and of his doctrine.

Jesus answered him, 'I spake openly to the world; I ever taught in the synagogue, and in the temple, whither the Jews always resort; and in secret have I said nothing. Why askest thou me? ask them that heard me, what I have said unto them: behold, they know what I said.'

That is what the high priest should have done. Without such witnesses, who were obliged by the law to accuse Jesus to his face, he ought never to have been brought before the high priest. In any case certainly not at night, much less bound, as if found guilty before the trial began. What they did was unlawful. The lawful procedure, was that to which Jesus pointed Caiaphas.

For doing this, one of the officers struck Jesus with the palm of his hand, saying with indignation at Jesus' response, 'Answerest thou the high priest so?' Jesus answered him, 'If I have spoken evil, bear witness of the evil: but if well, why smitest thou me?'

If Jesus had spoken evil, on which presumption the officer had struck him, what was the evil? But if he had spoken well, why strike him? He had spoken well. Where were the witnesses to testify to what they had heard, if they objected to his doctrine? Why ask Jesus, bound, and at night, without witnesses, to testify of his own doctrine? It is for the officers to establish the charge, out of the mouth of proper witnesses. Not for them first to bind the prisoner, then seek to manufacture the charge, and afterwards to strike him for telling the truth.

After having rehearsed the events of Peter's denial, following which the cock crew, John adds no more concerning that which passed in the house of Caiaphas. The stark brevity of John's summary emphasises the absurdity and lawlessness of the Jewish proceedings.

After this the Jews led Jesus from Caiaphas unto the hall of judgment, and it was early. They themselves went not into the judgment hall, lest they should be defiled; but that they might eat the passover.

Punctilious to maintain their exterior purity, the Jews refused to enter into the house of the uncircumcised. Pilate, the Roman governor, must needs go out to the entrance. So begins the coming and going between the judgment hall and the porch, backwards and forwards, four times over.

Nothing would move the Jews to cross the threshold. If that happened they would be judged unclean until even, unfit to eat the passover which must be killed during that same day, between the two evenings. Throughout all the manoeuvrings that followed, the ceremonially clean Jews remained outside the door of the judgment hall, fearful of losing title to the passover sacrifice: that is, the ceremonial slaying and eating of the passover lamb, re-enacted annually by the Jews to typify the sacrifice and blood of him that was to come.

But he had come. 'Christ our passover', as Paul the apostle calls Jesus, stood before them, bound with cords, that same passover day. The Lamb of God, typified in the feast ordained by Moses for ancient Israel in the land of Egypt, kept by countless succeeding generations, was the one whom they had rejected. But the darkness comprehended it not, and, with desperate anxiety about the figure, they stumbled in darkness over the true.

Pilate, the governor, obliged by their ceremonial rules, went out to the company waiting for him at the doors, with their prisoner held fast in bonds. He enquires what accusation they brought against the man. They reply, 'If he were not a malefactor, we would not have delivered him up to thee.'

But Roman law did not condemn a man for nothing, and Pilate was of sterner character than to bow to their dictates. If their law had condemned him, then let their officers execute the sentence.

This brought forth the answer, 'It is not lawful for us to put any man to death.'

At this, Pilate understood that far deeper issues lay beneath the surface, than they were prepared to reveal to him. Not for nothing did they stand there, with the dew still heavy on the ground, or ever the sun had risen in the heavens, fuming and fretting out their anxiety to put this man to death.

At the realisation, Pilate went into the judgment hall, and called Jesus. Out of earshot of the Jews, he asked, 'Art thou the King of the Jews?' But who had mentioned that? In the Gospel according to John, certainly not Jesus' accusers. Here Pilate himself raises the question.

In the cool of the judgment hall Jesus answered, 'Sayest thou this of thyself, or did others tell it thee of me?' Pilate contemptuously evades this query, and, referring to the accusers, asks Jesus what he had done.

Jesus replies indirectly, 'My kingdom is not of this world: if my kingdom were of this world, then would my servants fight, that I should not be delivered to the Jews: but now is my kingdom not from hence.'

Pilate therefore said unto him, 'Art thou a king then?'Jesus answered, 'Thou sayest that I am a king.' And so Pilate wrote.

But the truth transcended every earthly kingdom, and surpassed all human thought. The kingdom was spiritual, and stood in the revelation of his Person, and that of the Father, and of the words which he had been given to speak. For this cause he, who was before the world, came into it, to bear witness unto the truth. Everyone that was of the truth would hear his voice, by the quickening of the Holy Ghost, and by the inworking of the Father.

This brought in the kingdom. But such things had nothing to do with what comes by observation.

What could be observed Pilate understood, hence he comments, 'What is truth?'

Then Pilate, leaving Jesus within, went out again to the Jews, standing in the dawning light of the sun at the entrance. This is Pilate's second conference with the Jews.

He opened with the words, 'I find in him no fault at all.' Nevertheless for their sakes he proposed a compromise: 'But ye have a custom, that I should release unto you one at the passover; will ye therefore that I release unto you the King of the Jews?' This expedient presumed the exercise of clemency, and therefore officially would have justified the Jews despite their having delivered up the innocent.

However he reckoned without their implacable enmity. Then cried they all again, saying, 'Not this man, but Barabbas.' Now Barabbas was a robber.

At this response, Pilate went within, and took Jesus, and scourged him. Perhaps it was in his mind that the severe punishment of scourging might assuage the Jews' wrath. Having scourged Jesus, he gave him over to the soldiers, that they might mock him. This they did, plaiting a crown of thorns, and putting it on his head, clothing him with a purple robe, and saying, 'Hail, King of the Jews!' smiting him with their hands.

Jesus having been scourged, mocked, and beaten, Pilate went forth to the entrance from the interior of the hall for the third time, saying to the Jews, 'Behold, I bring him forth to you, that ye may know that I find no fault in him.'

Then came Jesus forth, wearing the crown of thorns, and the purple robe. Pilate, seeing the bruised and humiliated figure, cried out, 'Behold the man!'

Thus he hoped to mollify their unreasoning implacability, as, standing again upon the threshold, he pointed into the doorway at the pathetic condition and dressed-up appearance of the man whom, apparently, they feared to leave alive.

When the chief priests therefore and officers saw him, they cried out, saying, 'Crucify him, crucify him!' quite lost, carried away, in a passionate rage for the death of Jesus.

Pilate saith unto them, 'Take ye him, and crucify him: for I find no fault in him.'

The Jews then pointed to what they called the law. What law? Where is this law? The type of all legalists, they spoke great swelling words about the law, but they understood neither what they said, nor whereof they affirmed. There was no such law as that to which they pointed.

'We have a law', said they, 'and by our law he ought to die, because he made himself the Son of God.'

Pilate had forced them to confess the real reason for which they demanded his death. When Pilate therefore heard that saying, he was the more afraid. Now he knew what lay behind the tumult. Perceiving the presence of profound and powerful forces, unseen and outside of the appearance of things, he feared greatly.

Troubled, he entered into the hall again for the third time, taking Jesus with him. He said to him, 'Whence art thou?' But Jesus gave him no answer. This incensed Pilate. He had sought for the prisoner's release, and yet this Jesus appeared not to understand that he, Pilate, was the only hope of deliverance. Pilate therefore points him to his power and authority: 'Speakest thou not unto me? knowest thou not that I have power to crucify thee, and have power to release thee?'

Jesus answered, 'Thou couldest have no power at all against me, except it were given thee from above; therefore he that delivered me unto thee hath the greater sin.'

Power? Authority? It was Pilate who knew not from whence came power and authority. Nevertheless he that delivered Jesus to him, Caiaphas the chief priest, of the seed of Aaron, had authority from above, and knew it, and knew that Jehovah had given him this power, till the Son should come. Knowingly, wilfully, in the past hours, the high priest had demonstrated the worst abuse of power ever to see the light of day. Therefore he that delivered Jesus to Pilate had the greater sin.

And from thenceforth Pilate sought to release him, redoubling his efforts to deliver Jesus from the Jews. Outside for the fourth and last time, he pleaded for clemency. But the Jews cried out, saying, 'If thou let this man go, thou art not Caesar's friend: whosoever maketh himself a king speaketh against Caesar.'

Pilate, when he had heard that saying, brought Jesus forth, and sat down in the judgment seat in a place that is called the Pavement, but in the Hebrew, Gabbatha.

The Jews had trapped him. They sought the condemnation of a king contrary to Caesar, but Pilate sought his release. Who was Caesar's friend? They, who rejected the alien sovereign, as a threat to the Emperor: or Pilate, who would acquit him, and ignore the threat?

Pilate capitulated.

And it was the preparation of the passover, and about the sixth hour, that is, the sixth hour according to a system of time keeping other than that referred to in Matthew, Mark and Luke. It was about nine o'clock in the morning, and Pilate said to the Jews, 'Behold your King!'

Pilate's career, his profession, his position, perhaps his life: this was too much to give up for the ideal of justice, or for those strange, newly-awakened sensations concerning the man they hated, and hated because he said he was the Son of God. If he had but said it, why the disproportionate rage, unless they really believed it?

Nevertheless, for Pilate, the world, its honour, its glory, and the pride of life, were too high a price to pay. Enthroned upon the Bema, the seat from which was pronounced the final sentence, the death penalty, he prepares for the ultimate betrayal of both law and justice.

Pausing with cynical contempt to mock the Jews, Pilate requires them to behold the king whose title they had been forced to acknowledge in order to trap the governor. He obliges them to confess the absolute rule and authority of Caesar over Israel.

'Shall I crucify your King?' The chief priests answer, 'We have no king but Caesar.'

Then delivered he him therefore unto them to be crucified. And they took Jesus, and led him away.

Meanwhile the Jews, replete with the double satisfaction of having achieved the object for which they had prayed so earnestly, and having preserved themselves from defilement in the hall of the Gentile, approached the passover sacrifice with renewed zeal and untroubled conscience.

Jesus, bearing his cross, went forth into a place called the place of a skull, which is called in the Hebrew Golgotha. Death and headship combine at this place of humiliation.

In the event, John records simply that they crucified him, and two other with him, one on either side, and Jesus in the midst.

Pilate wrote a title, and put it on the cross. This title then read many of the Jews, together with the chief priests, who came themselves to see because 'they had a law, and by their law, he ought to die.' The place being near to the city, and out of doors, they were able to satisfy their desire without being defiled.

However, they objected to the wording of the title, com-plaining of it to Pilate. But this was their own wording, with which they had trapped the governor in his conflict of loyal-ties. And he was not about to change it for them. It stood, in Hebrew, Greek, and Latin, for all the world to see, fixed to the head of the cross: JESUS OF NAZARETH, THE KING OF THE JEWS.

This is the title that was set above the transfixed figure hanging on the cross over against the Holy City, the parch-ment fluttering now and then in the morning wind, nailed to the wood above his head.

The wording began with his name, 'JESUS'. Salvation of Jehovah. Is this their accusation? Man crucified the Saviour, the King that came unto them, lowly, and riding upon an ass, and upon a colt the foal of an ass. Jesus of Nazareth. Can any good thing come out of Nazareth? Yes, the Saviour of the world, crucified in weakness, came out of Nazareth. He who made the world, without whom was not anything made that was made, who became flesh, he was from Nazareth. Can any good thing come out of Nazareth? Come and see.

'KING OF THE JEWS.' They had named Jesus to Pilate as the Jewish King only to secure his crucifixion. Having secured it, they would disown the title. But Pilate requited them. The wording stood. Unknown to Pilate, however, providence guided his hand to declare the Messiah. This was the King of the Jews. God had sent forth his anointed, and they by wicked hands had taken and crucified him. Of this the title bears record.

This is he who was crowned with thorns, the symbol of the fall and the cursed ground. 'Thorns also and thistles shall it bring forth to thee.' The world, by the soldiers, thrust the thorns upon the head of the Lamb of God, which taketh away the sin of the world. Of old, the ram given to save Isaac was caught by its horns in a thicket: but there was none to save the Lamb of God, who should save others, from the thorns of the thicket of the curse, beneath which he was crucified. 'He was made a curse for us, as it is written, Cursed is every one that hangeth on a tree.'

In the place of headship and of death, alike indicated by the skull, he was crucified beneath the thorns. Under the threefold title, 'JESUS OF NAZARETH, THE KING OF THE JEWS', he was hung up to die on the tree.

Pilate wrote the title in three languages. As the thorns, so also the languages trace their origin to Genesis, the book of beginnings. Genesis 11:1 declares, 'And the whole earth was of one language, and of one speech.' And by it fallen man expressed the enmity and rebellion of his haughty heart towards God, rising up to the very heavens with exalted independance and wilfulness against the Creator of heaven and earth.

But God confounded their tongues, and scattered the proud in the imagination of their hearts. 'Therefore is the name of it called Babel; because the LORD did there confound the language of all the earth.' Beneath the three most significant tongues from the consequent babel of this world, Jesus was crucified.

The leading languages from mystical Babylon, the world, were those under which he was put to death. 'Now is the judgment of this world.' As the Lamb of God which taketh away the sin of the world, beneath its curse, and under its confounded languages, he wrought redemption, 'that he might deliver us from this present evil world.'

Truly, by three witnesses it is seen, The whole world lieth in wickedness. 'But God forbid that I should glory, save in the cross of our Lord Jesus Christ, by whom the world is crucified unto me, and I unto the world.' At the cross hung the ransom for all, to be testified in due time, condemned by the world, condemned beneath its principal tongues, yet, paradoxically, condemned for the world. 'He is the propitiation for our sins; and not for ours only, but also for the whole world.'

Hebrew was the first of the three languages. This is the language of man under revealed religion. The gods of the heathen are idols, and their hands have made them. But God revealed his holy covenant to Israel. This was expressed in the law, and written in Hebrew characters.

Now we know that what things soever the law saith, it saith to them who are under the law: that every mouth may be stopped, and all the world may become guilty before God.

Therefore by the deeds of the law shall no flesh be justified in his sight: for by the law is the knowledge of sin.

Wherefore then serveth the law? It was added because of transgressions, till the seed should come to whom the promises were made. For the scripture hath concluded all under sin, that the promise by faith of Jesus Christ might be given to them that believe. Wherefore the law was our schoolmaster to bring us unto Christ, that we might be justified by faith.

Then, was the law sin? God forbid. Nay, I had not known sin, but by the law, for without the law sin was dead. But when the commandment came, sin revived, and I died: for 'I am carnal, sold under sin.' By the law, the rule of righteousness for man, the world stood guilty, condemned, and under a curse.

This was the curse under which Jesus of Nazareth, the King of the Jews, hung vicariously, transfixed beneath the Hebrew letters.

The second language of the title was Greek. This was the language of philosophy. The world's great philosophers had come and gone. Greeks they were, and Greek was their language. It is therefore the tongue that stands for the wisdom of this world, the intellectual pretension to truth without revelation, the expression of the mind of man that ignores both the depth and the extent of the fall. This is the tongue that exemplifies the pride of life, the pride of learning.

But it is written, I will destroy the wisdom of the wise, and will bring to nothing the understanding of the prudent. Where is the wise? Where is the scribe? Where is the disputer of this world? Hath not God made foolish the wisdom of this world? For after that in the wisdom of God the world by wisdom knew not God, it pleased God by the foolishness of preaching to save them that believe. For the Jews require a sign, and the Greeks seek after wisdom: but we preach Christ crucified, unto the Jews a stumblingblock, and unto the Greeks foolishness.

As to this vaunted philosophy, it is called in the scriptures, vain deceit. As to those who seek after wisdom, the god of this world hath blinded the minds of them which believe not. As to the wisdom of the Greeks, their high sounding knowledge, and their fair speech, Christ was crucified under its characters.

And were he not to die for them, and under it, none of those blinded by this world's philosophy could ever be saved, the carnal mind being enmity against God. But he did die under it, to save all the proud helpers trapped in its haughty system: therefore it was that the deliverer which should come forth out of Zion hung beneath the Greek lettering, 'JESUS OF NAZARETH, THE KING OF THE JEWS.'

The third and last tongue in which Pilate wrote was Latin. This was the language of the Roman Empire, the speech proper to Rome. Beneath it the Saviour was crucified, for Rome was the prevailing world power.

Daniel had prophesied of a series of world powers, rising and falling in succession, each possessed of a determination to achieve world dominion. The penultimate of these powers was Rome.

But the heir is Christ, and the language of world dominion asserts, We will not have this man to reign over us. In such language stands earthly unity. In the reign of Christ, stands heavenly unity. Now these are irrevocably opposed the one to the other—see Psalms two and eighty-three—and, because the world power as such and by definition refuses the kingdom and rule of Christ, it is implacably against him: its spirit is against his. Pilate, the Roman governor, although inclined to justice, and favouring Jesus' release, found the principles and spirit of the system, the world system, to which he, Pilate, belonged, incapable of accommodating the King of the Jews.

The genius—the idea—of Rome was world dominion. The whole world as one, united in one great world brotherhood, under one world government, proclaiming, Peace on earth, good will toward men. But this is God's prerogative, this is a divine right, it is Christ's inheritance, it does not pertain to man.

Nevertheless, as the book of the Revelation teaches us, taking up the prophecy of Daniel, one vast world power after another must strive for the mastery, being inspired by the god of this world and assisted by his mysterious spiritual powers. However, each in turn would be frustrated by the Lord of Hosts.

That contemporary power was Rome. Rome ordered the crucifixion of the King of the Jews, but God raised him from the dead. Rome sealed the tomb, but the Almighty burst its bands. Rome put Caesar on the world throne, but he that sat in the heavens laughed, the LORD had them in derision, he set his King upon his holy hill of Zion.

How can any be saved, that belong to such a system? They cannot. Not without that one die in their place, delivering them from this present evil world. Not unless one lead them out as strangers and pilgrims upon the earth, looking for the world to come, for an heavenly country, for a city whose builder and maker is God.

And one did die, to deliver both from the world, and that worldliness, which is enmity against God, being hung up beneath the Roman words, 'JESUS OF NAZARETH, THE KING OF THE JEWS.'

After the superscription, the next part of the narrative concerns Jesus' raiment. Evidently they stripped those about to be crucified. Four soldiers were required to hold down each prisoner in turn, whilst the nails were being driven through both hands and feet into the wood. It was to these men that the discarded garments fell.

The soldiers, having crucified Jesus, made four parts of his raiment, to each a part. His exceptional coat, woven without seam, like the robe of the ephod, presented them with a problem. They solved it by casting lots. This fulfilled the ancient scripture to the minutest detail, whilst the brutal men remained oblivious of the significance of their actions.

Jesus hung there above them, conscious of the centuries-old prophecy being unfolded with such precision in the events taking place before his eyes.

Now there stood by the cross of Jesus his mother, and his mother's sister, Mary the wife of Cleophas, and Mary Magdalene.

When Jesus therefore saw his mother, and the disciple standing by, whom he loved, he saith unto his mother, 'Woman, behold thy son!' Then saith he to the disciple, 'Behold thy mother!' And from that hour that disciple took her unto his own home.

Two things appear: first, those who stood by the cross, all women, John 19:25. After this, the separate reference to the disciple whom Jesus loved, besides the things which he said to his mother and to that disciple, John 19:26.

First, those who stood by the cross. Note that the writer, that beloved disciple, omits any reference to himself. This is not modesty: it is the inspiration of the Holy Ghost. The careful omission in and of itself draws attention to the feminine nature of all those—John 19:25—who stood by the cross of Jesus. Here is a spiritual allusion. The feminine presence brings to mind the bride corresponding to the bridegroom, according to the revelation and purpose of God.

The emphasis on womanhood alludes to that female which should be taken out of the side of the male in the deep sleep of death. Here at the cross we are intended to see the second man, the last Adam, and, if so, not alone, 'And the LORD God said, It is not good that the man should be alone', Gen. 2:18. The bride was ever in the mind of God for his Son.

'And I John saw the Holy City, new Jerusalem, coming down from God out of heaven, prepared as a bride adorned for her husband.' 'For I have espoused you to one husband', says Paul, 'that I may present you as a chaste virgin to Christ.'

Three—or perhaps four, depending on interpretation— women are mentioned, John 19:25, and, for the spiritual purpose alluded to, no other person.

The first is Jesus' mother. She who bare the son of Abraham, the son of David. Then, typically, not only spiritual Sarah, but spiritual Eve, the mother of all living. 'And there appeared a great wonder in heaven; a woman clothed with the sun, and the moon under her feet, and upon her head a crown of twelve stars: and she being with child cried, travailing in birth, and pained to be delivered. And she brought forth a man child, who was to rule all nations with a rod of iron.' Rev. 12:1-2, and 5.

The man child referred to must be Christ, for none other is to rule the nations with an iron rod, Psalm 2:8-9. But who is the woman? Not Mary in a literal sense, obviously: yet Mary bare that man child. Then Mary spiritually, symbolically, seen as the faithful remnant according to the election of grace, travailing Zion, which should bring forth the Deliverer.

Thus appears Jerusalem above, the mother of us all. Spiritual Sarah, which bare the promised seed. In a word, Eve, whose seed—but not Adam's seed—should bruise the head of the serpent.

It is a heavenly view of the 'Mother of Jesus'—she who was at the wedding—the true Zion, which brought him forth: 'clothed with the sun, and the moon under her feet.' Here is a heavenly view, a divine conception, of all that led up to the mysterious and supernatural work in Mary. All that heavenly work, all that divine promise, all that spiritual heritage, all that was of God, from above, of the Holy Ghost, set forth in the mystical figure personified by Mary. Here is spiritual Eve who received the promise, and should bear the promised seed. Here is the barren that bare not, the daughter of Zion, the daughters of Jerusalem, the summation of the spiritual seed from the beginning, leading to and consummated in Jesus Christ come in the flesh, the seed of David, the seed of Abraham.

Why? Because that must come out of the cross. That is why he is viewed as the Lamb slain from the foundation of the world. This may be the womb that bare him, but it, itself, must come out of the cross. His mother was there.

Besides Jesus' mother, by the cross stood two others, both named Mary. This shows the bitterness with which the passover lamb must be eaten. In the book of Ruth, Naomi went down seeking for bread in Moab, after that God had sent a famine upon his own land. In Moab the hand of the LORD went forth against the woman who had fled from his judgments made known in Judah. At last, after much chastening, the woman returns, broken-hearted and penitent, saying, Call me not Naomi; call me Mara—Mary—for the Almighty hath dealt very bitterly with me.

Were he not to deal bitterly with us, every one of us, not one should be saved, for, Whom the Lord loveth he chasteneth, and scourgeth every son whom he receiveth. Of this the two Marys are witness. This, and nothing but this, brings in a tender, melted femininity suited by the Holy Ghost for such a bridegroom as the Lord Jesus Christ.

If all that is for God must come out of the cross, and it must, then it comes in the light of the bride. Feminine, subject, a complement of the bridegroom, she is enabled to show forth his glory. This subjective state is brought about by way of the interior operations of the Holy Ghost, and by the bitter dealings of God's providence. Nothing else will produce a broken and contrite heart that trembles at his word.

These spiritual truths are set forth in an allegory. The women provide the allusion to a mystical bride gathered from the four corners of the earth by the lifting up of the Son of man. The women, I say, are a figure, indicative of the femininity of the bride in the vision. This is a great mystery, but I speak concerning Christ and the church.

Having distinguished the group of women as an entity, the writer goes on separately to record the presence of the disciple whom Jesus loved, and to state Jesus' words to his mother, and to that disciple. This is a revelation of new relationships arising from the cross. Jesus sees the beloved disciple and his own mother standing beneath the cross on which he is crucified. Here is much more than natural sympathy. It is a sign, full of spiritual significance.

If only sympathy for his mother—as bereft of her son—were intended, let it be remembered that in no more than three days he should rise again from the dead. Of this he himself had lately foretold, and, if so, that would have been the time to make the provision which believers in human sentiment, but not divine resurrection, are so anxious about. Besides, the assurance of his resurrection was the comfort which he gave to all his disciples. Why not his mother? Why 'comfort' her as if there were to be no resurrection? After 'the little while' would have been the time for these words, not now, were sympathy for his mother intended. As if there were no Joseph, not to mention fleshly brothers and sisters. Mark 6:3, Matthew 12:46-50.

But as always the purpose is spiritual. The words, Behold thy son! and, Behold thy mother! indicate new spiritual relationships born out of the death of Jesus upon the cross. By calling his mother and the beloved disciple to view one another as son and mother respectively, he demonstrates that, from the elevation of the cross, Jesus and John are regarded as brethren.

As to the flesh, the old relationships have gone down into death. 'Touch me not', that is, not after the flesh, 'For I am not yet ascended to my Father.' But when he was ascended, having brought many sons to glory, he should send forth the Holy Ghost, and bring in divine relationships out of his death and by his resurrection from the dead.

It is a question of identification. Jesus identified John with himself on the cross. Behold thy mother! But she was not John's mother, she was Jesus' mother. But John was so identified with Jesus upon the cross by the work of God, that they were called brethren, in the divine mind. Then, his mother was John's mother. 'Behold thy mother!'

How could John and Jesus be brethren? 'Go to my brethren', said Jesus, 'and say unto them, I ascend unto my Father, and your Father; and to my God, and your God.' New relationships. Wherefore henceforth know we no man after the flesh: yea, though we have known Christ after the flesh, yet now henceforth know we him no more. Therefore if any man be in Christ, he is a new creature: old things are passed away; behold, all things are become new.

In death, out of death, Jesus would bring in the children of God, sons to the Father. He was identified with them. 'For both he that sanctifieth and they who are sanctified are all of one: for which cause he is not ashamed to call them brethren', Hebrews 2:11.

Far from the usual humanising of the passage, to suit the sentiments of the worldly, and appeal to the flesh, it is a place that is intensely spiritual. In his travail upon the tree, looking down, Jesus sees the very figure of that for which he is suffering. And in his suffering he speaks not of himself: in sublime, peerless composure he uses the circumstance to enlighten and instruct their hearts and minds with the revelation of divine consolation and encouragement.

Those for whom he died, whom he identifies with himself, were being smitten in him. And beyond death, when all was finished, this identification would remain: they would be one with him for ever in resurrection, his life their life, his place their place, his God their God, and his Father their Father. 'My brethren.' 'Behold thy mother!'

After this Jesus, knowing that all things were accomplished, that the scripture might be fulfilled, saith, 'I thirst'.

Now there was set there a vessel full of vinegar: and they filled a sponge with vinegar, and put it upon hyssop, and put it to his mouth. This, that the scripture might be fulfilled, Psalm 69:21, 'They gave me also gall for my meat; and in my thirst they gave me vinegar to drink.'

Thirst? What thirst? What is thirst? Thirst is caused by the drying up of one's moisture, creating a deep internal craving for the water essential to life. How spiritual these words appear when uttered by Jesus upon the cross, as he bore the iniquity of his people, being identified with them in vicarious atonement, so that their condition became his, that he might bare it away.

Then, all his moisture was turned into the drought of summer. For the great Sin-bearer slew all the spiritual enemies of his people, even their sins, their transgressions, their iniquities, their trespasses, yea, he slew a thousand foes, not with the jawbone of an ass, but with an equally unlikely and incongruous weapon, the cross. However, having slain a thousand men with the jawbone of an ass, it is written of Samson, 'He was sore athirst.'

Likewise the great Deliverer, foreshadowed by Samson, cried out, 'I thirst'. Of him David foretold, 'All my moisture is turned into drought.' Again, the psalmist, by the spirit of Christ, saith in prophecy, 'I opened my mouth and panted.' And again, of Jesus he could say, 'My strength is dried up like a potsherd; and my tongue cleaveth to my jaws; and thou hast brought me into the dust of death.'

Oh, he thirsted: as the hart panteth after the water brooks, he thirsted. The scripture was fulfilled, yes, in his very experience, and beyond all human experience, 'My skin is black upon me, and my bones are burned with heat; my bones are burned as an hearth.' 'Yea', saith the prophet, 'A burning fire is shut up in my bones.'

For now the sacrifice had been laid upon the white-hot lattice suspended in the midst of the raging fire in the brazen altar of the wrath of God. 'And', cried the psalmist, 'shall thy wrath burn like fire?' Yes, it shall, and the sacrifice must be consumed by the flames, and the flames by the sacrifice, or ever propitiation can be made for his people. 'I thirst.'

Like Jacob serving for his bride, Jesus could say, 'Thus I was; in the day the drought consumed me, and the frost by night; and my sleep departed from mine eyes.' But for love he endured. He could say, 'Thy reproach hath broken mine heart.' A broken spirit dryeth the bones.

He thirsted who had said, 'Ye hew to yourselves cisterns, broken cisterns, that can hold no water, and have forsaken me the fountain of living waters.' And again he spake to the woman of Samaria, saying, 'But whosoever drinketh of the water that I shall give him shall never thirst.' Once more he saith, 'If any man thirst, let him come unto me and drink.' But how can the fountain of living waters thirst?

How? He can thirst to do his Father's will, and to finish his work. He can thirst to make an end of sin, and finish the transgression. He can thirst to bring in everlasting righteousness, securing the justification of his people. He can thirst to fulfil his sufferings, and enter into his glory: Yes, and he can thirst until all these things be accomplished.

He can thirst beneath the wrath of God; thirst under the outpoured judgment; thirst above the sacrificial fire; thirst surrounded by the burning flames of the vengeance of the Almighty; he can thirst: 'I thirst.' He did thirst, until he had glorified God upon the earth, and until he brought his chosen people to everlasting glory. Till this was done, that the scripture might be fulfilled, he saith, 'I thirst'.

When Jesus therefore had spoken these words, and had received the vinegar, he said, 'It is finished'. And he bowed his head, and gave up the ghost.

It is finished. The work which the Father had given him to do was accomplished. What faith is seen in Jesus! Surely, the Just One shall live by his faith. Against every appearance, the blindness of the world, the rejection of Israel, the forsaking of his own, the hour of the wicked and the power of darkness, by faith Jesus went the way of the commandment which he had received from his Father. That word marked out the way of faith and gave him such interior, spiritual knowledge. 'By his knowledge shall my righteous servant justify many.' How should he do that? 'For he shall bear their iniquities.' Isaiah 53:11.

Jesus knew, by faith he knew, that the Father would lay those iniquities upon him, and punish them in him, until there was nothing left either of the iniquities or of the punishment. All that would remain was a crucified Saviour, hanging dead upon the tree. This is called, justifying many. And by the many it would be called, 'Being now justified by his blood', Romans 5:9.

The Son knew, his knowledge reached to this, and his faith answered to it, he knew that in death he would glorify God on the earth. Before the cross the mercy, the justice, the compassion, the holiness, the pity, the righteousness, the lovingkindness and the judgment of God all stood at variance.

The love that God was, appeared to be in conflict with the rectitude that he had manifested. His wisdom had been brought into question by apparently irreconcilable opposites, and opposites, seemingly, revealed within his own character.

The infinity between the nature of God and man, between heaven and earth, time and eternity, this world and the next, the promises and the realities, posed terrible questions that opened a vast gulf of immeasurable distance, of unfathomable depth, and of incalculable consequence.

All was in question: how could God be vindicated, enmity reconciled, mercy exercised, law vindicated, and righteousness satisfied, in a word, How could man be just with God? Jesus, the Son of God, knew. 'By his knowledge shall my righteous servant justify many.' And this vindication, this reconciliation, this satisfaction, brought about by the knowledge of God's righteous servant, found its answer in the crucifixion. This he called, Glorifying God upon the earth.

Reaching to God in his divine nature, to man in his humanity, Jesus, the mediator, knew the way, and followed it to perfection. By faith he went the way of his heavenly vision, the way of the corn of wheat falling into the ground and dying, the way of the cross. Denying himself, forsaking all, at last forsaken of God in the place of judgment, he knew that this way of substitutionary atonement and this way alone, would justify God in his righteousness, satisfy the law in its immutability, and vindicate the Father in bringing many sons to glory.

He believed God, and God answered that faith, the faith of Jesus Christ, by laying sin upon him, and letting down into his soul the iniquities which he trusted to bear, till none were seen in his people, and all were seen in their substitute.

He believed God, and God answered that faith, the faith of Jesus Christ, believing that all the everlasting wrath due against that sin and those iniquities should, in a mystery, be poured out upon him. That all the just vengeance incurred for eternity by his people should, by the power and operation of God, be visited upon his own soul. And according to his faith it was done unto him. Till he had glorified God in the place of sin and of judgment.

Then, and not till then, but then he could cry, and he did cry, 'It is finished!'

And he bowed his head, and gave up the ghost. Thus Jesus finished the transgression, made an end of sins, made reconciliation for iniquity, and brought in everlasting righteousness, to the praise of the glory of God's grace, world without end, Amen.

PART TWO
THE BLOOD

THE BLOOD

V

The Shed Blood

ALTHOUGH the blood of Christ was shed on the cross, the shedding of blood in itself is distinct from the crucifixion. It is the body that is crucified. Blood is shed. In the natural course of events, there would have been no blood shed at the crucifixion. In fact, in Matthew, Mark, and Luke, nothing is said about Jesus' blood at the cross.

One may say, What of the nails? It may be true that there would have been a certain amount of blood involved in the driving of nails through both hands and feet, but, first, it is not mentioned in any of the evangelists, and, second, this would not amount to what is known as 'shedding' blood, which means its being poured out. Besides, the nails are never mentioned until John, and then only after the resurrection. In the account of the crucifixion in Matthew, Mark, Luke, and John—the four evangelists—there is neither mention of blood on Jesus' hands and feet from the nails, nor on his head from the crown of thorns.

There is no record of blood being shed in connection with the crucifixion, or before it, until John, and then it is not the result of the crucifixion at all: it is the result of the spear thrust into his side.

One may object that there is mention of bloodshed in Luke, in the garden, where Luke records that when Jesus prayed his sweat was as it were great drops of blood falling to the ground. It may be said, There is the blood of Christ before the cross.

But the record states that his sweat—mark that, the subject is his sweat—was as it were great drops of blood falling to the ground. Not that his sweat was great drops of blood, it could not be, it was sweat, not blood. But it was as it were great drops of blood. As if it were that. It was not as one would sweat normally, this was extraordinary, it was sweat that formed and fell in great beads, as blood would form and fall.

Luke never suggested for one moment that that to which Jesus' sweat was likened, was what it was in fact. It was his sweat, not his blood, and that was what it was like. Or to be strictly accurate, what the formation of the drops was like. What exertion is set forth here! This is prayer.

Apart from the prophetic utterance in the context of John 6:55, or that at the last supper in connection with the cup, the first and only reference to the blood of Jesus in the gospels is at the cross, due to the spear thrust, the record of which is exclusive to John. His body was crucified on the cross. But his blood was shed by the spear. That it was shed whilst he was on the cross, though dead already, is not of itself in the least germane to the crucifixion.

The spear alone caused the shedding of blood. Not the cross. Without the spear thrust, the shedding of Jesus' blood would not have been recorded at the crucifixion. Neither the spear nor the blood are mentioned by the first three evangelists.

Only John records that the soldier, seeing that Jesus was dead already, thrust his spear into his side, and forthwith came there out blood and water.

The cross itself is simply a wooden stake, with or without a crosspiece. A crucifixion takes place when a body is fixed to that stake. The shedding of blood is another matter entirely.

In the apostolic teaching of the New Testament three parts constitute the whole of the doctrine regarding the death of Christ. First there is the fourfold record of the crucifixion. Next appears the revelation concerning the blood of Christ. Finally, there is taught a distinct body of doctrine respecting the cross.

In this present work we have passed from the teaching about the crucifixion, exclusive to the four evangelists, and are come to the revelation concerning the blood of Christ.

The English word 'blood' is derived from an old Teutonic word. It has no root either in the Hebrew of the Old Testament or in the Greek of the New. For that matter, the word owes nothing to Latin origins. It is rooted entirely in the Old German.

The Hebrew word for blood, transliterated *dam*, is derived from an ancient Hebrew root meaning 'red'. The reason for this root word being used to signify 'blood' goes without saying. Another word derived from the same ancient source is 'Adam', presumably because of the colour of the soil, God having made Adam—despite all conjectures to the contrary—from the dust of the ground.

The Greek word for blood, in the New Testament, when transliterated, reads *haima*. Now, whilst the English word 'blood' is not derived from the Greek, many significant medical words do owe their origin to this language, as, for example, haematology, haemorrhage, anaemia, anaemic, and haemoglobin. Here the Greek is seen to be the source of many cognate English words.

In the Old Testament the word 'blood'—*dam*—occurs some three hundred and fifty-six times. The word appears in twenty-seven of the thirty-nine books of the Old Testament.

Many wonderful types and figures foreshadowed the blood of Christ in the Old Covenant. The blood of beasts, sheep, goats, bulls, doves, pigeons, and even sparrows, all depicted the necessity of atoning blood, and each sacrifice pointed in its own unique way to the blood of him that was to come. All combined to show forth the virtue, necessity and application of the blood of that true of which they were the figures.

Just as many tiny rills, trickling into swelling streams, combine to magnify the roaring of a mighty river, so many texts, appearing in such a large proportion of the books of the Old Testament, unite to give forth the voice of many waters, declaring as one from the beginning of time to the end of the age, Without the shedding of blood there is no remission of sin.

The Greek word *haima* appears some ninety-nine times— excluding two compound words—on the pages of the New Testament. Forty-one of these occurrences apply directly to the blood of Christ. Out of the twenty-seven books of the New Testament, all references to the blood of Christ are concentrated in thirteen books.

Thirty-six times out of forty-one, either the definite article or some possessive form is used to designate the blood of Christ. Jesus describes the blood as 'My' blood seven times. It is referred to as 'The' blood seven times again. Six times it is 'His' blood. Four times 'His own'. Once 'Thy' blood is used, and, once again, 'This man's blood'. Four times the blood is

said to be 'Of Christ'; twice 'Of the Lamb'; once 'Of the Lord';
once 'Of Jesus'; once 'Of Jesus Christ'; and, once more, 'Of
Jesus Christ his Son'.

The importance of the possessive case can hardly be over-
estimated. The preciousness of the blood of Christ to the
Holy Ghost, the incalculable esteem in which it is held by the
Father, pass all that the most profound and sanctified mind
can possibly conceive. Then, when the Spirit gives possessive
titles in respect of that blood, or uses the definite article, in
view of the inestimable worth of him whose blood it is, one
may be sure that the designation is precise, and precise
because of everlasting and divine love.

The reason therefore that any article or possessive is used
of the blood of Christ must be of immense consequence to
the faithful, whose spiritual understanding will surely search
it out, as led into all truth by that Spirit who has come to
glorify Christ, take of his things, and show them unto the
disciples.

Fifteen times the blood of Christ is characterised in some
way or another in the New Testament. The blood, for example, pertains to the holy place. That place characterises it.
Again, it is described as being 'The blood of his cross'. Once
the blood is called 'Precious'. Again, it is 'Of God'. Once
more, the blood of Jesus is called, 'Drink indeed'.

The blood of Christ is characterised seven times as being
'Covenant' blood, although the precise description differs. It
varies, for example, from 'My blood of the New Testament',
through 'The New Testament in my blood', to 'The blood of
the everlasting covenant'. Once it is called, 'The innocent
blood'. Once again, 'The blood of this just person'. Lastly, his
blood is said to be 'Brought on the Jews and on their children'.

So precious is his blood, so profoundly, mysteriously, 'Of God', so does it give both foundation and seal to the everlasting covenant, and to all Christ's seed that are of it, that a solemn and awful responsibility is entailed. The flippant, the chaffy and trifling speaker in religion, all who lightly or superficially treat the holy things, all bear a terrible responsibility in respect of that blood of which they can sing so airily, and talk so blithely, whilst their vacant smiles and empty conversation declare plainly that they are strangers to what they profess.

The Jews were far more serious. Nevertheless, the blood of this innocent, this just person, lies upon them and their seed to this day. The blood is said to be brought down upon the heads, and upon the heads of the children, of all the guilty who, whether in mouth or not, in heart lightly esteem and despise what is called in heaven 'Precious'. Inestimable. To us therefore which believe he is precious, and we can truly say, from a heart made serious and solemn, so is his precious blood.

The blood of Christ is referred to as having been brought to light, or manifested, in various ways, seven times in all. First, the blood of Jesus was poured out of his side together with water. That was how it was seen. Four times his blood is said to have been 'Shed'. One of these references is a compound word, in which the Greek *haima* is joined with another word meaning 'outpouring', to form one new word.

Twice the blood of Christ is manifested as sprinkled. When it was shed, it was done to him: he was passive, his blood was shed by another. When it is sprinkled, he is active: he himself sprinkles that blood with his own finger, spiritually. What a wonderful thing this is: in a spiritual way he sprinkles in and from heaven the blood shed upon the earth.

How can these things be, says one? They know, who are in the secret, for they have felt it experimentally and powerfully upon the hidden man of the heart. This comes neither by observation, reason, nor study: it is by revelation. It is the revelation of the mystery, and it brings into the experience of the secret. Whoso is wise, and will observe these things, even he shall understand the lovingkindness of the LORD.

As to the application of the blood, Jesus, speaking to his own disciples, declares that his blood is shed for 'you'; for 'many'; and for 'many for the remission of sins.' The testimony of the voice of Christ, sounding by the Holy Ghost within the heart, brings consolation beyond all expression to his convicted people, when he saith to them, 'For you'. This is application in spirit and in truth. With water, blood shows his coming, and, by the Spirit, testimony is borne with a witness.

The blood brings justification. Nothing else does. Be not deceived. Many will come in his name and say otherwise. But they are liars. The word of God says, 'Being justified by his blood.' Not by the law; not by legal obedience, 'active' as they call it; not by a 'risen Christ', as others say; nor yet by union with Christ in ascension. The blood, and the blood alone, in and of itself, brings justification fully and freely. Whosoever looks elsewhere, believes a lie.

Redemption was wrought in and through Jesus' blood. Nothing else could pay the price, nothing else could bring remission of sins, nothing else could declare forgiveness, nothing else could free the ransomed, and hence, the blood brings redemption.

This means the loosing away of all that bound and held the people of God in insolvency, bondage and destitution. The blood of Christ clears the debt, cancels all arrears, and disolves every bond and chain. It sets free the prisoner, secures the inheritance, and seals a redemption that is both free and everlasting. That is the declaration of the blood of Christ, which, in truth, speaketh better things than that of Abel.

Propitiation is through faith in his blood. This expiates sin, and renders God propitious, or appeased, in respect of those who hitherto had gendered his wrath. But no more! Made nigh by the blood of Christ, they find a propitiation set forth through faith, peace having been made by the shedding and sprinkling of the blood of Jesus Christ.

What communion is brought in through the blood of Christ! The cup is the communion of his blood. This is the cup of blessing which we bless, which not only proclaims but, rightly administered, is the New Testament in his blood. The communion of his blood sets forth and shows an experimental union, in which his blood is drink indeed, bringing in everlasting life, for whoso drinketh his blood dwells in him, and he in him.

The blood of Christ purchased the church. It makes nigh, and is that which gives boldness to enter into the holiest. The blood of Christ makes election known; and it, itself, sanctifies the people of God, so that by it they are able to overcome the accuser of the brethren.

The blood of Christ removes otherwise ineradicable stains, blessed be his holy name. It purges every conscience to which it is applied, however polluted or filthy. By it all sin is cleansed, all sins are covered, all transgressions are blotted out, and every washed robe is made perfectly white.

It is most important to remember that the blood of Jesus was seen to have been shed. We have not followed cunningly devised fables. There were eyewitnesses, and, if so, to facts which took place. The very date predicates the truth that he which came by water and by blood, came into the world. And the observation of unimpeachable witnesses tells us how he went out of the world.

The crucifixion is an historical fact. 'He that saw it bare record', Jn. 19:35. That is his testimony. 'He'—that is, the writer, John—'that saw it bare record, and his record is true.' Look further at what he says: he is impelled to put this testimony on record. He adds, 'And he knoweth that he saith true, that ye might believe.' He says, I saw it; it is true; I know that it is true. What is true? That he saw the spear enter into Jesus' side, when he was dead already, and that blood and water came out forthwith.

If one dies naturally, blood is not shed. But Jesus was put to death, he was cut off out of the land of the living, his death was violent, not natural. And it ended with bloodshed. After he died, the blood that brings in so much, that achieves such abundant blessing, that underlines every doctrine, seals the sum of truth, establishes the everlasting covenant, brings in eternal righteousness, and lays the foundation for the world to come, forthwith came out of his side with water. John saw that. It is an historical fact.

There is another witness. By the mouth of two or three witnesses every matter shall be established. But the witness John calls to stand with him had been dead for nearly one thousand years. David, being a prophet, witnessed through the Holy Ghost things far ahead, and, by the spirit of prophecy cried out in vision, as seeing the death of Christ a thousand years before, 'A bone of him shall not be broken.'

And the soldiers came to the first, and brake his legs. They came to the third also, and brake his legs. But, coming to Jesus, they hesitated. He was dead already. 'A bone of him shall not be broken.' And they brake not his legs. How did David know? He being a prophet, spake beforehand of the sufferings and death of Christ.

Yet a third witness is called to establish testimony to the death of Christ. John summonses this witness from some five hundred years before the event of which he is to testify. It is the prophet Zechariah, who, being in a prophetic trance, saw visions of things to come appearing before him.

As the prophet dreamed dreams, and saw visions, he beheld the man upon the cross. He saw the figure with the spear. He saw the two come together, the spear thrust upwards, the figure drawing away. The prophet viewed the congregation mutely watching, and, involuntary, he cried aloud, 'They shall look upon me whom they have pierced.' Five hundred years later, what he saw, happened.

Facts, yes, but more than facts. Witnesses, true, but more than witnesses. Here is stupendous, breathtaking divinity.

Jesus' blood was shed after death. All was accomplished, the work had been done. To that the blood itself bore witness.

Four wounds were inflicted when he was crucified. When the spear was thrust into his side, he received the fifth. But between the four wounds, those in his hands and feet, and the fifth, that in his side, he died. When he died he said, 'It is finished.' By which he meant, all the work to atone for the sins of all his people, all the work to reconcile that people to God, all the work to declare to the world that God is love, all was finished.

He had finished his work and obtained eternal redemption for the elect. He had done everything, everything that was needed to take the beggar from the dunghill, the depraved wretch from the depths of iniquity, to bring the dead and putrifying through the resurrection unto eternal glory.

He had done everything necessary to deliver his people from the wrath to come, from the lake of fire. He had done everything for his people. Everything necessary to bring them to the heights of heaven, to triumph for ever in the glory of everlasting bliss. Everything that was needed was accomplished between the four wounds and the fifth.

Hence it was not until after death, with the infliction of the fifth wound, that his blood was shed, and that miraculously.

This witnessed to a finished work, and so does the scar. It was all over. He had covered sins, wrought redemption, finished salvation, conquered death, saved from hell, and bought the church with his own blood.

His blood was not shed in order that something might be accomplished. It had been accomplished. The blood testified to what was already finished and complete. 'It is finished.'

The faithful believe in blood once and for all shed for their sins, blood that has already purchased them to God, blood that, at the time at which it was shed, in and of itself, procured for them free and everlasting divine righteousness, whilst they were yet sinners. This, they believe, is reckoned to them by grace alone, without the works of the law. All the value and the worth of the death of Christ is in the blood. He 'died for our sins according to the scriptures.' That, the faithful believe.

But not only blood was shed. Miraculously, distinctly, there came out blood and water. That water should come forth with the blood is full of divine teaching.

We know that his work was finished, that all the worth was in the blood. Then why was there water with that blood?

Water? 'He that believeth on me', John 7:38, 'out of his belly shall flow rivers of living water.' 'But this spake he of the Spirit, which they that believe on him should receive: for the Holy Ghost was not yet given; because that Jesus was not yet glorified.'

Water in John is a figure of the Spirit. 'Whosoever drinketh of the water that I shall give him shall never thirst', John 4:14. The giving of this water is signified by that which came out of Jesus' side in death. The drinking of it appears when faith takes in the truth of Christ crucified. 'Received ye the Spirit by the works of the law, or by the hearing of faith?' What is this word of faith which we preach? Christ crucified. 'I determined not to know anything among you, save Jesus Christ, and him crucified.'

Many speak of wanting the Spirit, or of seeking spiritual experience. But the Spirit speaks not of himself. He has come to glorify Christ. He takes of the things of Christ and shows them to the disciples. If so, Where is the Spirit? In Christ. Whence comes the Spirit? Out of the side of Christ. The Spirit is sent in order to glorify Christ, and that by the truth. He is the Spirit of truth. He comes not for his own sake, much less man's, but to glorify Christ.

It is by believing the gospel of Christ that the Spirit is received. It is out of the pierced side of the Saviour. 'And forthwith came there out blood and water.' That is, out of Christ's death, as revealed by that gospel which declares the crucifixion, makes known the blood, and sets forth the cross. This is called, Preaching Christ crucified.

If any man therefore seek for the Spirit, that man must look into the death of Christ. How? By observing the law? 'Received ye the Spirit by the works of the law, or by the hearing of faith?' By the fear of God? But devils tremble. How? By faith alone. For 'without faith it is impossible to please him.' Therefore it is of faith. By faith alone the obscuring veil is removed, the darkness dispelled, and Jesus Christ appears 'evidently set forth, crucified among you'. As was signified at the crucifixion, the Spirit comes by the preaching of Christ crucified, with the blood, out of his death. Faith, however, comes by hearing, and hearing by the word of God. 'And this is the word which by the gospel is preached unto you.'

The issuing forth of the blood and water together teaches us that it is the Spirit of God who applies the blood of Christ, not the mind of man in the dead letter. It is not intellectual, in the head, this application, nor does it depend on the withered arm of free will. When the Spirit of God works, it is in the heart. This is called, The washing of water by the word, and answers to that which is written, 'With the heart man believeth.'

This work takes place in the deep, hidden parts, in the interior man. 'Behold, thou desirest truth in the inward parts: and in the hidden part thou shalt make me to know wisdom.' The consequence of this knowledge is, 'Ye have obeyed from the heart that form of doctrine which was delivered you.'

This is the faith that Jesus calls, The work of God. 'This is the work of God, that ye believe.' 'Who by him'—mark that: not by yourselves, but by him—'do believe in God.'

Such faith is ordained of God: 'As many as were ordained to eternal life believed.' It is inwrought by the Spirit: 'Who have obtained like precious faith with us.' Observe, they obtained it: they did not generate it of, for, from or by themselves. The Spirit wrought it: 'having the same spirit of faith', which faith came by hearing the truth, for, 'He shall lead you into all truth.' And, being led by the Spirit in the inward man, they really believed for themselves, and not another.

This faith is called, the faith of God's elect, and comes, with the blood, out of the side of the crucified Saviour. Those for whom he died, are those for whom the Spirit has already been procured.

It is all of one, blood and water, and all through the death of Christ. All of one: His redemption and their believing. His work and their faith. The blood and the water. Sins expiated and their trusting. All was settled in the counsels of God when Jesus bowed his head, and gave up the ghost.

It is not that God wrought a general work by the blood of Christ, leaving man to his own devices, natural religion, free will, native goodness, or other ludicrous fiction, to complete the work. If that were so, Christ need neither to have come, nor to have died, there being that still in man which might be improved, and be the basis of an appeal for righteousness from human ability.

The truth is, depraved and fallen man has become helpless by his own iniquity. If anything were left for him to complete, he would lose everything. But there is nothing to 'complete'. It has been completed. 'It is finished.' Not only the work of redemption, but the work needed to bring to faith in that redemption. Hence, by virtue of the Spirit having been procured for the elect in the death of Christ, it is said, by a threefold witness, 'And forthwith came there out blood and water.' And water. Everything has been accomplished to ensure the awakening, quickening, regeneration, faith, repentance and endurance of all believers to the end. Were it not so, none would be saved. But vast multitudes, a great myriad shall and must be saved, to cry aloud at last in Canaan's land, 'Salvation is of the Lord.' Amen.

VI

The Blood of Purchase

CENTRAL to the doctrine of the New Testament is the truth that the church has been acquired at the price of shed blood. The blood of Christ is spoken of as having 'bought' the people of God: 'Ye are bought with a price.' Moreover the assembly is said to be 'The church of God which he hath purchased with his own blood.' Acts 20:28. It is a matter of purchase, and if so, of a price.

This is often thought of as redemption, but it is not the same thing as redemption. It is the price of redemption. It is the cause of which redemption is the effect. The New Testament Greek is very precise about this, and for that matter, so is the Old Testament Hebrew. However this precision has been lost to the English reader due to the translators having put one and the same English word for two entirely different words in the original.

This ineptitude has made it impossible for the English reader to distinguish between things that differ in the Greek Testament, and, of course, the general perception of the truth has been blurred in consequence. Neither has the succession of modern versions—all taken from the slyly substituted Westcott and Hort text—made the least attempt to correct the real errors. On the contrary, with increasing abandon, the versions have made confusion worse confounded.

Thus it is that to the English reader there is but one concept, generally expressed by the word Redemption. But to

93

those who heard the apostles in the beginning, and who read what they wrote in the Greek of the New Testament, this was not so. Two distinct words were used, and, of course, they conveyed things that differ. One word showed the cause, the other the effect. One conveyed the foundation, the other the structure that rests upon that foundation. The first declared the fact of the purchase, the second the effect of the purchase having been made.

Two separate Greek words, or rather groups of words having in common the same root and stem, were used by the apostles to convey the whole truth of purchase and redemption. But in the English these two are confounded together, and made to appear the same, by arbitrarily putting one single English word for both. This is but another example of tradition being in defiance of apostolic direction, by those who improperly claim the apostolate for their authority. If the apostles were their authority, they would have done as they had been directed.

The first of the two groups of Greek words used by the apostles is that derived from the noun ἀγορά, *agora*, which occurs eleven times in the New Testament. From this word, and sharing the same root and stem, two verb forms appear—one a compound—which teach the truth of purchase and price in relation to the people of God. Both these verbs have been translated with gross inaccuracy 'redeem', a word which does not belong to the *agora* group.

In the Authorised Version the noun *agora* has been translated 'market', six times; 'market place', four times; and 'street', once. The root of this word denotes gathering, or gathering together, herding or assembling; or, if used of things, collecting or begging. From the idea of gathering, particularly in the market place, forum, or place of assembly, the word *agora* has developed, generally denoting the market place.

From this word the verb and compound verb forms are derived, but, whatever the form, it is sheer confusion to put 'redeem' for any of the *agora* class of words. It is thoroughly bad translation, doctrinally erroneous, and it blinds the reader. Nevertheless it is what the translators have done, and successive ages and versions have preserved: 'Full well ye reject the commandment of God, that ye may keep your own tradition.'

The simple verb form of this noun is ἀγοράζω, *agorazō*, which appears thirty-one times in the New Testament, and in the Authorised Version has been translated 'buy', twenty-eight times; and 'redeem' (sic), three times. Perhaps the most literal translation would be 'to market', as in marketing a product, or else simply 'purchase'.

More is entailed in marketing than 'buying' or 'purchasing' however. For example, selling is implied, both buyer and seller are involved, and, of course, there is the price, not to mention the article bought. In the New Testament Greek, all this comes into consideration.

Probably, all things weighed in the balance, despite the limitations of the word, 'purchase' is the best translation, with connotations of the market place.

An example of this is seen in Matthew 13:44, the parable of the treasure hid in the field. 'Again', said Jesus, 'the kingdom of heaven is like unto treasure hid in a field; the which when a man hath found, he hideth, and for joy thereof goeth and selleth all that he hath, and buyeth that field.' Five questions present themselves: What is the treasure? what is the field? who is the man? why does he hide the treasure? and what is the selling and buying?

The treasure is the kingdom of heaven, that is, dispensationally, the church: 'The kingdom of heaven is like unto treasure.' The field, we know, is this present world: 'The field is the world', Matthew 13:38. Some, including Calvin, have said that the treasure is the Lord. What, hid in the world? Despite the opening words 'The kingdom of heaven is like unto treasure'? In this dispensation the Lord is in glory, not hid in the world! He came into the world, and of that the parable speaks. He prays not for the world but for those given him out of the world. That is the treasure hid in the field. 'Thine they were, and thou gavest them me.' He found them, not they him.

If the treasure were the Lord, then believers individually, or rather the church collectively, gain the Lord for the payment of a price. Then the reward is reckoned of debt with a witness, and salvation must be by works after all. But the reward is of grace, we have nothing to pay, we are debtors in bankruptcy, and salvation is by faith alone. Then how can the treasure be the Lord? It cannot. The treasure hid in the field is the church, which he came to seek and to save, for it was lost. He found it: and if so, it was his treasure.

Christ gave all that he had for what he treasured: 'Christ loved the church, and gave himself for it.' Not only his possessions, but all that he had, that is, his life. 'For the life is in the blood.' That is the price. He obtains, he purchases—the word is *agorazō*—he buys the field to gain the treasure: 'Ye are bought with a price.'

As to his hiding this treasure, the church is called 'The hidden mystery', and 'The mystery hidden from ages and from generations.' But, 'All that the Father giveth me shall come to me.' This is certainly not all the world: 'Thou hast hid these things from the wise and prudent, and revealed them unto babes.' 'Ye are not of the world.' Of the field, and the treasure in it, hidden from the eye of man by the election of God, but called and revealed according to purpose in due time, Jesus says, 'As thou hast given him power over all flesh, that he should give eternal life to as many as thou hast given him.'

The present dispensation is the period of the revelation of the mystery, because the treasure already has been purchased by him who 'loved the church, and gave himself for it'. When he was in the world, in connection with Israel, the treasure was hidden. But now the purchase has been made, the mystery of his will is known, the gospel has gone forth, the Gentiles gathered in, and the church revealed in the purpose of God.

Once the purchase had been made, the veil was rent in twain from the top to the bottom, and it appeared that God had his own divine and heavenly possession in the world, but separate from it. This was a treasure indeed. And, despite all that has come in, it still is a treasure. This treasure, the church, already purchased, really belongs to the Man who paid the price for it, and to none other.

This is the teaching of I Corinthians 6:19-20, 'Ye are not your own.' Why not? For this reason, 'Ye are bought with a price.' Ye are marketed, purchased, with a price. Again, the word is *agorazō*.

'Therefore glorify God in your body and in your spirit.' This is what was purchased, and purchased in the plural: your body, not thy body; your spirit, not thy spirit. The saints are purchased, that is what made them saints, sanctified, separated; bought by blood, body and spirit, 'Which are God's.'

A man of wealth could go to market and purchase a slave. The slave became his property. But no one could buy a soul: 'For what shall a man give in exchange for his soul?' Blood. Ye are bought with a price, that of the blood of Christ.

97

To be a slave of men was no glory. But to be the purchased of the Lord was a glory, 'Therefore glorify God in your body, and in your spirit.' One was the Lord's, of his own choice, by his own purchase, at the price of his own blood, together with all who were likewise acquired. 'Ye are bought with a price; be ye not the servants of men', I Cor. 7:23. Ye are marketed: that is, his purchased possession.

Not only the purchase but the price appears clearly in Revelation 5:9, 'Thou wast slain, and hast redeemed'—sic— 'us to God by thy blood out of every kindred, and tongue, and people, and nation.' Although the translators used the word 'buy' twenty-eight times out of thirty-one, sheer prejudice mingled with temerity caused them to alter the apostolic meaning in three cases, of which Revelation 5:9 is one. Why put 'redeemed' when they knew it was 'purchased'? Because in their wisdom they chose to put redeemed, the passage being, they thought, improved by their tinkering. They thought it sounded better than the word which the Holy Ghost gave. They knew best. Otherwise, Why did they meddle?

All the versions in the King James' tradition have erroneously translated *agorazō* in Revelation 5:9 as 'redeemed'. The RV (ASV), however, has the correct 'purchased'. The following version, the RSV, has 'ransomed'; but ransomed is not the same thing as purchased. It is only when the price has been paid to free a party from bondage or captivity that the word 'ransomed' can be used properly, but *agorazō* is neither so limited nor confined in its meaning: it is purchase, as such, in any and every case. It is therefore not right to state in translation one's opinion of what the Holy Ghost meant by the word purchase. One should translate what is there, not impose one's interpretation of what is there.

Consequently the text should read, 'Thou wast slain, and hast purchased us to God by thy blood out of every kindred, and tongue, and people, and nation.'

Here the meaning is clear: He was slain, and, as a lamb, slain by another as a sacrifice, in consequence of which blood was shed.

The slaying of such a sacrifice is the work of Almighty God: 'I will smite the shepherd.' Again, 'It pleased the LORD to bruise him.' That is, as the substitutionary sacrifice in the place of those whom he came to save. In their place, to make atonement, he died. Of this, the shed blood is witness. Now, what is being said about that blood, further, is that it is the price of purchase.

'Thou hast purchased us to God by thy blood.' Then, the price is the blood of the Lamb. Those purchased are said to be a great number whom no man can number. These are the people chosen by him before the foundation of the world, and they are called God's elect. For these, as their Substitute, he died, and the witness of this is the shedding of the blood of atonement.

This was the price that 'purchased them to God.' Then, they must have been sold elsewhere to another. But now an atonement has been made, and they are actually and really purchased with the price of shed blood.

Thus it appears that the Lamb knew them, and how to ransom them, and what was the price of purchase: his perfect intelligence, denoted by seven eyes, perceived every last one of this vast number. The Lamb was worthy to answer on behalf of each one, and for the whole, as their Substitute, and his blood was equal and superior to the value of the whole. There was this power in him, described as 'Seven horns'. Perfect power to effect the purchase.

Moreover this same power was equal to the gathering in of all those for whom he died, that is, all those actually purchased when his blood was shed, for it is written, 'All that the Father giveth me shall come to me.' This work depends not on them, but upon him: 'Seven horns, which are the seven Spirits of God sent forth into all the earth.' Therefore they shall—not they may, or they might—they shall come to him.

You see clearly that it is not a general price, conditional on the subsequent action of man to make it effective. It is effective in itself. It is a particular price, one that actually purchased and really acquired all those 'bought with a price' the moment that price was paid: 'For thou wast slain, and hast purchased us to God by thy blood.' Observe the tense, 'wast', and 'hast'.

His blood was the purchase price for all the elect from every generation throughout time to the end of the age. They are gathered, who were thus purchased, out of the world: 'Out of'—mark that—'every kindred, and tongue, and people, and nation.' Nothing general here. Called out of the world, from the four corners of the earth, the Spirit draws every last one of those whom Christ purchased with his own blood when he died.

They were already purchased. In the nature of the transaction, they were acquired when the price was paid. The acquisition is 'Unto God'. It was the blood of the Lamb that acquired them for God, the moment that blood was shed. They were chosen from eternity by the Father, given to the Son before the world was, and purchased in time by the blood of the Lamb when he laid down his life for the sheep.

As having acquired his own, he presents them to God and the Father: 'Thou hast purchased us to God.' That is, he presents them in his own Person, 'Accepted in the beloved.' In all ages, in view of the election, because of the acquisition, the purchased are brought into the fold by 'the seven Spirits of God sent forth into all the earth.'

The verb *agorazō* has a second form, due to the addition of a preposition making the word a compound. The verb is exactly the same, save that it is qualified by a preposition: it is *agorazō*, yes, but in a particular way. The preposition is *ek*, (here, ἐξ) a complicated word, as are all Greek prepositions, because so many shades of meaning may apply, due to the variety of grammatical uses. But for our purpose, 'out of' or 'out from' may suffice. Hence ἐξαγοράζω, *exagorazō*, means, To purchase out of, to purchase out from. This compound verb has been used four times, and each time in the Authorised Version it has been mistranslated 'redeem'. But we have shown that the verb means 'purchase', qualified by 'out of'. It is, demonstrably, sheer confusion to put 'redeem' for any of the *agora* class of words. It is nothing but interpretation, and thoroughly bad interpretation at that. From the noun, Market, or place of gathering (to buy or sell), or forum, comes the verb To market, or purchase what is to be sold, and, in the case of the compound verb, To purchase out of the market, or from the forum.

That the act of purchase may or may not effect redemption is not the point. The point is the act itself. The cause, not the effect, is what is designated. The word describes the purchase, and nothing more nor less. It is as the blindness of the scribes and Pharisees to confuse together what the Holy Ghost distinguishes and separates, in order that he might glorify Christ and his work thereby.

The compound verb *exagorazō* is used to describe the purchase of the people of God from under the law, Galatians 4:4-5, 'But when the fulness of the time was come, God sent forth his Son, made of a woman, made under the law, to redeem'— sic—'them that were under the law, that we might receive the adoption of sons.' Once again the translators mislead and deceive the reader: it is 'To purchase out them that were under the law'; that is, purchase them out from under the law and from the servitude which it entails.

Here the meaning of purchase becomes clear, because the passage shows that to which men are under obligation: the law. It is not a question of the sanctions, or penalty, of the law, but the law itself. Whether broken or not, men were obliged to keep the rule of law, in the degree to which it was revealed. This obligation, or indebtedness, stood in the nature of moral responsibility. Men were responsible, and the law declared that responsibility, and defined it, and from this there appeared to be no escape. It was not a question of whether men broke the law, but of the existence of law, of obligation to it, and man's consequent indebtedness.

Men speak of the Gentiles not being under law, and, in the sense in which the law came by Moses, there is truth in that statement. But in the sense of the law as declaring the rights of God and man, written in creation, nature, and in the consciousness and heart of man, it is obvious that every accountable being must be under obligation to render that which moral relationships demand, according to what is due. Man is indebted. There can be no question about this. 'When the Gentiles, which have not—the Mosaic—law, do by nature the things contained in the law, these, having not —the Mosaic—law, are a law unto themselves: which show the work of the law written in their hearts, their conscience also bearing witness.'

Not every ceremonial or judicial precept, but every moral rule, is as clear to the Gentile as to the Jew, written in the heart. Of this conscience also bears witness, and if it be conscience, then the witness borne is that one ought to keep the rule. And that 'oughtness' is a debt. If not a debt, then there can be no responsibility, no accountability, no judgment, and no future punishment. Then, Christ died in vain, and God is found to be false. God forbid.

The truth is, however, the rule of law, and its inwritten work, morally, places the whole human race under obligation to keep it, that is, to render to each their due rights, whether it be to God, or whether it be to man. In this sense not the Jew only, but the Gentile also, is 'A debtor to do the whole law', Gal. 5:3.

Then, what does the law discover? Man's bankruptcy is dis-covered. 'I had not known lust, except the law had said, Thou shalt not covet.' It is this that awakens man to the inbred sin to which he is in thrall, by the discovery that 'The law is spiritual, but I am carnal, sold under sin.' The discovery to the awakened soul is, that righteousness is not by the law, for by the law is the knowledge of sin. Law, as a principle, is that to which man is under obligation, and from the nature of its immutability, inescapable obligation. In the nature of law, there can be no escape. But in the nature of man, no escape means certain condemnation.

This is not a question of breaking the law: it is a question of being under it. To be under law, is to be under bondage, and in debt, 'A debtor to do the whole law.' It is from this debt that man needs to be delivered. If so, a price must be paid. A price, here, not to deliver from the penalty of the law, but to deliver from the law itself. 'God sent forth his Son, made of a woman, made under the law, to purchase out them that were under the law.' It is a question of price.

Death is the price. The dead body of the crucified Substitute paid that price. Death puts the debtor beyond reach of law: 'I through the law am dead to the law.' 'Wherefore, my breth-ren, ye also are become dead to the law by the body of Christ.'

Observe that this is not being dead to the guilt entailed by breaking the law. For, however a man were freed from guilt, as long as law exists to that man, and he is found alive to the law, he will break it over and over anew, and it will condemn him again and again in the future. But Paul speaks here of being dead to the law in and of itself. 'Ye are become dead to the law.' As such. Why? Because the price of death, such a death, witnessed by the shed blood, has been paid on behalf of all the people of God. Hence, they are not under the law, but under grace.

By his death Christ paid the price for his people in respect of the law itself. That is, his dying for them purchased them from being under law. Of this, his cross gives evidence, and the blood testifies. 'And there are three that bear witness in earth, the Spirit, the water, and the blood: and these three agree in one.' The witness of his blood, testifying to all that was accomplished in death, shows that the condemned body hanging on the tree on behalf of his people has paid the lawful price: 'I through the law am dead to the law.' The broken body is clear evidence of full satisfaction rendered to the law. Then, it can require no more for ever from those for whom he thus died.

The Apostolic testimony is this: 'But now we are delivered from the law, that being dead wherein we were held.' 'For Christ is the end of the law for righteousness to every one that believeth.' In a word, by his death Christ has delivered us from being under the law, because that death places us beyond its reach, and does so in a way that satisfies every legal demand. The price of every lawful obligation was fully met, and the case altered in perpetuity: 'Ye are not under the law, but under grace.'

The compound verb *exagorazō* is found also in Galatians 3:13. 'Christ hath redeemed'—sic—'us from the curse of the law, being made a curse for us: for it is written, Cursed is every one that hangeth upon a tree.' Once again the translators have obscured the meaning by interpolating—without regard either to accuracy or authority—the effect for the cause, thus imposing their notion upon the page of holy writ. They have by so much misled the English reader. 'Christ hath purchased us out from the curse of the law.'

Here it is not a question of being in debt to the law to keep it, as responsible before its moral requirement, and accountable to the legal rule in and of itself. Here it is a question of guilt, of having broken the law consistently and totally, with the sanctions sounding forth against the transgressors in consequence. The sentence has gone against the law breakers, whose debt lies in the suffering they are due to pay to the outraged rule of law, which by its curse demands payment to the uttermost.

As opposed to Galatians 4:4-5, it is not the law itself that is in view in Galatians 3:13, but the law in its sanctions. Responsible man stands in obligation to the one, and under condemnation by the other. The latter verse does not speak of the law and man objectively held accountable to keep it, but of man having failed to keep it, therefore of man's sinful past life being brought to account for lawbreaking, before the outraged sanctions. It is the broken law that is in view, invoking the curse upon the transgressor's past, with the sanctions of the law calling down curses and imprecations upon the guilty.

This curse of the law sounds against every single trespass, against all abatement of strength or zeal in the performance of the precept, and it levels withal against any breach of continuity in respect of every least commandment. 'Cursed is every one that continueth not in all things'—notice that, continueth not in all things—'which are written in the book of the law to do them.' Indeed, all that are under the works of the law are under a curse, because, 'Every transgression and disobedience receives a just recompense of reward', which just recompense is the commensurate curse.

All Israel must needs hear the curses of the law roared out by the tribes stationed upon mount Ebal, echoing and re-echoing from mount to mount across the valley floor. So doth the curse echo from heaven to earth: 'And out of the

throne proceeded lightnings and thunderings and voices.'
'Which voice then shook the earth', sounding from 'The
mount that might be touched, and that burned with fire',
with 'blackness, and darkness, and tempest, and the sound of
a trumpet, and the voice of words.'

And if so, who shall abide the day of his coming, when
with fiery vengeance he shall strictly recompense every transgression, and fulfil the law to perfection, for its immutable
sentence is that which he will neither compromise nor
mitigate. What a sentence shall sound forth against sinners!
For, even if it be kept outwardly in form, as it was by the
Pharisees, still it is continuously broken inwardly in intention,
and actually in heart. It is debased by ignorance, profaned
by hypocrisy, condemned by self-justification, shamed by
covetousness, disgraced by lust, misrepresented by self-
righteousness, polluted by sin and defiled by the flesh. All
this will be set to rights in the day of judgment, when the
abusers of the law shall be judged by the law, under the
sentence of the Judge of all the earth.

Therefore by the deeds of the law shall no flesh be justified
in his sight, for by the law is the knowledge of sin. Whatsoever
things the law saith, it saith to them that are under the law,
so as to bring in the whole world guilty before God. It works
wrath, calls down the curse, shuts up to judgment, brings in
fear, stirs up rebellion, increases the transgression, and
genders straitness, bondage and condemnation. There is no
hope, but only bleakness and despair, for every soul of man
under the law, with an accrued debt that can never be repaid
world without end. It is this that shuts up to everlasting
misery, in the prison house of eternity.

Nevertheless, 'Christ hath purchased us out from the curse
of the law.' When did he do this? When he was 'made a curse
for us'. But who made him a curse, and for whom? God made
him a curse, as it is written, 'The LORD hath laid on him the

iniquity of us all.' And again, 'It pleased the LORD to bruise him, he hath put him to grief.' But for whom? For as many as 'believed our report.' Every one 'to whom the arm of the LORD is revealed.' For all those who spiritually 'make his soul an offering for sin', though once they did esteem him 'stricken, smitten of God, and afflicted.' Isaiah 53:1-10.

Christ being 'made a curse' by Almighty God for those law-breakers in whose place he hung, means that he suffered in full measure, enduring all that the law required as punishment to cancel the arrears of debt owed by every one of the guilty transgressors. This curse God himself called down from heaven upon him, causing him to bear their stripes, enduring in his body the buffetings and pangs demanded by the broken law from them, even unto death. The cursing which he bore, having been made a curse, fully removed the curse directed against those who had incurred it, and wholly discharged the debt which was to their account in the debt-book of heaven.

By his blood Christ paid the price. The shed blood was witness to his sufferings in death, by which the curse was silenced, and the Lawgiver and Judge fully vindicated in righteousness. Moreover his blood was witness to the blotting out of debts from the Accounts of the great Creditor of heaven. Of this the Spirit is the seal.

Christ purchased out the elect from the debt of misery owed by them to the penal sanctions of the law. The curse was removed by the pain which he suffered and the death which he died. His agony and passion fully met the last demand of the law. That was the price, and he paid it, purchasing out all the elect seed from both the curse and the sanctions of the law at the cost of his own precious blood.

Thus it was that 'Christ suffered for sins'. He suffered for sins, enduring the price to be paid, that is, the price of pain and misery. Christ paid the demand in full when he died on the tree. It was the price of sins which he paid, who knew no sin, who was without sin, and who did no sin. 'The just for the unjust.' That is, he suffered as a just and perfect Substitute in bearing the sins of the unjust, receiving the curse of the law against that which had been transferred to him, and the price of those debts which he took upon him as his own.

He suffered not only the physical agony of the cross, and of death, but, beyond all conception, the unbearable torment of an innumerable company in everlasting punishment. That was where the curse left them, and, beyond death, that is the unending destiny of bankrupt debtors to the law, trapped by an immeasurable debt to eternal justice which their immortal souls can never repay. But 'Christ also suffered for us.' He paid.

Because of Christ's divine nature—which bore up his substitutionary humanity on the tree—he could, and he did, in a mystery, bear the equivalent of what was due from all the chosen seed to the law and its sanctions in his own body. He discharged every debt, removed the entire curse, and cleared from all obligation. This is called, purchasing out his people from under the law, and, purchasing them out from beneath the curse. He paid the price, and paid it in blood. And delivery of the purchased possession is what shall and must follow of necessity upon payment.

This work is finished. All the children of God were purchased when the price was paid. That is the nature of the transaction. It is not effective provided they believe. It was effective when the price was paid. They believe because it was effective.

The transaction is completed. It is in the past tense: 'Hast purchased us to God by thy blood.' And again, 'Hath purchased us out from the curse of the law.' He has not made that work possible. He has done it.

Christ is not made ours, neither is that work conditionally applied, in the event of our believing. The reason that we believe is because we were already his from before the foundation of the world. The work was effective, and the purchase was made, or ever the Spirit was sent forth to call in all those whom he had 'bought with a price'.

The effect of the payment of that price was that the elect seed were then and there brought to God. 'Thou hast purchased us to God by thy blood.' Far from it being that they came to Jesus when they believed, the truth is that Jesus brought them to God when he died. Neither is it that he brought them to the law, nor by the law to God. The true doctrine is that Christ purchased out from under the law and its curse an elect people foreknown and predestinated, at the price of his own precious blood.

This great company, the purchased possession, receive the adoption of sons. They are brought to throng the Father's house, and are called, true worshippers. These are they that worship the Father in spirit and truth, and to them pertains not only the Spirit of adoption whereby they cry Abba, Father, but the everlasting glory of an eternal inheritance, world without end, Amen.

VII

Redemption Through His Blood

THE word Redemption is of immense consequence in the scriptures. It is a word of profound meaning, its roots going back through the Bible to the beginning of the world. In the Greek of the New Testament the word ἀπολύτρωσις, *apolutrōsis*, translated 'redemption', belongs to a family of great and complex significance. The scope of the word is vast, encompassing grand sweeps of doctrine, reaching to the horizons of time, yet stemming from the death and shedding of the blood of Christ.

The source of the Greek word *apolutrōsis*, 'redemption', is found in the verb λύω, *luō*, meaning, To loose, that is, to loose any person or thing tied or fastened. This word has been used to signify the loosening of bandages, of shoes, or to loose one that is bound with chains, or held in prison. It has been translated Loosen, dissolve, break up, destroy, nullify or make void.

From this single source comes a variety of related words, the most significant for the present purpose being λύτρωσις, *lutrōsis*, a noun forming the basis of the word for redemption. Traditionally it has been translated A redemption, a ransoming. It has also been used to denote variously A deliverance, a setting free, a release, or a discharge from an obligation.

To the noun *lutrosis* the prefix *apo* has been added to form the compound ἀπολύτρωσις, *apolutrōsis*, the word properly meaning 'redemption'. So that from the source *luō*, through the stem *lutrōsis*, gathering up the increase of expression and application, comes the essential concept of the word. However, finally the developed meaning is qualified in turn by the *apo* prefix, which, here, broadly signifies 'away from', or 'forth from'. The final sense of *apolutrōsis* therefore is that of a loosing, yes, but it is 'away from'; a release, but 'forth from'; a redemption 'away from'.

The compound word occurs ten times in the Greek Testament, having been translated Deliverance, once; and Redemption, nine times. As is true to a certain extent of other related words in the same family, here is a word which has a vast doctrinal scope. It is applied to the soul, the body, Israel, the church, the land, the inheritance, and the creation.

This word is in a sense negative. It is 'from', not 'to'. The preposition *apo*, 'away from', both illustrates and enforces this. Redemption has in view that with which the people were bound, from which they are now released; that by which they were enslaved, from which they are at length set free; that in which they were imprisoned, from which they have been delivered. They are redeemed forth from bondage; released out of servitude. Their deliverance is described in terms of their being set at liberty from all the things by which they were once bound.

Hence redemption looks backward rather than forward. It sees what the redeemed were freed from, rather than what they are freed for. They are delivered from all their enemies, yes, but the promised land has still to appear. Redemption therefore is not the description of the prospect before the people, but of their release from the captivity behind them.

And yet whatever the direction in which the doctrine requires one to look, however great the breadth of the deliverance may be, it is the relationship of redemption to the blood of Christ, and that relationship alone, that concerns the present work. And the truth is, redemption is rooted and grounded in the shedding of the blood of Christ. It is the foundation of all the doctrine. 'We have redemption through his blood.'

It is not only significant but absolutely vital to grasp that the shedding of blood is that indispensable condition without which redemption cannot be accomplished. The first principle of redemption is that it is 'Through his blood'. Redemption is secured by the shedding of blood. When Christ's blood was shed, the essential work was done. Any doctrine or teaching that omits this, or vitiates it, strikes at the heart of the faith. There can be no fellowship with those to whom these things are not vital.

The shed blood of Christ was the price of redemption. Redemption is not the price: blood is the price; redemption is what the price has secured. I Peter 1:18-19 'Ye were not redeemed with corruptible things, as silver and gold, from your vain conversation received by tradition from your fathers; but with the precious blood of Christ, as of a lamb without blemish and without spot.'

Here the English 'redeemed' is used to convey the Greek verb *lutroō*, one of the *luō* family, better translated Freed, loosed, or delivered. Nevertheless, the passage shows that deliverance is wrought by the blood of Christ alone, and that nothing else can set free the people of God. Blood is the indispensable condition for the release or loosing of the people of God from bondage.

This is precisely the teaching of Eph. 1:7, 'In whom we have redemption through his blood, the forgiveness of sins, according to the riches of his grace.' This passage is confirmed by the testimony of Col. 1:14, 'In whom we have redemption through his blood, the forgiveness of sins.' The word 'redemption', common to both verses, correctly renders the Greek *apolutrōsin*. The original in both cases has the definite article, 'the' redemption.

A difference exists between Ephesians 1:7 and Colossians 1:14, not apparent in the Authorised Version. I do not refer to the alteration of the Greek Text itself by Westcott and Hort, deliberately omitting the words 'through his blood' from Col. 1:14. This was because their 'scholarship', which had no liking for the redeeming blood of Christ, conveniently found the best manuscripts dubious, and the worst a wondrous discovery, to suit their theory. I refer to the word 'sins', common in the English to both texts.

Whereas in Col. 1:14 the word 'sins' correctly translates the Greek— ἁμαρτιῶν, *hamartiōn*, To err, miss the mark—that in Eph. 1:7 does not. The word there is παράπτωμα, *paraptōma*, a difficult and complex word variously translated Fall, fault, offence, trespass and sin. This variety indicates that the translators could not make up their minds. The word is a compound, literally meaning To fall beside, or fall from beside, with strong suggestions of death.

The truth is that there is no English equivalent, but certainly the translators could have done better in Ephesians 1:7 than 'sins', weakly leaning on the association with the parallel text in Colossians for authority. Nevertheless the literal 'fall (dead) beside' is far too cumbersome, so is 'mortal fall', though that is the implication. Perhaps 'fall' is nearest, which the translators have given twice out of the twenty-three occurrences of the Greek word in the New Testament. The word in Eph. 1:7 is in the plural.

The great range given by this word in Ephesians, and 'sins' in Colossians, would show how vast and dire was the terrible bondage in which the people stood under guilt and condemnation. What a range is encompassed by the two words:

outward action, inward intention, ruling principles, all deliberate, wilful and rebellious, gendering the wrath and the fury of Almighty God, besides the curse of the law.

Not only so, but the fall is implied, a being fallen, with innumerable and continuous falls in consequence. Here is indicated a state of death wholly obnoxious to the living God, a condition of inbred corruption long given up by the holiness of the Most High, who is of purer eyes than to behold iniquity.

What a fall! What continual evidence of it in fallen conduct. The wrath of God is revealed from heaven against all such unrighteousness of men, aggravated by formal, outward and legal religion to furious indignation and anger. The curse sounds continually from heaven, and the righteousness of God is revealed in wrath against the day of wrath and vengeance of Almighty God, men, the meanwhile, being given up to a reprobate mind, unclean affections, and a perverse heart.

The fearful guilt of accumulated sins, the dreadful condemnation of the fall, lay man under the worst of tyrannies. Here is the foundation, the bottom and the substance of all his bondage: release him from this, and the rending asunder of chain after chain shall echo from the gates of hell to the heights of heaven. Deliver man here, and prison door after prison door, thrown open in ascending triumphs of deliverance, shall reverberate from the ends of time to the ages of eternity. Redeem man from sin and the fall, and redemption is secured from every enemy, all iniquity, from the law and its curse, from Satan and the powers of darkness, from the world and the bondage of corruption, from the judgment to come and the great assize, from the wrath of God and everlasting punishment.

But this is precisely the redemption that has been accomplished, and which is preached in the gospel: 'We have redemption through his blood, the forgiveness of sins.' The forgiveness of sins. No wonder Paul the apostle calls this 'the' redemption.

This is a redemption in which the elect are seen as 'Accepted in the beloved'. How? By the work of God and the Father: 'Wherein he hath made us accepted in the beloved.' It is the Father's doing, 'He hath made us'. And made us what? 'Accepted in the beloved.' That is, the nearness of the beloved Son of God to the Father, is the nearness of the entire adoption.

Those whom the Father chose in Christ are given the place of sonship, a nearness in love exclusive to the only begotten Son in the bosom of the Father. That is their place, exclusive still, yet in Christ they have been made to share by the Father himself. They could not be nearer. There is nothing nearer. Accepted in the beloved.

The redemption shows what a mighty release, what a tremendous loosing, took place at the cross: for sinful man could not have been further away. The distance appeared infinite, the guilt immeasurable, the barrier insurmountable, and the difficulty insuperable. Yet the Redeemer, equal in riches to the infinite debt that had bankrupted the chosen people, overcame all, paid the price, and by his own precious blood brought in the redemption.

In the proper sense, sins are not forgiven. Sins are remitted. It is sinners that are forgiven. The effect of remitting sins is to ensure the forgiveness of the sinner. To 'forgive' sins is to imply that they may be forgotten, treated as if they had never occurred. The law for ever stands against such an illegal notion. The righteousness of God perpetually bars up the way against such false and universal charity.

Every transgression must receive the just recompense of reward. Sin earns wages, and justice demands payment. But the sins of God's elect people were paid, and paid by the blood of Christ. 'We have redemption through his blood.' This, and this alone, remits sins. And this, and this alone, gives just and lawful title to forgive sinners.

Matthew 26:28 declares, 'For this is my blood of the New Testament, which is shed for many for the remission of sins.' Notice, it is shed for many. The remission of sins was not made possible for all. Here, the Lord Jesus teaches categorically, it was made effectual for many.

The shedding of the blood of Christ is never said to be conditional for all. That is the evil of the Arminian system, of universal charity, which is the real basis of popery, on which multitudes stand who would recoil from becoming professing Roman Catholics. The truth is that the shedding of the blood of Christ really effected redemption, because it actually remitted sins, and assuredly secured the forgiveness of sinners. When he died. Then, when his blood was shed.

When the price was paid, the purchase was obtained. Otherwise, where is the value in the currency? If the currency had the value required, then the purchase must have been effective upon payment. Otherwise the currency was not equal to what was to be purchased. But it was equal to what was to be purchased. Then the purchase can never be said to be conditional upon some further transaction. As if additional currency could be required from the object being purchased!

The price actually acquired the possession when the payment was made. Then if the blood of purchase was shed indiscriminately for all mankind, it follows that all were purchased when payment was made, and universalism is true. But if for 'many', it follows that, when payment was made, many were purchased, and election is true.

The blood of Jesus Christ was shed for many for the remission of sins, Mt. 26:28. When Christ died, in dying, he brought many sons to glory. We, that is, those chosen in Christ before the foundation of the world, predestinated to the adoption of children by Christ Jesus to himself, made by him to be accepted in the beloved, 'have redemption through his blood'. We have it; no conditions. We have it through his blood. When that blood was shed.

Everything else, like believing and receiving, follows from that. That does not follow from believing and receiving. How could it? Then it must needs read, We have redemption through our believing in his blood. But it does not. It reads, We have redemption through his blood.

How many Christ redeemed with his precious blood! 'I beheld, and, lo, a great multitude, which no man could number, of all nations, and kindreds, and people, and tongues, stood before the throne, and before the Lamb, clothed with white robes, and palms in their hands; and cried with a loud voice, saying, Salvation to our God which sitteth upon the throne, and unto the Lamb.' A great multitude: many.

Utilising the verb *lutrōsin*, but omitting the prefix *apo*, Hebrews 9:11(12) illustrates the work of deliverance by the blood of Christ in a remarkably graphic series of contrasts. 'But Christ being come an high priest of good things to come, by a greater and more perfect tabernacle, not made with hands, that is to say, not of this building; neither by the blood of goats and calves, but by his own blood he entered in once into the holy place, having obtained eternal redemption for us.' Heb. 9:11-12.

In the Old Testament the priests officiated in the tabernacle called 'a worldly sanctuary'. This tabernacle is said to have been made with hands and pitched on earth, being served by a priestly service that could not make the comers thereunto perfect, due to the fallibility and inadequacy of the tabernacle, themselves, and of the sacrifices which they offered.

The tabernacle was divided into two parts by a veil. Into the first part the priests went always, accomplishing the service of the Old Covenant. Into the second, the tabernacle beyond the veil, called the Holiest of all, went the high priest alone once every year, not without blood, which he offered both for himself and for the errors of the people.

By this the Holy Ghost signified that the way into the Holiest was not yet made manifest. That is, the entrance of the high priest alone once a year did not make it manifest. Mark that well. Even more remarkable is the fact that the rending of the veil from the top to the bottom did not make it manifest. The way into the Holiest was not made manifest by either of these events.

This is easily demonstrated in that, notwithstanding the rending of the veil, the priests never once served in the second part of the tabernacle. In fact thereafter the whole system fell into disuse. What the rent veil made manifest was the conclusion of the Old Testament. It had served its purpose. Then, what did make the way into the Holiest manifest?

The ascension made it manifest. When Christ came 'an high priest of good things to come.' The perfection of his own humanity, and the spotless offering up of himself to God by the eternal Spirit, showed the only acceptable Substitute and sacrifice to God. But it was his ascension and reigning priesthood in heaven that manifested his entrance into the Holiest of all.

The Old Testament priesthood was of necessity clad with symbolic priestly vestments, to depict what was not inherent. But Christ possessed within himself every priestly quality. He was a priest, and that for ever, in virtue of the perfection of his Sonship. He needed no symbolic and outward vestments, whose inward character shone with divine radiance.

The old priesthood had first 'to offer for themselves'. Then how could such priests be effective in offering for others? If they could only offer for others provided they were purged themselves, who was to offer for them? There was no one. Then they themselves must offer for themselves. But they were unclean. How then could their offering on their own behalf, before they were purged, count for anything? And if that could not count for anything, why should their offering on behalf of others count for anything?

Moreover, those priests aged, corrupted, and died, and their sons must needs take the place of the dead. But death is the wages of sin. Of sin. Death came by sin. How can such sinners offer for sinners?

Besides, they offered up goats and calves: how could these count as substitutes for men? They are not equivalent to men. They are equivalent to brute beasts, and at that, neither better nor worse than other brute beasts. What was needed by sinful men was a Substitute possessed of perfect manhood. Which is what the levitical priesthood could never provide. Notwithstanding, it is what Christ, and Christ alone, possessed in and of himself.

'But Christ being come an high priest of good things to come, by a greater and more perfect tabernacle, not made with hands, that is to say, not of this building.' Christ proved to be the perfect priest, one who could offer the suited sacrifice. Not in the first tabernacle, no, nor in the second, beyond the veil. But by a greater and more perfect tabernacle altogether, one made higher than the heavens, in the glory, in eternity, where 'the LORD is in his holy temple: the LORD's throne is in heaven.' There, in what the earthly pattern so feebly depicted, there Christ entered, and entered by the ascension, with his own blood.

He entered, yes, in the power of an endless life, in the virtue of an everlasting priesthood, having risen from the dead, being the other side of death, raised to glory in eternal life, he entered into the heaven of heavens, into the tabernacle not made with hands, 'And a cloud received him out of their sight.'

Neither did Christ enter the heavenly glory of this taber-nacle which the LORD pitched, and not man, by the blood of goats and of calves. No, he ascended up into the temple of God in the very heavens with his own blood. Blood of a perfect Substitute, blood of an acceptable sacrifice, blood of an effective atonement, blood that had actually purchased and already redeemed every last one of his people.

Neither did he enter oft to repeat the entrance, as did those high priests on earth every year in the worldly sanctuary with the blood of beasts, annually re-enacting the form of an atonement that could never take away sins. No, leaving the world, ascending far above all the visible firmament, Christ entered in once. Wherefore? Because the blood was effective before God. 'Having obtained'—not annual redemption— 'eternal redemption for us.' Save only, the word *lutrōsis* should really be rendered, 'deliverance', or else, Release, freedom, or loosing.

Release from a carnal priesthood that can never be effective for men before God. Liberty from an old law that can only reveal sin, increase the transgression, work wrath, stir up rebellion, and bring down despair. Loosing from the body of sin, the old man, the fall itself, and the first creation. Freedom from uncertain, fallible, useless sacrifices offered by men, oft to be repeated, never to be effective, enslaving in the bondage of guilt, fear, and a conscience continually distressed by piercing accusations. O what a release! And not for a while: eternal release. Deliverance world without end, Amen.

Just as it is eternal, this deliverance, so it is absolute. There are no ifs, buts, conditions or qualifications. If there were, it could not be called eternal. But it is called eternal. By his own blood he obtained eternal deliverance for us. By his own blood, and by nothing else, before or after, on earth or in heaven, in time or eternity. The work is finished. Blood finished the work.

That is the nature of redemption. We are loosed away from everything that bound us. This total deliverance begins to be administered when we are called, continues throughout our pilgrimage, carries us through death to life, and is consummated in the resurrection and glory of the world to come. That is redemption. It is that which rests in its entirety upon the blood of Christ, and is founded in this truth: 'We have redemption through his blood, the forgiveness of sins.'

The price of redemption is the precious—the priceless— blood of Christ. Redemption is not the price: it is what is brought in as a result of the price having been paid. Redemption is the effect of the payment made: the unloosing of every band, bond, chain, and entanglement; the opening of every prison door, every gate of brass, all the bars of iron, yes, and the sending forth of the prisoners out of the pit wherein is no water. Redemption is the being set free from every enemy in the body and out of the body, every foe on earth and in heaven, and every accuser before God and man. It is a deliverance from the body of corruption, from a groaning and travailing creation, and from a present evil world of sorrow and darkness, corruption and death.

When the redeeming blood was shed, that loosing away from every hindrance was actually achieved. Redemption was wrought when he died, sealed when his blood was shed, ratified when he rose from the dead, and promulgated when he sat on his Father's throne in the glory.

Redemption was accounted with the shedding of blood, declared in the preaching of the gospel, ministered by the forgiveness of sins on earth, inwrought through the Lord of glory, and it is sealed by the Holy Spirit of promise.

Redemption is sure to all the seed, shall be fulfilled in the day of redemption, and must claim with impeccable title the purchased possession, that is, the redemption of the body. Redemption secures the inheritance, pays the price, sounds the jubilee, and ensures the entering into everlasting glory free from every enemy and from the hand of all the hateful foes, of every last one of the redeemed.

By the blood of Christ, redemption releases us from all our sins, and it delivers us from the place where sin is imputed. Redemption acquits us from the sentence of death by a free pardon, and it opens the prison doors to life, light and liberty.

Redemption stands in the effectual worth of the shed blood, and releases seal after seal of the door of the prison-house shut by the hand of seven implacable enemies. Remission opens the seal of unatoned sins, ransom opens the seal of bondage to the law and its curse, forgiveness opens the seal of a trembling and accusing conscience, deliverance opens the seal of the devil and all his works, liberty opens the seal of the body of sin and death, freedom opens the seal of a fallen world, of a present evil age, and, finally, redemption blows the trumpet of jubilee to open the seal of the tyranny of the last enemy, the bankruptcy of a lost inheritance, and the punishment of everlasting wrath. Every seal is broken, and the ransomed of the Lord shall return, and come to Zion with songs and everlasting joy upon their heads: they shall obtain joy and gladness, and sorrow and sighing shall flee away.

Redemption does not propose such a discharge. It proclaims it. The discharge that has been effected is what is preached in the gospel. It can never be shaken. 'We have redemption through his blood, the forgiveness of sins, according to the riches of his grace.' Amen and Amen.

VIII

The Blood of Sprinkling

THE Epistle to the Hebrews declares that the people of God are come to 'Jesus the Mediator of the New Covenant, and to the blood of sprinkling', Heb. 12:24. But, today, how many professing Christians can tell us what this means inwardly, or can declare how they came spiritually to Jesus the Mediator, or speak of what it is to come experimentally to the blood of sprinkling? These things are not preached to them, this does not concern them, and they know nothing in consequence, least of all by the Holy Ghost from heaven.

Many will speak of coming to Jesus, but few of coming to him as the Mediator of the New Covenant. Many will pay lip service to the blood, but very few actually will come to the blood of sprinkling.

What is a Mediator? Why is one needed? What is the New Covenant? What is the blood of sprinkling? What is it to come to the blood of sprinkling? Evidently the apostles preached these things in the gospel as an essential part of that gospel, otherwise this would not be written. It is equally evident that the early church heard, believed 'and experienced what is written, for the writer testifies 'Ye are come'.

In order to declare this doctrine properly, and particularly to testify of 'The blood of sprinkling', it is necessary to look at the context of the verse. The 'coming' is not confined to the things spoken of in Hebrews 12:24. Nor is it simply a matter of coming. There is also a question of not coming. In fact 'Ye are not come' precedes 'Ye are come' in the exposition of the passage. And every real and experimental believer knows that this is and must be true both in doctrine and experience.

The argument of the writer of the Epistle to the Hebrews is one of contrasts. In the context of Hebrews 12:18-24 two groups of things are contrasted. The first group appears in vv.18-21, and the second in vv.22-24. The one is set over against the other, things in the Old Testament are contrasted with things in the New Testament, what is under the law is seen as opposed to what is under grace. That is the argument concerning which the writer admonishes the people, Ye are not come to those things, but ye are come to these things.

Two mountains are contrasted: Ye are not come to this mount, Heb. 12:18, but ye are come to that mount, 12:22. In divine things, spiritually, there are two mountains, Galatians 4:24-26, which answer to the two covenants, the one from mount Sinai, and the other from mount Zion. These two mountains each beget a kind of religion, of which the one is utterly opposed to the other. Because of this begetting, the two mountains are likened to the two women from whom Abraham begat children. Firstly Hagar, who begat bondchildren; secondly Sarah, who brought forth free-born sons. 'One from mount Sinai, which gendereth to bondage, which is Agar.' 'But Jerusalem which is above is free, which is the mother of us all', that is, of all the freeborn sons.

Addressing these freeborn sons, the writer to the Hebrews states, Hebrews 12:18, 'Ye are not come unto the mount that might be touched', that is, mount Sinai. 'But ye are come unto mount Sion', Heb. 12:22. Two mountains in contrast.

There are certain things about the two mountains which are grouped together respectively and set in contrast. Certain

125

opposing things pertain to each mountain. But perhaps the greatest and the most striking contrast is between the mountains themselves, and this the writer emphasises as being central to the difference between the Old Testament and the New Testament. The difference is that the one mount is upon the earth, but the other mount is in heaven.

Those addressed by the writer are said to have come to a mountain in glory called mount Sion. They have no earthly inheritance, they are not come to mount Sinai. No, they have an heavenly inheritance, everything for them is in glory. The saints' portion is not on earth but in heaven. If a mountain is on earth, one can see it, one can touch it. But if it is in heaven one can neither see it, nor touch it, the senses avail nothing at all, it is a matter of faith, and faith alone.

Hence the epistle teaches 'Ye are not come unto the mount that might be touched', to apprehend which requires the carnal senses. 'But ye are come to mount Sion', which is in heaven, invisible, and must be apprehended by faith. It is an heavenly mountain: 'And I looked'—that is, into heaven— 'and, lo, a Lamb stood on the mount Sion.' Rev. 14:1. In the book of the Revelation the Lamb is in glory, he is in heaven. The angelic host, the four and twenty elders, the living creatures, all are about him, and praising him in glory. 'And with him an hundred forty and four thousand.'

Mount Sion is always spiritual, always invisible, always heavenly, and it always pertains to the glory. To it the people of God have come—'but ye are come'—and must come. Just as all the bondchildren are come and must come to the mountain that begat them, which is mount Sinai. All professing religion will sooner or later resolve itself into one or other of these two opposites, nothing more nor less.

In the larger context of Hebrews 12:18-24, there are four things to which we, the freeborn sons, are not come, vv.18-21, and ten things to which we are come, vv.22-24.

Not infrequently in recognisable places, numbers are used in scripture to convey ideas, and teach spiritual verities. Four is used, for example, in this place, as the number of the earth: north, south, east and west, speak for themselves. This indicates spiritually what is of the earth, earthy. Of the first man, Adam. What is carnal and outward, sensual and visible.

Ten, on the other hand, is the number of completeness: a round figure, it is indicative of fulness, of realisation, of consummation. This fulness is in Christ, the second man, the last Adam, the life-giving spirit, the Lord from heaven. This speaks of all that is satisfying to God, complete in purpose, and ultimate in realisation. Mount Sion: 'We look not at the things which are seen, but at the things which are not seen; for the things which are seen are temporal, but the things which are not seen are eternal.'

Four things are seen in connection with the first mountain, Hebrews 12:18-21. The first is 'The mount that might be touched, and that burned with fire.' It might be touched, yes, but if so much as a beast did touch this mount, vv.20-21, 'It shall be stoned or thrust through with a dart: and so terrible was the sight, that Moses said, I exceedingly fear and quake.' It might be touched in the sense that it was material, temporal, visible, answering to the natural senses, but it might not be touched answering to the commandment of God, and the holiness made manifest thereby.

Mount Sinai discloses the majesty and justice of God. The wrath of God is revealed from heaven upon this mount, and his holiness made known. Here God appears to men as they are in the flesh, revealing himself to them as they stand by natural birth, without a new birth: as they are in Adam, not in Christ. God came down on mount Sinai, showing his character to men full of sin and born in sin, in consequence of which there is a fiery exhibition of flaming vengeance. This reveals what may be known of God under the law, made manifest on the old mount. We are not come to that.

Secondly, we are not come unto 'blackness, and darkness, and tempest'. The natural man, under the old mount, thinks that he sees all that there is to see of God, but it is all blackness.

Filled with fleshly zeal for the law, such a man is sure that he has the message for the people, gazing as he does into the blackness with amazement at the revelation confided to him. What eludes him is that God is light.

On the old mount man sees nothing at all of God, the veil is upon his heart, thick darkness lies heavy upon him. He is quite blinded to his own state, he can see nothing at all of his interior sin, hardness or unbelief. Oblivious of true religion, he is full of self-righteousness and pride in the form and works of the law. In consequence, he cannot conceive that he is the captive of Satan, bound with chains, gripped by illusion, and held fast in the prison-house of bondage, whilst the storm rages tempestuously within and without his soul. We are not come to that.

Thirdly, 'The sound of a trumpet.' The trumpet is blown as a warning of judgment, as we see in the book of the Revelation when the seven trumpets are given to the seven angels, the sounding of which brings down the judgment of God. The last trump is reserved for the day of judgment. Those under the law, though they cannot stand the judgments of God sounding continually in their own ears, yet hold forth nothing but judgment to the ears of others. It is all fear, death, and condemnation. It is a ministration of death, their ears ring with it, whilst their mouth is full of it. Though they cannot bear the sound from the mount to their own conscience, which works in them rebellion, desperation, and a spirit of fear, yet they cannot refrain from storming at others with the same sound of condemnation, laying them under the bondage that they cannot bear themselves. We are not come to that.

Lastly, there sounded 'the voice of words'. The people however intreated that the word should not be spoken to them any more, for they could not endure that which was commanded. Even Moses himself exceedingly feared and shook. For the voice shook the earth. Who then can endure the day of his coming, or who shall stand when he appeareth?

The law, promulgated by the voice from the old mount, is what the flesh cannot endure. Wherefore? Because it reveals the corruption and native rottenness of the old man, and his carnal enmity against God. How then can anyone willingly abide under the law for a moment? Properly, one cannot. But the self-righteous will take the dead letter from the living Spirit, the form from the power, and pretend to an outward righteousness in order to justify themselves before men. They are highly desirous of being known as teachers of the law, but they understand neither what they say nor whereof they affirm. Thanks be to God, we are not come to that. It is all earthly, sensual and devilish.

Nevertheless, God brings his people by this way to Sion, and they know full well what it is to be under the old mount. There they were slain, there they learned deep and humiliating lessons of sin, death, and judgment. There the sinew of their thigh was made to shrink, and there they were taught to say to corruption, 'Thou art our mother', and to cry from the dust, 'I am vile'. The old mount was the very place where they learned that Christ must be all in all, first and last, Alpha and Omega, beginning and ending, and that they must find him upon another mount altogether, if ever they were to be saved.

Hence they are come to mount Sion. They come knowing that God cannot be found in the things which are to be seen. They know experimentally that he dwelleth not in temples made with hands. He is reached by no earthly priesthood. He cannot be known by tables of stone. This they know by experience, and none teacheth like him. 'Blessed is the man whom thou chastenest, O LORD, and teachest out of thy law.' They have learned that God cannot be found in the things which were revealed under the Old Covenant upon mount Sinai. But then they have also been taught of God that they shall find him in things that are invisible, heavenly things, spiritual things which faith apprehends, and apprehends upon mount Sion.

These are the things which are complete, and there are ten of them in number, Hebrews 12:22-24. Heretofore 'Ye are not come to the mount that might be touched.' Now in contrast altogether, 'Ye are come to mount Sion.' Not on earth, we have seen that mount Sion is in heaven. He that sitteth in the heavens shall laugh, the LORD shall have them in derision: 'I have set my king upon my holy hill in Zion.' The LORD is there, it is the mount of grace, of justification by faith, of divine righteousness freely imputed to faith. This is the mount of his dwelling, where the King reigns in right-eousness, and peace is within the gates of the city. It is Jerusalem above, the mother of us all, the regenerate know it by revelation, 'This man was born there.' Birth establishes title.

'Ye are come', secondly, 'Unto the city of the living God.' In Hebrews 11:9-10, we read, 'By faith Abraham sojourned in the land of promise, as in a strange country, dwelling in tabernacles with Isaac and Jacob, the heirs with him of the same promise: for he looked for a city which hath foun-dations, whose builder and maker is God.' Abraham did not see it, but he looked for it. All through the path of his pilgrimage, he looked for the city of God and he looked for it above, by faith.

Thirdly, verse 22, 'The heavenly Jerusalem.' This is the city that is even now in heaven, 'Jerusalem above, the mother of us all.' It is the city that shall be revealed coming down out of heaven in the world to come: 'And I John saw the holy city, new Jerusalem, coming down from God out of heaven.' Then, it is the heavenly city, and God alone is the builder and maker thereof. We are come to that, who are of Abraham's seed, and shall yet come to it in the glorious resurrection, in the new heavens, and the new earth.

Fourthly, we are come to 'An innumerable company of angels.' How spiritual and heavenly these things appear, which never entered into the head, much less the heart, of the carnal in religion. What do they know of angels? Absolutely nothing. They have never known nor experienced their work, nor had the least thought of their existence. Yet to the freeborn it is said, 'Verily, verily, I say unto you, Hereafter ye shall see heaven open, and the angels of God ascending and descending upon the Son of man.' Ye shall see it. But spiritually, for, 'He maketh his angels spirits.' Then they see it in spirit. Angels keep the saints, ministering to the heirs of salvation, Yet they are as invisible as they are heavenly.

Angels fill the glory. We see this. 'And I beheld, and I heard the voice of many angels round about the throne and the beasts and the elders: and the number of them was ten thousand times ten thousand, and thousands of thousands; saying with a loud voice, Worthy is the Lamb that was slain to receive power, and riches, and wisdom, and strength, and honour, and glory, and blessing.'

Jesus has his own angel, there are the seven angels of the churches, seven angels with trumpets, and seven angels with vials. We are come to an innumerable company of angels, which are ministers of his, who do his bidding, and by them he does great things for his people. The angel of the LORD encampeth round about them that fear him. Angels have charge over the elect, keep them in all their ways, bear them up in their hands, and preserve them in their goings. We never knew they were there before, but now we are come to them, and come to them in an innumerable company in heaven.

Fifthly, we are come to 'The general assembly', and, sixthly, the 'Church of the firstborn'. It is written, Heb. 12:23, as though it were all one, but it is not, these two things are different. The words are distinct in the Greek. Actually, the description, 'The general assembly', stands more in relation to 'An innumerable company of angels', than it does to the 'Church of the firstborn', according to the text in the original.

The general assembly, or 'universal gathering', *panegurai*, was a word used distinctly for the assembly of the States of Greece, particularly on festive occasions. Here, it is applied to the great heavenly gathering of diverse bodies, such as the innumerable company of angels, the four and twenty elders, the great multitude which no man can number, the four living creatures, and the spirits of just men made perfect. The latter refers particularly to the faithful enumerated in Hebrews 11. Because of course there can be no confounding together of Israel and the church.

When the Spirit speaks of 'The general assembly', the common factor is that of being assembled in heaven, in the glory. This heavenliness transcends all else: it is the gathering of the various companies pertaining to the glory, not their distinctiveness, that is stressed. Ye are come to that. What wonderful grace this is, to come to such an assembly!

The writer next refers to one company of that assembly in particular, namely the 'Church of the firstborn'. This expression, *ekklesia prototokon*, clearly points to a part of the gathering of the general assembly. And it does so by a figure taken from the types and shadows under the Old Covenant.

When Israel was called out of Egypt, every firstborn male of each household was chosen to constitute the priesthood. The firstborn were to be set apart for divine service: they were sanctified, they were the LORD's, they were to be his priesthood. It was only after the corruption of the people at the foot of the mount, when the Levites went in and out among their brethren, slaying every man his brother, that Levi was chosen in place of the firstborn, who must of course, pay ransom money for their excess in number over the Levites, Numbers 3:44-51.

But in the divine mind the firstborn of all the tribes were to be the priests. This is fulfilled in a spiritual way in the church. All those called into this heavenly company are reckoned as firstborn children, crying Abba, Father, these sons are a royal priesthood, they have been made kings and priests unto God. They stand as the firstborn in life from the dead, in sonship. The whole church is that, and that is the whole church. A spiritual priesthood in the first begotten from the dead. Ye have come to that.

Seventhly, ye have come to 'God the Judge of all'. What fear this expression strikes into the legal heart and con-science! But not with the saints. They are come, already, to the Judge. And the pronouncement from the judicial throne is on this wise, 'It is God that justifieth: who is he that condemneth?' The Judge is the Justifier of his people. 'A just God and a Saviour.' The people of God are come with joy and rejoicing, with praise and thanksgiving, to the Judge, the Judge of all, to the God of all comfort, and the Father of mercies. To God the Judge of all. And to them, Christ is all in all. Thence, ye have come.

Next the writer states the eighth thing to which the people of God are come: 'The spirits of just men made perfect.' Of the earthly pilgrimage of these men one may read in the eleventh chapter. Their names roll sonorously from the pages of the Old Testament: 'of whom the world was not worthy.' Abel, Enoch, Noah, Abraham, Sarah, Isaac, Jacob, Joseph, Moses, Israel, Rahab, Gideon, Barak, Samson, Jephthae, David also, and Samuel, and the prophets. All of these, every one of whom obtained a good report through faith, endured to the end, and died in faith. These, Christ hath perfected. In spirit. The spirits of just men made perfect. Ye are come to them.

And, ninthly, to Jesus the Mediator of the New Covenant. Observe, first, that this coming is to Jesus in his office of Mediator, and, secondly, that it cannot be separated from all the things to which 'ye are come'. The 'comers thereunto' have come, in brief, to a mount, a city, Jerusalem, the company of angels, the general assembly, the church, to God, the spirits of just men, and to Jesus the Mediator. All heavenly things, and all inseparable. Nothing can be isolated from the rest, least of all from Jesus the Mediator. He is found on the mount to which 'ye are come', and nowhere else. All these things give heavenly character to those that have come to him in consequence of what they have been taught of God. 'Every one that hath heard, and hath learned of the Father, cometh unto me.' What they had heard, and learned, set them on the pilgrim path of glory indicated in the eight things which preceded coming thus to him, and consonant with that coming he says, 'I know my sheep, and they follow me.'

This coming to Jesus is nothing to do with carnal feelings, excited emotions, or human sentiment. Nor with coming to 'the front'. It is a coming out of inward and spiritual exercises, to the Mediator. Not, I say, to the front, to fill in a card. But to the Mediator of the New Covenant, written not with pen and ink, but with the Spirit of the living God, in fleshy tables of the heart. To Jesus the Mediator, who reaches to God in his divine nature, and to man in his human nature, and who in the union of both natures in one person, is able to bring the estranged parties together in harmony as a result of the covenant sealed with blood. This is a covenant made between the Father and the Son before all worlds, in eternal ages, which can never fail, and concerns every last one of those about whom it is said, 'Ye are come'.

Next, and lastly, the writer shows the completeness of this consummate work of Father, Son and Holy Ghost. This is seen in that 'Ye are come' unto 'the blood of sprinkling that speaketh better things than that of Abel.'

This brings together and concludes the ten things to which 'Ye are come'. Heavenly things, divine things, spiritual things. Things invisible. These follow on after the experimental knowledge of the four things to which 'Ye are not come'. Earthly things, carnal things, visible things, temporal things.

First appeared the way in which God manifested himself to man in the flesh; then, lastly, the way in which God reveals himself to man in Christ. In connection with the latter revelation, and in indissoluble union with every step of it, is the 'blood of sprinkling'. This is made known to all who hear his voice from heaven, commanding them to come. 'For if they escaped not who refused him that spake on earth, much more shall we not escape, if we turn away from him that speaketh from heaven.'

Four things were spoken on earth. Ten from heaven. In connection with the latter appears Jesus the Mediator, and also the blood of sprinkling. Neither of these can ever, possibly, be taken out of context. As to the speech from heaven, what is it? 'The blood of sprinkling.' This 'speaketh', and, evidently, speaketh better things than that of Abel. However, I have taken pains with the general and particular context, because none will hear that voice save he who comes to it in God's way. That way—and the steps which constitute the way—is what has been set forth in the preceding pages.

The blood of sprinkling is contrasted with that of Abel, Heb. 12:25. Notice that the writer does not say 'the blood of Jesus', but 'the blood of sprinkling'. If it were the former, Jesus himself would be the emphasis, his blood, and therefore the mind would be drawn to the cross where it was shed. But the thing that is emphasised about his blood is that it is sprinkled, and this draws the heart to heaven.

Notice further that it does not say 'the blood' of Abel, though this is of course implied. It says 'that' of Abel, as if the allusion were merely to provide a contrast. Sprinkling is deliberately emphasised, that is one thing. Abel's blood is not mentioned, but implied, and that is another. Again, the speech of each one is opposed, and attention is drawn to this in the verse.

The blood of Jesus was not sprinkled on earth. His blood was shed on earth. It is sprinkled in heaven. In John we read that when Jesus' side was pierced 'forthwith came there out blood and water'. Blood was poured out: it was shed when his side was thrust through by the spear as he hung on the cross in death. His blood flowed out, it was shed, but Heb. 12:25 speaks of sprinkled blood.

When blood is shed, it pours out of itself from the dying body. Once such a wound is inflicted, the blood gushes out of its own accord, no one makes it gush. When blood is sprinkled, however, another must perform the sprinkling, blood cannot sprinkle itself, nor of course can the one whose blood it is sprinkle the same blood. It required another to do that. Yet the unique truth of Jesus the Mediator of the New Covenant, raised from the dead, ascended into heaven, I say, the unique truth of Jesus is that he does sprinkle his own blood.

Sprinkling, in the figures under the Old Covenant, is something the priest did with the atoning blood of the sacrifice. Therefore it follows that the blood of sprinkling refers not to Jesus' blood when it was shed on earth in death, but to his taking it up into heaven, after death. All the worth and value of that precious blood was carried by Jesus into glory, and sprinkled before the throne of God. 'For Christ is not entered into the holy places made with hands, which are figures of the true; but into heaven itself, now to appear in the presence of God for us.'

From this high and holy place in heaven, God speaks peace to his people. By what voice? By the voice of the precious blood of Christ, sprinkled by that great high priest in the glory upon the propitiatory not made with hands, which sprinkled blood speaketh better things than that of Abel.

Abel's blood was not sprinkled. Cain, whose rotten religion was condemned by that of his righteous brother, slew Abel in the field. It was said to Cain, 'The earth which hath opened her mouth to receive thy brother's blood from thy hand.' Now if the earth must needs open her mouth to receive his brother's blood, then that was blood shed indeed. Cain struck so violently that the earth must needs open her mouth to take in the blood that gushed forth. 'The voice of thy brother's blood crieth unto me from the ground', Genesis 4:10-11. If so, it cried out because of the unrighteous act of murder, crying for judgment against Cain.

Jesus' blood, though shed on earth, was taken into heaven, Heb. 12:25. There it was sprinkled by the great high priest, and from thence its voice is heard. This is the teaching of Heb. 9:12, 'By his own blood he entered in once into the holy place', that is, the holy place made without hands, high in the heavens. First he took the blood in, then he sprinkled it. 'Having obtained eternal redemption for us.' Hence it is said, 'For this cause he is the mediator of the new testament.' And thus ye are come 'To Jesus the Mediator of the New Covenant, and to the blood of sprinkling.'

On the day of atonement, once every year, all the tribes of Israel were gathered in their hundreds of thousands, ordered in vast ranks, tribe upon tribe, about the tabernacle. The priest, clothed in pure white, was seen by that great multitude as little more than a remote and distant figure. This was the day on which Israel's high priest slew the goat of atonement, and entered into the first part of the tabernacle with the bowl of atoning blood.

The curtain having parted at his entrance and falling shut behind him, the distant figure passed from the sight of the children of Israel. Hidden from view, he entered within, the candlestick on the one side and the table of shewbread on the other. Before him, and in front of the veil, stood the golden altar of incense. Carrying the golden censer with burning coals from the altar, full of incense, the high priest approached with fear and trembling. Parting the curtain of the second veil into the Holiest of all he went through in clouds of incense, sprinkling the blood from the bowl with his finger seven times before the mercy seat and seven times upon the mercy seat.

Still enveloped in incense, still upon the blood sprinkled way which he had made to the mercy seat, the high priest turned, reversing his direction, and, passing through the veil, retraced his steps past the golden altar, the table of shewbread, and the golden candlestick.

Outside, the vast multitude, profoundly still, watched the curtain of the outer tabernacle, waiting with bated breath. At last the curtains stirred, the high priest parted the hangings, and, emerging, face shining, blessed the people because atonement had been both made and accepted on behalf of all Israel. The words rang out in the stillness: 'The LORD bless thee and keep thee: the LORD make his face shine upon thee, and be gracious unto thee: the LORD lift up his countenance upon thee, and give thee peace.' Amen.

The Blood

This atonement, made on earth, in the worldly sanctuary, by a carnal priesthood, with the blood of goats, stood for a year, till re-enactment was required at the hand of that—or the next—high priest, because of the annual repetition.

But Jesus the Mediator of the New Covenant, having obtained not annual but eternal redemption for us, has entered into heaven itself, into that greater and more perfect tabernacle, not made with hands, and not of this building. The outer curtain fell behind him: 'a cloud received him out of their sight.' Beyond the veil of time and sense, in the ascension, he entered into glory. The second curtain, rent asunder in the body of his flesh through death, has passed away for ever. He has sprinkled the heavenly pathway, he has sprinkled with his own finger and by his own blood, the glorious propitiatory. The mercy seat in glory being covered by the sevenfold atoning work, from henceforth the blood of sprinkling speaks out of heaven to every believer upon earth.

'Having therefore boldness, brethren, to enter into the holiest by the blood of Jesus, by a new and living way which he hath consecrated for us, through the veil, that is to say, his flesh, and having an high priest over the house of God, let us draw near with a true heart in full assurance of faith.'

This blood of sprinkling speaketh better things than that of Abel. It does not cry out, Murder! It does not require vengeance. This blood speaks peace. It requires mercy. It calls not for condemnation, but declares free justification.'

With all the spiritual value of his priceless blood shed on earth, Jesus entered into the excellent glory, as heaven opened to receive him, and closed as a curtain behind him. He entered the very temple of God in the heavens, this perfect high priest, and sprinkled the propitiatory seven times with his finger, over the thundering and lightning and voices of the law. All became silent. There was a great calm. Ransom had been paid, redemption sealed, and sins remitted. What a voice of blood! Blood, the priceless sprinkled blood of Jesus in the glory, speaks peace, pardon and forgiveness, and cries for mercy upon the sinner.

By hand he sprinkled the blood, not as the uplifted hand of Cain which slew his brother, but the passive nail-pierced hand of Jesus who died for sinners. This is he who offered up himself a perfect sacrifice, so that from heaven his blood declares the remission of sins to all believers.

In the sacrifices under the Old Covenant, the blood might be shed, poured out, put on, or sprinkled. This might be done with an instrument, out of the slaughtered body, from a bowl, by the hand, finger, or with hyssop. All this had deep spiritual meaning and typical significance.

If blood were shed, then it was poured out quickly, the swift flow streaming out into a widening pool, wet upon the ground at the foot of the altar. The swiftness of this blood shedding answered in appeasement to the burning fire of wrath gone forth against rebellious and guilty sinners.

But if blood were sprinkled, then the work was not quick. Blood that had been poured out at the altar was caught in a bowl and carried within the holy place. There the priest exposed that blood little by little, drop by drop: that is sprinkling. The blood is exposed to view in its entirety, by sprinkling. No swift darkening opacity as the blood is poured out and the body drained in the sacrifice. Slow sprinkling exposes every last drop of that blood. The voice of law sounded against every one of the sins of the guilty. The wrath of God exposes every transgression. Here it is not fiery wrath and vengeance demanding swift bloodshed. Here each successive sin is held remorselessly in remembrance, just as each had been committed, one by one. Yes, and remitted drop by drop. Blotted out. Thus, and thus alone, sins are covered in atonement.

The hand stands for labour, but the finger represents precise, refined work. The finger of Jesus, the Mediator of the New Covenant, will miss not one single sin of his own people, no, not in the whole of their lifetime, not one sin of all his covenant people. Every one shall be covered. And covered by sprinkling, the only acceptable atonement before God. Precisely covered. Blessed is the man whose sin is covered.

This sprinkled blood, which speaks pardon, mercy and peace from heaven, is put in perfect cover over every and all sin remembered at the throne of judgment by everlasting justice, in respect of all the people of God. Every offence having been covered by the precious drops of priceless blood, God saith, and, in view of his ordaining such an atonement by such a high priest, saith of necessity, 'Their sins and their iniquities will I remember no more.'

This sprinkled blood is in the glory. This glorious high priest is in heaven at the throne of God. It is from thence that the voice of mercy sounds. 'My sheep hear my voice.' Ye are come to that.

IX

The Blood of the Covenant

THERE are some seven references in the gospels and the epistles to the blood of the covenant, or to the blood of the New Testament. What characterises the blood in these references is that it is covenant blood, it is his blood, yes, but it is 'of the New Testament'. From this, two questions arise. First, what is a covenant, or testament, and, second, is there any difference between the two?

The English words 'covenant' and 'testament' both serve to translate one word in the original, namely, $\delta\iota\alpha\theta\dot{\eta}\kappa\eta$, diathēkē. This Greek compound is made up of the preposition $\delta\iota\dot{\alpha}$, dia, meaning very generally 'through', and $\theta\dot{\eta}\kappa\eta$, thēkē, a rather obscure word derived from the well-known root $\tau\dot{\iota}\theta\eta\mu\iota$, tithēmi, To lay down, lay out, dispose, arrange, put in place, put in order. Hence diathēkē, Covenant, testament, arrangement, disposition, or, more literally, 'an arrangement through'.

Diathēkē occurs thirty-three times in the New Testament, and is translated 'covenant' twenty times, and 'testament' thirteen times. Both words are suitable, the meaning of the original 'an arrangement through' not being quite covered by either. If diathēkē were translated 'testament' consistently, this would be inadequate where 'covenant' is implied, and vice-versa.

Diathēkē therefore may mean either an arrangement 'through a covenant', or an arrangement 'through a testament', according to the stress required in a given place. Neither English word is adequate for the full significance of the Greek. The context must determine the emphasis, and the translators have used both terms to answer to the wide range of the original word.

Consider firstly the use of the word 'covenant'. A covenant is an arrangement made through or between parties. Two sides bind themselves to each other through this arrangement: they make a covenant.

When two parties covenant together, they agree on what is due each from the other, as binding them through this contract by mutual consent. The arrangement between the parties is written down, signed and witnessed: this document then constitutes the terms of reference as to what was covenanted. It is binding. If one party fails, the other is not only released from obligation, but entitled to damages.

In the Old Testament, the covenant was between God and man, under the terms of the law. The people bound themselves through the commandments to an agreement with the LORD. 'And Moses took the book of the covenant, and read in the audience of the people: and they said, All that the LORD hath said will we do, and be obedient', Ex. 24:7. God would do this: they would do that. It was written and sealed. It was arranged.

But the covenant failed, utterly, hopelessly and irrevocably. The law could not bring in obedience, though the people bound themselves to render it. 'What the law could not do, in that it was weak through the flesh.' The law could not produce the obedience it required and Israel promised. The law failed because man put under trial always breaks down in divine things. 'The law is spiritual: but I am carnal, sold under sin.' Man proved to be a covenant breaker under the law, 'for by the law is the knowledge of sin.'

The law brought to light the inbred corruption and depravity of man under the fall. It took that covenant or agreement to bring out what was hidden in the heart, to which man is blinded by his own conceits, and by the delusions of Satan. 'I was alive without the law once.' Yes, but at the same time dead toward the dormant corruption within. Alive to man, the world, outward things, formal religion, but dead towards God, the glory, inward things, spiritual and experimental religion. A form of life, it is true, but it is all a delusion. 'When the commandment came, sin revived, and I died.' Dead in trespasses and sins.

Man always fails in the covenants, bonds, and agreements into which he enters with God. Israel failed, worshipping the calf or ever Moses came down from the mount. The priesthood failed, even before the consecration was concluded. The kings failed, and the kingdom divided and fell. The prophets failed, and the prophetic office became prey to the multitude of false prophets. As to the true, 'Which of the prophets have not your fathers persecuted?' They slew the true prophets, who called the people back to the covenant.

In all man's bargains and arrangements he fails and breaks down before God. The old world broke down. World government, in Daniel, broke down. Yes, and Israel broke down. 'He came unto his own, and his own received him not.' Man under covenant? 'Who both killed the Lord Jesus, and their own prophets, and have persecuted us; and they please not God, and are contrary to all men.'

Neither will the substitution of a 'Christian' system for a legal one, as in the Arminian scheme, alter this in principle. Of this vital truth neither modern evangelicalism nor contemporary Christianity has any idea whatever: the Christian religion is not the substitution of the gospel for the law, the Gentiles for Israel. The covenant itself is changed: it is a new covenant.

The vast majority, overcome in practice by infatuation with the Arminian principle—even though many call themselves Calvinists after the modern fashion—really think of Christianity as an agreement between themselves and the Lord Jesus. If they do this, he will do that.

But the substitution of Jesus for Moses, Christianity for law, Gentiles for Israel, makes no difference when the terms of the covenant are still on the old bargaining principle. The covenant principle 'All that the Lord hath spoken will we do' remains. But this is not the New Testament. It is the Old Testament in sheep's clothing.

The truth is that whenever man is under responsibility towards God, he fails. The very idea that the New Covenant is on this principle or basis is not only error but heretical error. As if there were some sort of an arrangement with God, and if man does his part, God will do his, but if man fails on his part, God will not keep his. That is the legal principle of covenant, and the substitution of gospel for law, whilst retaining this principle, destroys the foundations of the New Testament. And yet it is the Arminian principle. Precisely because this principle failed, God brought in the New Covenant.

It is not only that the gospel is new, the covenant is new: the principle changes entirely. The New Covenant is not a covenant between man and God. It is a covenant between divine Persons. The New Covenant is between the Father and the Son, and it is sealed by the Holy Ghost. That is the difference.

The New Covenant was in the deity, hidden in the Godhead, 'Kept secret since the world began, but now is made manifest' Rom. 16:25-26. 'The mystery which hath been hid from ages and from generations, but now is made manifest to his saints' Col. 1:26. The revelation of this mystery, is the making known of the New Covenant.

What a mystery! In the Old Covenant, the great cry was 'The LORD our God is one LORD'. One God: one LORD. It had not entered into the heart of man that in one Godhead there were three divine Persons. But when man utterly broke down, having been tried out under all circumstances, God made known in love the revelation of the mystery, and the veil of the temple was rent in twain from the top to the bottom.

When God brought in a new thing, this utterly transcended man's highest thoughts. The revelation of the deity in the giving of the Son of God, the child born of the virgin, the making known of the Father, the manifestation of the Holy Ghost, all pass understanding. The truth that there are three divine Persons in one God, and one God in three divine Persons, and that the New Covenant is between these divine Persons, is a mystery which nothing but interior revelation can convey.

That is where the New Covenant stands, between the Father and the Son, in one Spirit. It must be so. Everything else had been tried out, everything with man had been tested, and there was nothing but failure. Unremitting failure. To change the terms of agreement, to put gospel for law, would not alter the principle. Man could not be trusted: he always failed. Then, a new thing was required, if God was to be glorified. But God has been glorified, and, if so, upon another principle. 'I have glorified thee on the earth.'

The Father gave a people to the Son before the foundation of the world. 'Thine they were, and thou gavest them me.' These are called, Christ's sheep. For them, he gave his life: 'I lay down my life for the sheep.' Not for the world: 'Ye are not of my sheep.' But for his own flock, Christ shed his own blood—'for thou wast slain, and hast purchased us to God'— thereafter sending forth the Spirit from the Father to bring them to himself. 'All that the Father giveth me shall'—mark that, shall—'come to me.' For this covenant cannot fail.

146

Man will fail and must fail. But God shall not fail. Nothing divine fails. 'No man is able to pluck them out of my Father's hand.' 'Of them which thou gavest me I have lost none.' It stands in grace, this covenant, and grace stands in almighty power. 'Thou hast given him power over all flesh, that he should give eternal life to as many as thou hast given him.' That was the covenant, and it shall surely be fulfilled to the uttermost.

The New Covenant is all God's work. Otherwise it would fail. If it were God's work dependant on man's choice, or free will, it would be the Old Covenant principle but with altered terms. But it is not. It is a New Covenant entirely. All is of God. Because nothing that rests on man in any degree whatsoever can prevail. When God looked, there was none to help; and he wondered that there was none to uphold: therefore his own arm brought salvation unto him. God has taken in hand the salvation of helpless, depraved sinners, to save them: and save them he shall. 'He shall save his people from their sins.'

That is the covenant.

However the word 'testament' also is used by the translators to render the Greek *diathēkē* into English. Now a testament is an arrangement that comes into force as a result of the death of the testator. A testament may be filed away for years. But death activates it, causes it to be brought forth, and makes it effective.

'For where a testament is, there must also of necessity be the death of the testator.' Mark that: of necessity be the death of the testator. A last will and testament in the vault of a bank, or the safe of a solicitor, is just so much mouldering paper. It might as well be rubbish for all the use that it is. But then the testator dies, and, suddenly, that paper assumes immense importance: it is a testament indeed, giving directions, as it were, from beyond the grave.

147

Christit t Crucified

Now, in the gospels Jesus refers to his blood as that 'Of the New Testament', Mt. 26:28, Mk. 14:24. Again, in Lk. 22:20 he speaks of 'The New Testament in my blood'. This is the blood of the *diathēkē*, the testament. In the epistles, I Cor. 11:25 repeats the words from Luke, 'The New Testament in my blood'. Every one of these references concerns the Lord's supper, at which Jesus said, 'This is my blood of the New Testament, which is shed for many for the remission of sins.' The cup manifests that, and it is identified with it. 'This cup is the New Testament in my blood.' The blood of the testament, or covenant, is also mentioned in Heb. 10:29, 12:24, and 13:20.

Seven times the blood of Christ is said to be of the covenant, or of the New Testament. Seven; perfect: the blood perfected for ever them that are sanctified. The covenant is perfect, nothing can come in to undermine it. The testament brings in perfection, it makes the comers thereunto perfect, and, if so, for ever. Hence it is called, The blood of the everlasting covenant, Heb. 13:20.

The force of the word 'testament', is that whilst it is also a covenant, an arrangement between parties through a written agreement, it has a unique character: this arrangement comes into force only when one of the parties dies. Death activates the arrangement. 'For where a testament is there must of necessity be the death of the testator. For a testament is of force after men are dead: otherwise it is of no strength at all while the testator liveth', Heb. 9:16-17.

Before death, it was just so much fine vellum covered with script. There was this vellum, if I may so speak, in the safe of the bank of heaven, a last will and testament in the vaults in the glory. Until death came in. Before that, though God had promised to all the seed of Abraham a sure inheritance, there could be no possession. It was death that made the inheritance a reality.

148

And what a death it was: 'Whereupon neither the first testament was dedicated without blood: This is the blood of the testament' Heb. 9:18,20. Here is death, yes, but what kind of death is it? 'This cup is the New Testament in my blood', said Jesus. Weigh the words well. Why is this death extraordinary? Because it is 'in my blood': This is the New Testament 'in my blood'. Then it is a death of violence, a death of bloodshed; it is not a peaceful death.

If a man dies naturally, as men say, there is no blood. When blood appears, violence has come in by some means; blood is shed. What Hebrews is teaching is that the words, 'This is the blood of the testament' indicate a violent death on the part of the testator, a death by bloodshed.

If it be so, enquiry must follow: What was the cause of death? The answer is, Sacrifice. Substitutionary sacrifice. It was an atoning death.

Why was this necessary? Because the beneficiaries of the testament had that within them, and that to their account, which effectively prevented them from entering into inheritance. They were sinful, and they were sinners, the children of wrath even as others. Heirs of glory? Impossible! As such, yes. But not if a peerless Substitute, equal to the task, ordained of God as a Lamb without spot or blemish, be made sin by Almighty God to atone for that sinfulness, and bear those sins in his own body, so that he might meet the innumerable charges of guilt for which they were accountable.

With men it was impossible, but with God all things are possible. Because what stood between the heirs of promise and the promised inheritance as an insurmountable barrier, that is, their own sin and corruption, God removed in a sacrificial Substitute. But the price was death. Violent death. A death marked by bloodshed. Then, having taken away what prevented the beneficiaries from inheriting, his death became precisely that of a testator. Upon his dying, they inherit. 'This is the New Testament in my blood.'

His death was violent because by wicked hands he was crucified and slain. Yet the greatest violence was unseen. 'It pleased the LORD to bruise him.' But who saw those blows fall? 'By his stripes we are healed.' But who marked that sore chastisement? 'He was wounded for our transgressions.' Yes, but who observed the piercing sword? He was 'stricken, smitten of God, and afflicted', and, as the Lamb of God, suffered the death of vicarious sacrifice at the hand of the LORD, his blood being shed. 'He was cut off out of the land of the living.'

Since that death was on behalf of the heirs of promise, the seed of Abraham by faith, everything that prevented their inheritance was removed in his vicarious and atoning sacrifice. If so, it effected exactly what is effected by the death of a testator. And, since it was all that he had, everything he possessed, that was freely given to them, their inheritance is exactly that of the beneficiaries of a will. 'For this is my blood of the New Testament which is shed for many.'

What comparison can there be between the New Testament and the Old? What have the two covenants in common? There is no comparison. They have nothing in common. 'For the law was given by Moses, but grace and truth came by Jesus Christ.' The LORD hath created a new thing in the earth: 'Behold, ye despisers, and wonder, and perish: for I work a work in your days, a work which ye shall in no wise believe, though a man declare it unto you.'

The Old Covenant was a covenant of works, it was a legacy of sin and death, a killing testament. The New Covenant is a covenant of faith, an inheritance of righteousness and life, a testament of glory. The old is past and finished, and the new shall stand for ever: 'The blood of the everlasting covenant.'

This cannot pass away, because it is an everlasting covenant, by definition it must stand and cannot be altered, any more than the everlasting gospel or eternal life. If these things were conditional, they could not be eternal. If they were mutable, they could not be everlasting.

After the death of the testator, there is no delay before the testament becomes effective: it is already effective. The inheritance has already passed to the heirs. That was Paul's teaching to the Corinthians, 'All things are'—notice the tense, are—'yours; whether Paul or Apollos or Cephas or the world, or life or death or things present or things to come, all are yours, and ye are Christ's and Christ is God's.' All things that are Christ's were theirs through a death which took out of the way everything that stood between them and their inheritance. 'This is the blood of the covenant.'

All things are yours: from the glorious throne in the heavens flows down the fulness of justification, sanctification and redemption; the heavenly ministration of the doctrine, the discipline and the ordinances; the abundant fulness of the Spirit for the Christian, the church, and the ministry. The remission of sins, the ransom of the sinner; the forgiveness of the guilty, the pardon of the condemned; the appeasement of wrath, the propitiation of the deity, the righteousness of God; reconciliation and substitution, sacrifice and atonement, all is not only secured but all is administered from heaven to the heirs of grace and of glory.

The prophecies, the two great promises of God to Abraham and to his seed for ever, the resurrection from the dead and the inheritance of the world to come, all is sealed to the heirs of promise by the blood of the testator. The beneficiaries of such a testament not only hope that they will be raised to glory: the glory is theirs, it is already secured by the blood of the New Testament.

'Whom he did predestinate, them he also called: and whom he called, them he also justified: and whom he justified them he also glorified.' Observe the tense: it is the past tense. It has been secured, and it is assured to the heirs: 'them he also glorified.' It is in the past tense. That is in the nature of the testament.

If so, Who shall lay anything to the charge of God's elect? The time for that is past! That time was at the cross, where all the charges from time and eternity, heaven and earth, from birth to death, from devils and men, were laid to the account of the Substitute on the tree. 'It is God that justifieth. Who is he that condemneth? It is Christ that died, yea rather, that is risen again, who is even at the right hand of God, who also maketh intercession for us.'

Who shall separate us from the love of Christ? A love which brought him from heaven to earth, from deity to manhood, from the glory to the world; a love which brought him to shame and ignominy, to buffeting and tribulation, to the suffering of death itself, even the death of the cross. A love which moved him to give all that he had for the lost, everything he possessed for the destitute, his life for the sheep. A love of devotion, self-denial, of sacrifice; a love that rejoiced not in iniquity, but rejoiced in the truth, bearing all things, believing all things, hoping all things, enduring all things. A love that never failed. Here is the love that brought in the New Testament for all the heirs. A love that is called 'everlasting'.

Tell me, now that he is risen, now that he is glorified, now that he has almighty authority, now that all power is given unto him, now that he is at the right hand of the Majesty on high, now that he is both determined and able to bring every one of the heirs by resurrection into the glory of the world to come, tell me, I say, What shall separate us from the love of Christ?

The heirs of promise receive the Spirit of promise, Jesus now being glorified. That same Spirit is 'the earnest of our inheritance until the redemption of the purchased possession.' He shall not depart from us. Filling us, blessing us, indwelling us; sent forth, poured out, he is the anointing that abideth in all the elect. He is the Spirit of grace and of glory. He is the Spirit of truth. He never ministers, fills, leads, blesses, anoints, nor quickens apart from the truth. Through him the heirs receive the love of the truth that they may be saved. The Spirit witnesses with their spirits. 'And the Spirit beareth witness, because the Spirit is truth.'

Such is the character of the New Testament in his blood. It is absolutely secure. The Father chose the heirs in eternity, and gave them the inheritance or ever he formed the world. This is that same 'eternal life, which God, that cannot lie, promised before the world began.' It is as the ordinances of the heavens, being 'according to his own purpose and grace, which was given us in Christ Jesus before the world began.' Eternal before the world began.

It is this that has been secured by death, the death of the testator, sure to all the seed when Christ died on the cross in the midst of time. For the blood of the New Testament, shed for many, removed every barrier, and all the hindrances to the heirs' inheritance for ever.

Such an inheritance is certain in glory, when the world is no more: 'An inheritance incorruptible, and undefiled, and that fadeth not away, reserved in heaven for you.' It is everlasting, the blood of the 'everlasting' covenant. When the world is no more, this must by definition abide for ever in eternity to come.

It is an everlasting covenant. It was agreed in eternity, ratified in time, sealed to all the heirs in succession, and shall

153

Christ Crucified

be consummated in glory, world without end, Amen. What is time? Brackets, a parenthesis, soon to pass away, lost for ever in an eternal context.

When one comes to brackets in a sentence, to keep the sense, one reads to the first bracket, then immediately on from the last. That is the real flow, the true narrative. And so eternity, and the determination of the inheritance, and the everlasting purpose, swell up to and around the parenthesis of time, for ever to resume uninterrupted their majestic and undisturbed flow of glorious life and liberty, light and love, the present world being no more than a memory.

In Galatians, the Apostle Paul declares that Christ 'gave himself for our sins, that he might deliver us from this present evil world.' The word 'world' in this place, Gal. 1:4, means 'age'. We are delivered from the age, the age Paul calls evil. Call it time. It is the same thing, and that is what he meant: αἰών, aiōn, Age, indefinite time, dispensation. Indefinite time, the age, as from creation to the end of the world. 'Who hath delivered us from this present evil time.' Out of time, into eternity. Out of penury into riches. Out of bankruptcy, into solvency. Out of shame, into glory. Out of the first man, into the second. Out of this world, into the next. Out of Adam, into Christ.

How will you describe such an inheritance as this? We are not in the parenthesis, we are in eternity. We are not of the earth, we are of heaven. We are not in the flesh, we are in the Spirit. We are not in the brackets, we are in the everlasting covenant. This was secured, when the covenant blood was shed. It happened then. That was the time when everything that was decreed in eternity was secured for ever.

We are lifted out of time. We are of an everlasting covenant that was given to us before time began, before the world existed, and which will be when time has passed away for ever.

154

This is the character of the covenant, of the testament, which has been left to us in love. It is the *diatheke*. It is what gives to the people of God a sense of the divine certainty that belongs to the New Testament in Jesus' blood, an assurance of the things which can never, no, never be taken away, because of the blood of the covenant which God promised before the foundation of the world was laid.

'Who shall lay anything to the charge of God's elect? It is God that justifieth. Who is he that condemneth?'

Now the God of peace, that brought again from the dead our Lord Jesus, that great shepherd of the sheep, through the blood of the everlasting covenant, make you perfect in every good work to do his will, working in you that which is well-pleasing in his sight, through Jesus Christ; to whom be glory for ever and ever. Amen.

PART THREE
THE CROSS

THE CROSS

X

The Doctrine of the Cross

WHILST by the blood of Christ believers are said to be forgiven and made nigh, by the cross of Christ their enmity is said to have been removed and abolished. By the blood access is gained into the holy place, and communion enjoyed at the blood-sprinkled propitiatory. But by the cross the bitter enmity of the flesh has been condemned, and sin itself judged in the body of Jesus hung up upon the tree.

It is the flesh, and sin in the flesh, that has been judged of God at the cross. That is what the cross teaches: the irreconcilable enmity of the flesh, the implacable evil of fallen nature, has been transferred, judged, and taken away in the Substitute. It is not a question of forgiveness. The irrecoverable and the incorrigible cannot be forgiven. It is a question of condemnation: 'Condemned sin in the flesh', Rom. 8:3. The cross took sinful flesh, and sin itself, out of the way. It was utterly condemned and removed from view by the righteous judgment of God at the cross.

The total depravity and malevolence of the flesh to all that is of God, all that is divine, heavenly, and spiritual, all that is of light, life, and love, is clearly seen in the terrible finality of the judgment upon the Substitute. 'Now is the judgment of this world', and how total that judgment was. The cross took out of the way vicariously under the wrath of God the obnoxious, execrated, and unforgivable fallen nature of the flesh. This is what was typified in the scapegoat led out into the howling wilderness, or in the ashes laid up in a clean place outside the camp.

Both the scapegoat and the ashes depicted the removal under judgment, the taking out of the sight of God and his people, of what was irreconcilable, inconvertible, unforgivable. The question was, How could a people, born of the flesh and dwelling in it, be saved? The divine answer appears in that the flesh was condemned in Another, and condemned to total extinction. 'For what the law could not do, in that it was weak through the flesh, God sending his own Son in the likeness of sinful flesh, and for sin, condemned sin in the flesh.'

Yet this doctrine, which ought to cause men to leap for joy, is offensive to mankind, because it shows the total depravity of human nature towards God. Man justifies the flesh, arguing good and bad in all men, entertaining Pelagian fantasies and Arminian daydreams. The Pelagians suppose that each man in turn is formed in a state of innocence, just as was Adam. The Arminians presume a latent virtue in man, a power in the flesh, sufficient to serve God. Then why the cross, a total condemnation of sin in the flesh? Why, if the state of man in the flesh be not totally reprehensible—or, as it is said, totally depraved—why the cross? That total depravity is what was wholly condemned in the Substitute, in order that sinners might be saved consistent with God's just and righteous judgment.

If one sees the cross aright, one sees how awful is the state of man in the flesh. The cross shows how bad is man's state before God, how rotten, filthy, and utterly corrupt in his sight. There is no staying this corruption: it is total. It is not that there is some latent goodness. Towards God, the state of man is only evil continually. 'Corrupt are they, and have done abominable iniquity: there is none that doeth good. Every one of them is gone back: they are altogether become filthy; there is none that doeth good, no, not one.' It is in this state of total corruption that man has trapped himself, from which there seemed to be no possible deliverance. But God had an answer, and that answer was the cross. How wonderful this is!

Here it is not a question of sins, what men have done, but of sin, inbred sin, the state in which man exists. It is the state of the flesh—sin in the flesh—into which the whole human race was plunged at the fall, passed on by natural generation. 'Behold, I was shapen in iniquity; and in sin did my mother conceive me.' And again, 'By one man's disobedience many were made sinners.' Once more, 'By one man sin entered into the world, and death by sin.' How could the life and soul of lost sinners be delivered from this body of death? The cross, the substitutionary death of the cross, provides the only possible answer.

From this it is clear that there is a distinctive doctrine in respect of the cross. There are things taught about the crucified body exclusive to it, just as this is true of the teaching concerning the blood. Our sins, though borne in his own body on the tree, are not said to be remitted through that crucified body, but through his blood. Our old man, the state of sin in the flesh, is not said to be washed in the blood of the Lamb, although our persons are, but our old man is said to be crucified with him.

Sins are covered, and that by blood. Sin is condemned, and that through the cross. We are washed, but sin is crucified. It is this, the cross, that is, and has been, so neglected in preaching. Where is 'The preaching of the cross'?

161

Crucifixion in itself does not involve shed blood. The blood of Jesus was shed after death at the cross. The shed blood was certainly a witness of death, and what was accomplished in death. But the crucified body itself is a witness, and this witness is recorded in the New Testament epistles by the doctrine of the cross. Quite apart from the blood, it was the body that was crucified. The flesh, vicariously, was hung up to die, in disgrace, under judgment. This is the truth of the cross.

Just as it was a divine work to which the blood gave witness, so the disgraceful shame of the crucified body testified also to the same death of Christ in a way that showed the tremendous breadth of God's work in salvation by Jesus Christ. It is this apostolic doctrine that systematic theology, with its legal and constricting bondage of human wisdom and philosophy, quite misses. This is a system which traps itself in the tradition of the elders and the seeking of human praise and honours, whilst quite failing of the revelation of the Spirit, and the approbation of God.

The spiritual reality is that the blood witnesses to all that was done in the body, whilst the cross witnesses to all that was done to the body. The observation of this truth in the reading of the New Testament opens up the nature of the work of God in the death of Christ. Yet the cross, in the doctrinal sense of it, is what has been left out of the modern gospel, even by those who speak much of the blood. It is the cross that has been neglected, the cross of which the apostle testifies, 'We preach Christ crucified, unto the Jews a stumblingblock, and unto the Greeks foolishness.'

There is that which was wrought in the death of Christ which is particularly revealed and taught by the blood, as it is written and set forth in the New Testament scriptures. Equally, in those doctrinal passages which speak of the crucifixion of the body, and of the body of sin being destroyed in the vicarious Substitute, there is that teaching which is unique to those scriptures which declare the truth of the cross.

The death was one. The Person was one. But to expound the fulness of that work wrought in death, a death seen typically in the sacrifices under the Old Testament, required that the body and the blood respectively set forth the whole truth of what was accomplished at Golgotha. There is that which was wrought of God in the body of Jesus as such, declared in the truth about the cross in the doctrine. And there is that which was effected of God through the blood of Jesus itself, made known in the truth about that blood in the New Testament epistles.

It is only by the teaching of the Spirit through the apostolic doctrine, in which things that differ are carefully distinguished, that the people of God are enabled to see into the revealed depths, and view the profound realities of the wonderful death of Jesus.

The length, the breadth, the depth, the divinity, the spirituality, the finality, and all the riches of that death were taken by the Holy Ghost and revealed to the apostles according to promise. He who is led by the Spirit, who is humbled to learn from those apostles, who is in meek submission to the holy scripture and its divine order, he it is to whom these mysteries are revealed.

The apostle teaches us that we are made nigh by the blood of Christ, and reconciled in one body by the cross. The questions arise, What was it that was wrought in the death of Christ for the people of God? What was accomplished for the saints by that body hung up upon the cross? What was it that was effected by the blood of Christ shed by the spear-thrust after he had died? The blood testifies to all that was done in the body: the cross to all that was done to the body. But it is the cross and the crucifixion that are so often left out of what passes for the gospel. What modern evangelism presents is a Jesus without a gospel. They have no preaching, no doctrine. Preaching has fallen in the streets. But there is no salvation without preaching. 'It pleased God by the foolishness of preaching to save them that believe', I Cor. 1:21.

The crucified body of Jesus was a spectacle of shame. It is shameful, a disgrace, that his body was hung up upon the tree. His crucified, naked, humiliated and scourged body was a spectacle of shame. Yet, he despised the shame. Nevertheless it is true that he was hung up to die in disgrace. The flesh was hung up. The cross respects that flesh: in the counsel of God it was hung up in dishonour. The body was transfixed by nails, elevated in shame, and left to die, that this might show forth the judgment of God on the one that hung accursed upon the tree.

Why? Because there is that in the bodies of his people which stood in the way of their redemption. The crucified body of Jesus removed this for ever from the sight of a holy God. Without such a work as this, that is, the judgment of sin in the flesh, the body of sin would effectively have prevented redemption, no matter what else was done to save the people. The body of sin itself was so obnoxious to the wrath of God, that, unless it were utterly removed from the sight of God in judgment, and the sinner justly seen as delivered and separated from it, none could be saved. But it was utterly removed in judgment. This is manifest in that the body of the Substitute was hung up in ignominy and shame.

There are eighty-six references to the cross in the New Testament, and six different words in the Greek from which these are translated. Of the six Greek words, four belong to the *stauroō, σταυρόω,* group, two of them being the verb and noun form respectively, and the other two being compound words. The verb occurs forty-six times and the noun twenty-eight. The two compounds are both adapted from the verb form *stauroō*, one being used five times, the other once.

Another word altogether, used only once in this connection, is the Greek word meaning 'to fix unto', translated 'crucified' because it refers to the fixing of the body of Jesus to the cross. Again, five times the Greek word for 'tree' is used, as, for example, with the text 'Whom ye slew, and hanged on a tree.'

The main word, *stauros*, means, An upright pole or stake, a pile which serves in a foundation, an instrument of crucifixion, or a pole which impales a corpse. This is the word chiefly used for the cross, about which the facts are in the four evangelists, and the doctrine in the New Testament epistles.

Resting upon the foundation of the cross, the apostolic doctrine of the gospel stands for ever sure. Justification by faith, embracing the doctrine of ransom, remission, forgiveness, reconciliation, substitution, propitiation, expiation, and atonement, appears as the sum of all the parts relating to his death, being firmly established upon the one foundation of Jesus Christ and him crucified.

Sanctification, the work of the Spirit, anointing, baptism, quickening, renewing, filling, washing, regenerating and sealing, all rest upon the death, shed blood, and broken body of the Lord Jesus. Take away the cross, and the foundation of the work of the Holy Ghost is removed at a stroke, everything being thrown into confusion, darkness, and uncertainty.

Redemption likewise is founded on the cross. Without that foundation there can be no church, no bride, no Zion, no kingdom, no heavenly country, no city, and no world to come. The cross is that upon which rests the hope, the inheritance, the resurrection and the glory.

The cross takes away, in the judgment of God, what otherwise made all these things, justification, sanctification, redemption and the glory, utterly impossible to realise. Take away the cross, and you take away everything of worth, with God or man, in heaven and upon earth, for time and eternity.

Of the eighty-six references to the cross, some occur when Jesus prophesied of his own crucifixion. 'Behold, we go up to Jerusalem; and the Son of man shall be betrayed unto the chief priests and unto the scribes, and they shall condemn him to death, and shall deliver him to the Gentiles to mock, and to scourge, and to crucify him', Mt. 20:18-19. Again, 'The Son of man is betrayed to be crucified', Mt. 26:2.

Other places speak of the crucifixion before it took place. 'Let him be crucified', Mt. 27:22. 'He delivered him to be crucified', Mt. 27:26. 'They led him away to crucify him', Mt. 27:31.

Next there are references to the event itself. 'And they crucified him', Mt. 27:35. 'And it was the third hour, and they crucified him', Mk. 15:25. 'The place where Jesus was crucified was nigh to the city', Jn. 19:20. 'The soldiers, when they had crucified Jesus, took his garments', Jn. 19:23. 'Then were there two thieves crucified with him', Mt. 27:38.

Again, certain texts tell of the crucifixion having been accomplished. 'I know that ye seek Jesus, which was crucified', Mt. 28:5. 'Ye seek Jesus of Nazareth, which was crucified', Mk. 16:6. 'The chief priests and our rulers delivered him to be condemned to death, and have crucified him', Lk. 24:20. 'Now in the place where he was crucified there was a garden', Jn. 19:41. 'Him ye have taken, and by wicked hands have crucified and slain', Acts 2:23. 'God hath made that same Jesus, whom ye have crucified, both Lord and Christ', Acts 2:36.

Then there are passages which refer to the actual stake upon which Jesus was hung up to be crucified. This is, of course, the noun form of the same word. 'Pilate wrote a title, and put it on the cross', Jn. 19:19. 'If thou be the Son of God, come down from the cross', Mt. 27:40. 'Now there stood by the cross of Jesus his mother', Jn. 19:25. 'Whom they slew and hanged on a tree', Acts 10:39. 'He became obedient unto death, even the death of the cross', Phil. 2:8. 'He endured the cross, despising the shame', Heb. 12:2. 'The God of our fathers hath raised up Jesus, whom ye slew and hanged on a tree', Acts 5:30.

All these occurrences, whether of Jesus foretelling the crucifixion, or of others speaking of the crucifixion before the event, or of the crucifixion itself, or of its having been accomplished, or else of the stake on which he was crucified, all these texts, I say, summarise the crucifixion itself, as such, and speak of it as a fact. It is the actual cross itself, or else Jesus' being crucified upon it, to which these passages refer.

Further to the various places which speak of the crucifixion itself, however, there appears a group of twenty-one texts which refer to the cross in a doctrinal way. These passages reveal what could never be known or deduced from the facts of the cross and crucifixion recorded in the gospels. These are texts that set forth the revelation given by the Holy Ghost to the apostles concerning the divine realities which were hidden from the eye of man at Golgotha. After the ascension, with the coming of the Holy Ghost, these things were revealed spiritually to the apostles, and written down by them in the scriptures of the New Testament.

All twenty-one doctrinal passages in the epistles properly constitute the mystery of the gospel concerning the cross, confided to the holy apostles by the revelation of the Holy Ghost sent down from heaven. It was impossible even for them, though they had witnessed the crucifixion, and had heard the words from the cross, to have known the invisible divine work then taking place, simply from what they had witnessed and heard when Jesus was crucified. All the doctrinal texts on the cross pertain to revelation and mystery, things utterly outside the realm of the senses, the powers of deduction, or the wisdom of man.

It is in these epistles therefore that the doctrine of the cross, properly so-called, must be discovered and understood. Here the apostles experienced what the Lord Jesus prophesied about the coming of the Holy Ghost, and the revelation of the gospel, 'When he, the Spirit of truth, is come, he will guide you into all truth.' For it is certain that though they witnessed the cross, saw the crucifixion, meticulously recording both words and events, yet of themselves they could perceive nothing at all of the truth that lay behind what they saw and heard.

The spiritual reality of the cross stands in what passed between the Father and the Son. The doctrine reveals the mystery of the sacrificial Substitute who by the eternal Spirit offered himself up without spot unto God. To the apostles it was given to receive the revelation of what was heavenly, spiritual, and divine, that lay behind the earthly, visible, and human. This they set forth in the twenty-one doctrinal texts in the epistles. And this is the doctrine of the cross.

This doctrine, then, came not by observation at the event, but by revelation after the event. The revelation manifested the unseen and invisible mysteries of the cross. It was communicated immediately and infallibly by the Holy Ghost to the spiritual consciousness of those chosen disciples to whom Jesus had prophesied of these things. Speaking of the Spirit of truth, Jesus taught the men whom he had called to be the vessels of this heavenly treasure, 'He shall glorify me', that is, after the ascension, 'for he shall receive of mine'—first and foremost of that which was wrought at the cross—'and shall show it unto you.'

That, in particular, which was 'shown' by the Spirit of truth to the apostles, inwardly and spiritually, when he descended to abide within them, is called The doctrine of the cross. Set forth in twenty-one passages in the apostolic writings, this doctrine could never otherwise have been known. It is saving doctrine: that without which one could never be saved. 'For the preaching of the cross is to them that perish foolishness; but unto us which are saved it is the power of God.'

The first reference from the group of passages which declares this doctrine is that in Romans 6:6, 'Knowing this, that our old man is crucified with him.' 'Knowing this', says Paul the Apostle, but how did they know it? By 'the preaching of the cross', I Cor. 1:18. That is, such was the preaching of the cross, that the believers knew, knew by faith, and knew experimentally, that their old man was crucified with him. Such spiritual knowledge preached to modern churches and religious groups today would be greeted with a mixture of scorn, derision and incredulity. Nevertheless, this is the knowledge that saves.

This was the knowledge that was received by all the faithful brethren at Rome, who obeyed from the heart the form of doctrine delivered unto them. They knew by the preaching of the cross the invisible realities that took place at the crucifixion, the hidden mystery of the divine transaction between the Father and the Son. And they knew it by the apostolic doctrine of the gospel. They knew that their 'old man was crucified with him, that the body of sin might be destroyed.' But who could know that except by the doctrine of the cross, by which the revelation of the mystery was made known at the beginning through preaching?

The apostles did not preach the gospel with the wisdom of words, I Cor. 1:17. That is, not with the wisdom which pertained to the outward and visible, the seen and heard, which corresponded with the five senses and the natural intelligence, even though these faculties could comprehend the outward events of the crucifixion. What would have happened had they preached the gospel with the wisdom of words? The cross would have been nullified. 'Not with wisdom of words, lest the cross of Christ should be made of none effect.' They preached the revelation, that is, the doctrine of the cross.

The apostles spake the wisdom of God in a mystery, 'Even the hidden wisdom', I Cor. 2:7. Had the princes of this world known the spiritual reality of the crucifixion, and, if it could have been discovered by outward observation, natural senses, and worldly wisdom, they would certainly have known it, 'They would not have crucified the Lord of glory.' But they did crucify the Lord of glory. Then, natural senses, outward observation, earthly wisdom, avail nothing at all when it comes to the revelation of the mystery in the doctrine of the cross.

Who could know it? Who could know in the heart, by the Spirit, experimentally, that which Paul expressed in Gal. 2:20, 'I am crucified with Christ'? Who could say, with him, 'The cross of our Lord Jesus Christ, by whom the world is crucified unto me, and I unto it'? No one could say this, save he that had received the doctrine of the cross.

How spiritual this doctrine appears, and how necessary it is that the preaching of the cross should flourish once more, the mystery being opened and expounded by those sent of God through our Lord Jesus Christ, filled with the Holy Ghost from heaven. Then believers would no longer be terrified, but rather comforted, by such doctrine as this: 'They that are Christ's have crucified the flesh with the affections and lusts', Gal. 5:24. Then the people of God would walk in the comfort of the Holy Ghost, in communion with Christ, who died for

all the seed, whether Jew or Gentile, that 'He might reconcile both unto God in one body by the cross', Eph. 2:16.
Since this is saving truth, why do we not hear it constantly
expounded?

Another example of the doctrine concerns the 'handwriting
of ordinances' which Christ took, 'nailing it to his cross'. But,
outwardly and visibly, Christ took no such thing at the
crucifixion, much less did he nail handwriting to the cross.
Nevertheless, the apostle says he did, and hence the meaning
must be both spiritual and doctrinal, and the burden is upon
those who profess to be Christ's ministers, who should be
preachers of the cross, continually and consistently to give us
the meaning. 'How shall they hear without a preacher? And
how shall they preach, except they be sent?'

Again, Heb. 6:6 speaks of those who 'Crucify to themselves
the Son of God afresh.' How can they do this? Not literally,
but doctrinally. Then, who, today, does this doctrinally?
And who, today, leads others to do so, beguiling them with
fair speeches? Let this be discerned, and the whole religious
edifice will tremble, if not crumble.

A final example of the twenty-one texts that make up the
group concerning the doctrine of the cross may be found in
Rev. 11:8. 'Their dead bodies', that is, the dead bodies of the
persecuted ministers of the word of the cross, 'shall lie in the
street of that great city, which spiritually is called Sodom and
Egypt, where also our Lord was crucified.' But our Lord was
crucified at Jerusalem. Yet John says, he was crucified at
Sodom, Egypt, and that great city. Then where was it? The
meaning is spiritual, it is a question of the doctrine of the
cross. When that is understood, all these mysteries will
instantly become clear.

XI

The Cross and the Body of Sin

IN the epistles the cross does not mean simply the wooden
stake, as it does in the gospels, nor is the crucifixion limited
to the outward event which the evangelists describe. There is
much more to it than that. Inherent also are the invisible
realities lying behind both the cross and the crucifixion,
accomplished by God for his people. These spiritual, immaterial and intangible verities, that passed between the
Father and the Son, things that belong to another dimen-
sion, are revealed by the words 'cross' and 'crucify', used
doctrinally in the epistles.

The doctrine of the cross reveals the meaning of Jesus'
crucified body. This revelation is distinctive, and brings to
light truths nowhere else taught. Much is taught about the
death of Jesus through the apostolic teaching on the blood,
but that is not the same thing. The blood speaks of what was
accomplished in his body, but the cross reveals what was
done to that body.

Before his people could be saved, there was that which
God, consistent with the divine nature, required to be judged
according to the strict judgment of his own righteousness.
That righteous judgment was fulfilled in the vicarious sufferings of Christ. Accepting the sacrifice of the body of Jesus
in the place of his people, the righteous judgment of God
demanded and obtained the condemnation of the flesh in the
crucified Substitute.

Not only was this accomplished, but it was seen to have been accomplished in the flesh of him whose body was hung up to die in ignominy and shame. The real truth about the shocking disgrace, the shameful humiliation of the cross, comes to light in the doctrine set forth in the apostolic epistles of the New Testament.

The opening up of this divine teaching first appears in Romans 6:6. 'Knowing this, that our old man is crucified with him, that the body of sin might be destroyed, that henceforth we should not serve sin.' In the earlier part of the epistle the apostle declares the revelation of God's wrath from heaven against ungodly men. For sinners burdened with the guilt of their sins there was a propitiatory, an appeasement, 'Through faith in his blood', Rom. 3:25. As to the dreadful sentence of condemnation passed upon the sinner, there was an acquittal, and more than an acquittal, 'Being now justified by his blood', Rom. 5:9, in which God justifies the ungodly through faith.

After this comes the question of sin itself. The fall of Adam and its consequences occupy the apostle's attention from chapter five and verse twelve. Sin in the flesh, the state of man in the fall, not what man does, but what he is, appears. Man is born in sin, that which is born of the flesh is flesh, the fallen race being seen in a state of corruption and enmity, under bondage to sin and death. Here the cross comes in. It is a question of crucifixion. Not of forgiveness by the blood, but of condemnation through the cross. The body of sin must be destroyed before wrath can be appeased. That is, the 'old man', begotten by and in Adam, must be condemned, judged, and put away in the Substitute, and the value of that substitution put to the account of the people of God or ever they can have to do with a holy God.

And that is what has happened, it is what the doctrine of the cross declares: 'Our old man is crucified with him, that the body of sin might be destroyed.' God can have to do with a people in Christ, because they are no longer considered to be in the flesh. The 'old man' was transferred to and condemned in another. It is a question of the place and standing that is theirs, of what has been gained for them by the Saviour, so that they are seen in the good of it: all that he gained is to their account. It is reckoned to them.

This is the position of which the Apostle Paul speaks in Romans 6:6, when he says, 'Knowing this'. This was what they knew, what he had taught, and what they believed. 'Our old man is crucified with him.' This refers to the truth of reconciliation in Rom. 5:12-21. There, two men are seen, one Adam, and the other Christ. The correct meaning of the Greek word translated 'reconciliation' appears not in the effect of the substitutionary atonement—which the English word describes—but in the cause, that is, the thorough exchange of places between Christ and his people. Not in the consequence of the action of substitutionary atonement, but in the action itself. Hence the accurate translation of the word rendered 'reconciliation' is 'substitutionary exchange'.

This exchange was wrought in relation to two men, Adam and Christ. The saints were born in the first man, Adam, but an exchange has been effected, an exchange that justice required should be substitutionary, an exchange by sacrifice, in which Christ took our place so that 'our old man is crucified with him.' That took us out of the old man, Adam, consistent with justice and judgment, according to the righteousness of God. There was only one way out, and that way was death. The riches of God's grace stand in this: It was not we that died, to be shut up to a black eternity, but Christ who died for us, opening up the prospect of everlasting glory.

This exchange is so thorough, in that if Christ took our place, and took it completely, then he also gives to us his place, and gives it to us wholly. What a contrast exists between the old man and the new! Here are two men, Adam and Christ, each seen as begetting a seed after himself, one carnally and the other spiritually, for, 'The first man is of the earth, earthy: the second man is the Lord from heaven.' 'The first man Adam was made'—mark that, he was made—'a living soul.' Yes, but, 'the last Adam is'—observe, he is—'a quickening Spirit.' As the Father hath life in himself, so hath he given to the Son to have life in himself. And by this life the Son shall surely quicken every last one of those for whom he died in that sacrificial exchange upon the cross.

What a difference between what is in Adam, and what is in Christ, between the old and the new! Flowing down from the ignominious earthly fountain-head of the old man, Adam, proceeds the foul stream of inbred sin, and upon this has been passed the judgment of God, death. Flowing down from the glorious heavenly ascension of the new man, Christ, is the free gift of justifying righteousness, and God's judgment upon the worth of that righteousness, everlasting life. Sin and death are in Adam, but righteousness and life are in Christ. The law and works are in the old man of this present world, but grace and faith are in the new man of the world to come.

Everything is in contrast. To Adam belongs the oldness of the letter, a killing ministry, the sentence of condemnation, and that which waxeth old, ready to pass away in dissolution and death. In Christ appears the newness of the Spirit, a life-giving ministry, the sentence of justification, and a new heavens and earth wherein dwelleth righteousness world without end, Amen.

In the present world, to which pertains the old man, there is the old law of Moses, the old garment, the old wine, old bottles, an Old Testament, a decayed covenant, old traditions, the old religion, and an old creation. In the world to come, of which Christ is the heir, there is the glorious gospel of the blessed God, the new garment, the new wine, new bottles, the New Testament, an everlasting covenant, the word of God, true religion, and a new creation.

To the first belongs darkness, despair, hopelessness, an accusing conscience, self-justification, self-righteousness, hypocrisy, bondage, fear, the tormenting of Satan, and a certain fearful looking for of judgment. To the last pertains light, life, love, hope, peace with God through our Lord Jesus Christ, the accounting of the righteousness of God through the faith of Jesus Christ, a broken and a contrite spirit, self-judgment, honesty, liberty, boldness in the faith, the overcoming of Satan by the blood of the Lamb and the word of our testimony, and a settled inheritance of everlasting glory.

What an exchange! And an exchange dependant upon substitutionary sacrifice: it was this that brought in the reconciliation, the 'thorough exchange' of one place for another in the Substitute. That, saith the apostle, is what we know. 'Knowing this', Rom. 6:6.

'Our old man is crucified with him.' Paul sees not only Jesus, but with him, 'our old man' upon the cross. He gives the underlying cause of this extraordinary vision: 'That the body of sin might be destroyed.' Paul sees the old man, the body of sin, in Jesus' crucifixion. Here is doctrine with a witness.

This is not a question of seeing the blood. John saw the blood. 'One of the soldiers with a spear pierced his side, and forthwith came there out blood and water.' John saw that. 'He that saw it bare record, and his record is true.' Paul received that, and preached it, but it is not what he is preaching here. Here he saw, merging with the body of Jesus, a crucified old man. 'Our old man is crucified with him, that the body of sin might be destroyed.' Paul saw, in vision, by

176

revelation, a crucified body. And not the body that was there literally in the crucifixion, but that which was there as a result of the work of God.

When the sacrifice for sin was made in the Old Testament, the blood was taken into the holy place, but the carcase was taken outside the camp. That is the crucifixion that Paul saw: The carcase outside the camp. 'The bodies of those beasts, whose blood is brought into the sanctuary by the high priest for sin, are burned without the camp. Wherefore Jesus also, that he might sanctify the people with his own blood, suffered without the gate.' His blood was taken in and sprinkled, but his body was crucified without the gate in a way typified by those beasts whose carcases were burned without the camp.

This consumption by fire of the body of the substitutionary sacrifice, the blood of which had been brought before the presence of God and sprinkled, shows that there was that which could not come before God, which must be burned up and condemned. This is what Paul the Apostle calls 'The body of sin', or 'Our old man'. It is the flesh, or man in the flesh, and we know that 'flesh and blood cannot inherit the kingdom of God.'

The crucifixion shows the utterly obnoxious state of man in the flesh. Fallen man, the old man, is given up of God, in the condition in which he stands by natural birth. He is 'born in sin', and 'conceived in iniquity'. He is 'estranged from the womb', before birth, in his very conception from the corrupt and sinful seed of Adam. He 'goes astray as soon as he is born, speaking lies.' Full of iniquity, children of wrath, sons of disobedience—wrath and disobedience having fathered and mothered the fallen race—it is no surprise to hear the withering truth that 'Ye are of your father the devil, and the lusts of your father ye will do.'

'Wherefore God gave them up' to the lusts of their own hearts, to a reprobate mind, and to vile affections. Fallen man is said to be 'Filled with all unrighteousness', and nothing else. He is totally depraved. The works of the devil, such as denying the word of God, misrepresenting the truth of God, persecuting the servants of God, and hating the people of God, these works fallen man will do, and must do. 'They are all gone out of the way, they are together become unprofitable; there is none that doeth good, no, not one.' There is no fear of God before their eyes.

Then what passes by natural generation, and what fills the body, of such a race as this? Sin, and nothing but sin. 'I know that in me, that is, in my flesh, dwelleth no good thing', saith Paul, confessing himself by nature, for all his religion, 'Carnal, sold under sin'. As to the body, he says, 'Who shall deliver me from the body of this death?' It is full of seething, inbred corruption, wholly objectionable to God's righteousness, and offensive in the sight of him who is of purer eyes than to behold iniquity.

Such is the blindness of man in the fall, that man is wilfully ignorant of his state, the world itself being a system built up to hide the truth of the fall and the fact of eternity. Man is, himself, said to be 'darkness' because of this, walking in an obscurity described as 'The vanity of the mind, having the understanding darkened, being alienated from the life of God through ignorance because of the blindness of the heart.' This deceitful state is called 'Being alive without the law once.'

When the commandment comes however, that is, by the Holy Ghost from heaven, with quickening and awakening power, how soon the sinner realises his condition. He cries, 'O LORD, rebuke me not in thine anger, neither chasten me in thy hot displeasure.' God's arrows of conviction stick fast in him, and his hand presseth him sore. There is no soundness in his flesh—there never was any soundness, but before he was blind to it, now he realises it, and ascribes his awakening to this—'Because of thine anger'. 'My wounds stink and are corrupt, my loins are filled with a loathsome disease: and there is no soundness in my flesh.' This is the conviction that can only come from God's awakening a man to his true state.

How can that state be forgiven? It cannot. How can it be improved? It cannot. The sinner can be forgiven, the state of sin in the flesh cannot. The old man cannot be improved, the old man is incorrigible: 'given up'. Nevertheless, a vast multitude, whom no man can number, are found in a new man altogether, who delivered them from that wherein they were held. How? Through the 'reconciliation', the sacrificial exchange of places, in which he took upon himself all their state and place in the old man. 'Our old man is crucified with him.'

This is not the forgiveness of the old man, it is his condemnation. He is crucified, 'burned without the camp.' Christ was 'made sin for us', made it, that he might bear its judgment in his body, taking it out of the way. When the work was finished, and the fire of God's everlasting wrath was assuaged, the object of execration was reduced to ashes, the body of sin was destroyed, and judgment was fully satisfied.

The body of sin is that which passed from Adam by natural generation from the fall. That is the consequence of man's fall in Adam, the consequence of headship. But now another head appears, a second man, the last Adam, head of another order of manhood altogether, of another realm, a new creation. To deliver his people from under the fallen head, the old man, from the body of sin, from the whole realm of the first man, of sin, death, the present world, the present age, Christ took their place by the exchange of places, called the reconciliation.

In the place of judgment, sin was condemned in the flesh, in Christ. Sin was not pardoned, it was condemned. 'Condemned in the flesh.' But the sinner was pardoned. The flesh being seen as condemned, the old man judged, the body of sin destroyed, in the eye of God's righteous judgment none for whom Christ died could ever again be perceived outside of that crucifixion, outside of that condemnation, outside of that destruction. In the sight of God, it was their crucifixion. 'I am crucified with Christ.' 'But ye are not in the flesh.' 'For ye are dead.' 'Dead with Christ.'

That is the position of the saints: the body of sin condemned already, awaiting the body of glory. Meanwhile, the crucified body of the believer's Substitute is that in which he is viewed by the eye of divine justice, and, because of the verity of the reconciliation, this is no more than just. 'For he that is dead is freed—justified—from sin.'

This is not the truth of Christ dying for the believer, but of the believer having died with Christ. It is not only Christ in the believer's place, but the believer in Christ's place when he died, 'planted in the likeness of his death.' This is dying with Christ when he died. Then, our old man was crucified with him.

This freely justifies us from the body of sin and death. This brings in the life of faith whilst yet in the world and what Paul calls our 'vile body'. And this lays the foundation of the hope of the resurrection, the redemption of the purchased possession, and the assumption of the body of glory. Then, at his coming, the work done on the cross will be consummated. It was effected, it is accounted, but it must be consummated. And it shall be, by him who 'shall change our vile body, that it may be fashioned like unto his glorious body.'

The disciples change places with Christ in the resurrection, just as before Christ changed places with the disciples in the crucifixion. This is the work of God. The fall had been judged, and sin condemned in the flesh. In another man of righteousness and life, brethren are justified from all things from which they could not be justified by the law of Moses.

Delivered by substitution, taken out of the old man Adam, from under the law, yes, and from under the law of sin and death, the saints stand justified by faith under the headship and in the realm of the Lord Jesus Christ.

This is the consequence of the truth that 'our old man is crucified with him.' Under Adam, chained, bound, and helpless in the fall, we were 'without strength'. Dead in trespasses and sins, without life, there was found no power to perform even the least act of desperate self-preservation. How wonderful then appears the love of the Saviour, pitying us in our deep distress, taking our condition upon himself, and dying for us, taking us in himself through death and out on the other side. 'Crucified with Christ.' Christ changed places with his own in the place of judgment, taking away all that which stood between God and the people. Being made sin, destroying the body of sin, bearing the judgment against it, he completely satisfied divine righteousness in respect of those for whom he died.

Thus the body of sin is destroyed. Not destroyed in us, but for us. Destroyed, that is, in him who died in our place, that we, dying with him in the counsel of God, might be seen as dead, and, by faith, might reckon ourselves dead indeed unto sin. So that the present effect of our old man having been crucified with him, is that the body of sin might be 'annulled', rendered 'of none effect', no longer possessed of the power of destruction that would have brought us to ruin. It is 'of none effect', καταργέω, *katargeō*, 'made void'. That is what has been brought in by the cross to the good of all the people of God.

The same doctrine is taught and applied in Ephesians 2:15, 'having abolished in his flesh the enmity.' The enmity is not forgiven, it is not changed, it is 'abolished', *katargeō*. How was it abolished, or destroyed? 'In his flesh.' That is, by his taking the place of his people in the substitutionary exchange, the reconciliation, when he was made sin, the very root of the enmity, that sin might be condemned in the flesh. Then all was judged and put away, yet the sinner himself distinguished from that which was judged, so that he himself might be brought nigh in Christ.

This work was wrought both for Jew and Gentile, for all the spiritual seed of Abraham, though by nature these were at enmity one against the other in the flesh. What enmity was this? The flesh at irreconcilable enmity with God, and Jew and Gentile in the flesh relentlessly at enmity one with another. But God in the place of judgment laid all upon Christ, made him to be sin, made over to him the body of sin in the flesh, and condemned it utterly in the sacrifice thus offered up. In this way sin was judged, abolished, and destroyed in the Substitute, once and for all, on behalf of all the elect. They are therefore henceforth not in the flesh: death has taken them out, to live in Another raised from the dead by the glory of the Father.

As to their old nature, that is, what they were in the flesh with its ancient enmity towards God and between each other, Christ died that 'he might reconcile both unto God in one body by the cross, having slain the enmity thereby.' The old enmity in Adam, the ancient enmity by the law, all was crucified. They themselves were dead, crucified with Christ. But Christ being raised from the dead, glorified by the Father, henceforward would show forth his headship and spiritual power to quicken and bring in a new order of sonship, a new manhood, destined for the world to come. 'For ye are dead, and your life is hid with Christ in God.'

How alienated we were: 'And you, that were sometime alienated and enemies in your mind by wicked works, yet now hath he reconciled', Col. 1:21. And what a reconciliation, so thoroughly to take our place, as it stood in Adam, under the man of sin and death, the head of fallen manhood, the spring of corruption, iniquity and inbred pollution. To take our place so thoroughly, I say, that he might not only bear the judgment of all that we had done, but bear to judgment all the state that we were in, bringing in forgiveness for the one and condemnation for the other, setting us wholly free in himself.

And not only so, but, having cleared and put away everything that was against us before the righteousness of God, now raised from the dead and reigning in glory, he constitutes us as his body, under his head, giving us his place. 'And ye are complete in him, which is the head.'

What of all the flesh, that clung even to our very soul, in which we were inextricably and inescapably trapped? He released us. How? First, by taking that flesh upon himself, really in our place and in our state at the altar of God. Next, by removing the body of sin in the flesh with the circumcising knife of God's judgments, separating, cutting it away, so as to cast it off for ever in the place of condemnation. 'In whom also ye are circumcised.' Not circumcised in yourselves in your life, but in him in his death. Not the circumcision of a piece of flesh, the foreskin, but of the whole body of the flesh in which we dwelt, a body of sinful flesh which was fused with our inmost life in an inextricable union.

But Christ separated the two, condemning the body of sin, and releasing the pardoned sinner, when he died, making the good of that death over to those on whose behalf he was crucified. This separation, wrought by the circumcising knife of God, is called the 'Circumcision made without hands', Col. 2:11. That is, made without man's hands, though wrought by the hand of God. 'The circumcision made without hands, in putting off the body of the sin of the flesh'—it is not sins, in the original, but sin, or, it may be, body of the flesh—'by the circumcision of Christ', Col. 2:11.

'Circumcision of Christ'? Not that performed outwardly in his infancy, to the Jewish child, taking away the foreskin. But that performed in his agony, in his substitution, when there had been transferred to him the body of the flesh, the old man, the body of sin, so that he was 'made sin', really in the place of sin by substitutionary sacrifice.

'Without hands'? Not man's handling a knife, nor the cutting away of a loose fold of flesh, but the invisible hand of God, the power of the operation of God, in taking away the whole body of the flesh in judgment.

At the cross the edge of the sword, the sword of the Lord, the flaming sword of divine justice, turned every way of vengeance upon the sacrificial offering of the Substitute. This thoroughly removed for ever the whole body of sin and death on behalf of all his people so as to put away that condemned body once and for all.

As with the scapegoat, so this work of God consigned the judged body of sin into the place of everlasting forgetfulness and destruction, never to be seen again, world without end, Amen.

XII

The Cross and the Carnal Mind

THE stake, or cross, was the instrument of crucifixion. It was upon the cross that the mystery of the exchange of places between Christ and his people took place. Because it was wrought of God, this work could only be known through revelation, it was unseen by the eye of man. In the death of Christ God's people were made nigh by the blood of Christ, whilst the body of sin was taken afar off, being condemned by the righteous judgment of God.

The crucifixion was foreshadowed by the sin offering, in which the blood was sprinkled seven times before the LORD, before the veil of the sanctuary, to show the acceptance of the people in the blood of atonement. The body, however, was burned outside the camp, demonstrating the judgment of God against sin in the flesh, borne away in the carcase of the substitutionary sacrifice.

In the death of Christ, we who were born of and in the flesh, the irreconcilable enmity of which was so utterly offensive to God, were made nigh by the blood of Christ. As to that sinful flesh, and sin in the flesh, it was condemned in his body on the tree. Our old man was crucified with him, even as sin was condemned in the Substitute. Because this work was wrought on behalf of the people for whom Christ died, it follows of course that what happened to him is counted as having happened to them. If the exchange was effective in the Substitute

185

on the cross, and it was, then it must be reckoned effective also in them on whose behalf it was made.

The bread and wine in the supper, which shows forth the Lord's death, illustrate the same thing. The death of Christ—bringing in for the people of God so great and manifold a deliverance—is set forth distinctly in the bread and cup. 'And as they were eating', that is, eating the flesh of the passover lamb, the blood of which was sprinkled upon the door posts and the lintel, 'Jesus took bread, and blessed it, and brake it, and gave it to the disciples, and said, Take, eat; this is my body. And he took the cup, and gave thanks, and gave it to them, saying, Drink ye all of it; for this is my blood of the New Testament, which is shed for many for the remission of sins.' Mt. 26:26-28.

Jesus, having eaten of the passover in that place the entrance to which was overshadowed by and surrounded with the blood of the lamb, next instituted the Lord's supper, which would show forth his own death by the breaking of bread and partaking of the cup. Just as the passover was a sacrifice that anticipated his death, so the supper is an ordinance which remembers it. And just as the flesh and blood of the lamb distinctively illustrate the extent of the sacrifice, so the bread and cup separately show the full measure of the death of Christ, reaching to God and man, sin and sins, the sentence of the law and the righteousness of God, the bringing near of a people and the taking away of the offence.

It is from the body of sin, by natural generation, that the corruption of the fall of Adam pollutes the whole race. But God has reserved for his people a body of glory for the world to come, by the resurrection, through Christ the firstbegotten from the dead, in whom righteousness and life are secured to all the seed. This same Jesus, raised from the dead, ascended to glory, proclaimed both Lord and Christ, has been made the head, the second man, the last Adam, from whom another race, a new creation after the order of sonship, shall be quick-ened into being out of the corruption and fall of the old man.

'As is the earthy, such are they also that are earthy.' Here is seen the likeness of the first, or old, man, of this present world, standing under condemnation and judgment. 'And as is the heavenly, such are they also that are heavenly.' Thus appears the likeness of the second, or new, man, the Lord from heaven, the quickening spirit, heir of the world to come, standing in righteousness and life. Of those whom he quickens the apostle saith, 'As we have borne the image of the earthy, we shall also bear the image of the heavenly.' When? 'Christ the firstfruits', afterwards, 'they that are Christ's at his coming.'

But by what means shall they that shall bear the image of the heavenly—who are of the new man, who are already quickened within—by what means shall they be delivered from the condemned 'old man', the outcast 'body of sin'? By the body of Jesus. 'This is my body.' At the cross his sinless, impeccable body was made sin, so that sin might be con-demned in the flesh, that it might be thoroughly, utterly taken away, by no less a judgment than that of the righteous-ness of God. Here is the deliverance. 'Except ye eat the flesh of the Son of man, and drink his blood, ye have no life in you.' Well may he, who suffered in the flesh, say to his own, 'Take, eat; this is my body.'

In the first Epistle to the Corinthians, the first chapter, the Apostle Paul brings home and applies the truth of the cross. It is not that it is different teaching from that given in the Epistle to the Romans concerning the body of sin, but it is a particular application of that teaching. Here he takes the general truth that 'our old man is crucified with him', and applies it precisely to the state of mind of those at Corinth. It is not a new truth further to Romans 6:6, but a distinct use of that truth in relation to the Corinthian mentality.

Unlike the Epistle to the Romans, which is purely didactic, the Epistle to the Corinthians is also corrective. Certain things had come into the church, which must be corrected by the apostolic doctrine. It is not a question of correction by exhortation, or admonition. Rather, the premise of the exhortation, the ground of admonition, must be laid down: it is a question of doctrine. Paul first postulates the doctrine, on the basis of which he then exhorts and admonishes. That is the apostolic method: the truth concerning Christ comes first.

To expose what had come in at Corinth, the apostle reveals the spiritual wickedness of being carnally minded. Because 'the carnal mind is enmity against God.' It fulfils 'the desires of the flesh and of the mind.' Therefore, 'to be carnally minded is death.' It was true that once they had been 'enemies in their minds by wicked works', but now they knew that in Christ the 'body of sin' had been crucified, and if so, the head had been judged, the old mentality, the carnal mind, condemned on their behalf in their Substitute. So objectionable to God was this 'mind of the flesh', and the 'minding of earthly things', that, in order to save them from judgment, it had been crucified in Another. And will they now return to that which had been judged and put away on their behalf?

Yes, they will, and that return to what they had once judged and put away became the occasion of this epistle. The apostle could not speak unto them as spiritual, but as carnal, as those who had fallen, who with the mind served the law of sin, and walked again in the vanity of their mind, and worse, for now it was mixed with the profession of the gospel of God. But to be carnally minded was death, no matter how high the Christian profession, and solemn warnings attend the epistle. Rather, they should be transformed by the renewing of their minds, having their hearts and minds kept by the peace of God through Christ Jesus.

Such was the effect of the Apostle Paul's having applied the doctrine of the cross in the first Epistle to the Corinthians, that he was able later to give thanks for their recovery in the second letter. The corruption from which afterwards they were delivered by the cross, had been the work of Satan. 'But I fear, lest by any means, as the serpent beguiled Eve through his subtlety, so your minds should be corrupted from the simplicity that is in Christ.' How could such a thing come to pass? 'If he that cometh preacheth another gospel', saith Paul, searching out the root of the matter, and finding that they had been seduced by false preachers, full of spiritual-sounding speeches, pleasing to the ear, but devoid of the doctrine of the cross.

It had been reported to Paul by them which were of the household of Chloe, that the brethren at Corinth were divided, and had fallen into contention, one party with another. This was the carnal mind in its strength, the negation of the truth that the old man, with all his mentality, the whole head, all that pertained to the carnal mind, had been crucified. If crucified, why were they carnally minded? If they had been crucified with Christ, if the body of sin had been destroyed, how could they dwell in the mind that pertained to that body? The Spirit of truth supported the cross: in what spirit, then, were they dwelling?

If they had the mind of Christ, if, in support of this, the Spirit dwelt in them as one body, how could they be divided? The mind in Adam was divided. But is Christ divided? No he is not. Then in him there can be no division. Brethren must of necessity put away all carnal mindedness, and, having the mind of Christ, must 'be perfectly joined together in the same mind and in the same judgment.'

But it was not so at Corinth. They all spoke different things, there were divisions among them, they were forming parties on the basis of personality, opinion and preference. The wisdom of words, intellectual and oratorical, prevailed. The love of argument, of worldly reasoning, the 'wisdom of the wise', the 'understanding of the prudent', rose up in the pride of life, so that the will of man ruled in the church.

The result was disputing, contention, debate, and consequently heated striving and schism. Not one vestige of this was in the mind of Christ. It was all in the mind of Adam.

'Now I beseech you, brethren, by the name of our Lord Jesus Christ, that ye all speak the same thing, and that there be no divisions among you.' But Paul's entreaty for the unity of brethren in the church bears no relation to the deceptive 'church unity' of today, in which denominations agree to form one 'church'. That is not church unity in the mind of God. It is an unauthorised agreement of denominations, in themselves improper, grouped to form a loose subordinate structure that never was nor ever could be the church of God. No such thing as 'the unity of churches'—by which they mean denominations—was envisaged in the New Testament, for the simple reason that churches as such were not then divided into denominational fragments as they are now. Then, it was a question of the unity of brethren in one church properly so called.

If those in the denominations, whether Roman, Protestant, or Sectarian, really desire unity, they must, who are of God, who seek his face, come out of their divisions, into the unity of one body. Being thus rightly gathered by the cross and in the unity of the Spirit, brethren will then be in a position where the New Testament teaching on unity applies: within the church. There, all must speak the same thing. There, there must be no divisions.

Why not? Because it is the house of God, where brethren are not in Adam, but in Christ. Where the old man with his carnal mind is seen to have been crucified. Where the saints put on the new man, raised from the dead. Where brethren show forth the mind of Christ. There, carnal mindedness, which is death, has been put away, the body of sin destroyed, and the mind of the Spirit is life and peace.

At the beginning, abiding in the love of God, led by the Spirit, in communion with Christ, brethren were seen to be dwelling together in unity. All spoke the same thing. Outside was the mind of Adam with its contentions. Within, the cross was effective to shut out all that was of the flesh. The Spirit, the mind of the Spirit, which was life and peace, filled the unity of the body, expressing in one the mind of Christ.

However, false teachers had come in, uncalled and unsent, with their false doctrine, to undermine the cross, and to seduce the brethren from the simplicity which was in Christ. But Paul knew nothing among them, save 'Jesus Christ, and him crucified.' Were some following him in the flesh? What flesh, in the church? 'Was Paul crucified for you?' No he was not, Christ was crucified for them, that they might dwell in him, in one body, by the cross. Then, Paul brings in the doctrine of the cross again, declaring to the people fallen from grace, 'The preaching of the cross is to them that perish foolishness, but unto us which are saved it is the power of God.'

The cross was foolishness to them that perish. That is, to the world. Why? Because they, the worldly, considered themselves too wise to believe it. Worldly wisdom, in the eyes of the world, was superior to the cross, and the worldly, in their wisdom, thought that they could see through this foolishness. But, I Cor. 1:25, 'The foolishness of God is wiser than men.' As to worldly wisdom, saith God, 'I will destroy the wisdom of the wise, and will bring to nothing the understanding of the prudent.' This destruction, this bringing to nothing, was wrought at the cross.

Why then is the cross foolishness to the world? Because the wisdom of it cannot be seen by the natural eye, it demands faith alone, it evades the senses, it lies outside of the rules of natural intelligence, in a word, as men say, there is no proof. But then, mysteries are beyond 'proof'.

What mysteries are these, that lie beyond proof? First, the mystery of the one who was crucified. The mystery of his Person was hidden from the world, for, 'had they known it, they would not have crucified the Lord of glory.' The divine Person of the Lord of glory was hidden behind the apparent weakness of his human nature. No amount of worldly wisdom, natural perception, or human intuition could have penetrated this mystery. Then why does the world boast of its wisdom? In divine things its wisdom is not only inadequate, it is disastrous.

The mystery of the cross lies beyond all understanding of men to comprehend. Who could comprehend the eternal, the immortal, the invisible God, smiting the Son of man, the human nature of his own Son? Who could understand that 'it pleased the LORD to bruise him', when no bruising discoloured his skin? That 'by his stripes we are healed', when neither whip nor rod appeared, and neither beating nor lashing occurred, as he hung upon the cross? How can the world, trusting in a wisdom dependent upon natural observation, understand that 'The LORD hath laid on him the iniquity of us all', when nothing whatsoever was seen to have been laid on him during the whole of his passion? Even the Jews could not believe it, religious as they were, because it was so contrary to reason. 'Unto the Jews a stumblingblock', I Cor. 1:23.

The mystery of God was hidden from human wisdom. Who can understand the mystery of the invisible God? To the world, it cannot be seen, therefore cannot be proven, ergo, it cannot be. But it is: there is one God in three Persons, and there are three Persons in one God. The Father did smite the Son, the church of God was purchased with his own blood,

God did make him to be sin for us, our old man was crucified with him. All this is the truth, the whole truth, and nothing but the truth.

It is the truth, but, being a divine mystery, it must be received by revelation, and made known by preaching, even the preaching of the cross. To the wise, who reject what they call uncertain and unproven assertions, this is 'foolishness'. That is, it is foolishness to 'Them that perish', I Cor. 1:18. But what kind of wisdom is this, that causes its advocates to perish?

The mystery of the power of God lies beyond proof also, and hence is denied by human wisdom. What folly! The wisdom of the world denies the power of God, because it cannot be proven. Since by its wisdom the world rejects the preaching of the cross, and since, I Cor. 1:18, the preaching of the cross is the power of God, how can the world complain of lack of proof? It denies to itself the only means of proving the power of God, that is, by experience, because it refuses the gospel which brings that experience.

But the world cannot see the power of God. No, it cometh not by observation. It is inward, this power. It is wrought in the interior, it is experienced in the inward man. It is the power of the Spirit of truth, 'Whom the world cannot receive, because it seeth him not, neither knoweth him: but ye know him; for he dwelleth with you, and shall be in you.' Hence, 'The world by wisdom knew not God', I Cor. 1:21.

To them that perish the cross is foolishness. The world is too wise, its knowledge too great, its learning too vast, to embark on such vague speculations. It did not please God by the foolishness of preaching to save the world. But to save them that believe. The preaching of the cross is insufficient for the religious. They want signs to settle the question, I Cor. 1:22. Such preaching is also insufficient for the intellectual. He wants tangible proof. 'For after that in the wisdom of God the world by wisdom knew not God, it pleased God by the foolishness of preaching to save them that believe', I Cor. 1:21.

Observe, it is preaching that saves. The preaching of the cross, which, of course, means doctrinal preaching. It is the preaching of the mystery. 'Unto me, who am less than the least of all saints, is this grace given, that I should preach among the Gentiles the unsearchable riches of Christ: and to make all men see what is the fellowship of the mystery.' This preaching, by which the mystery is made known and the power of God communicated, is called variously, The preaching of the gospel, I Cor. 1:17; The preaching of the cross, 1:18; The foolishness of preaching, 1:21; and, The preaching of Christ crucified, 1:23.

The preaching of the gospel divides mankind into two. It divides the world and the church asunder. When the preaching of the cross sounds forth, it appears 'Foolishness to them that perish', but becomes 'The power of God unto us which are saved', I Cor. 1:18.

The preaching finds out the wise, the scribe, the disputer, the sign-seeker, the mighty, the noble, and the understanding, and it finds them out to be too wise for the gospel, and too knowledgeable for the cross. The preaching finds out believers also, who are the called, the chosen, the brethren. These are unwise after the flesh, foolish in the world, the weak things of the world, the base things of the world, the despised, the nothings. Nevertheless, they are saved by the power of God, called by the grace of God, and destined for the glory of God.

When Christ crucified is preached to such poor creatures as these, whom the world despises but whom God chooses, whom the world rejects but whom God calls, God is magnified. He is glorified because 'no flesh shall glory in his presence.' Since by definition they can do nothing, it is very plain that God has done everything. The whole work is of himself. The glory is God's alone. In such brethren the gospel is effectual, the cross is saving, power attends the word, revelation accompanies the preaching, and, behold, the fellowship of the mystery is let down from heaven. They have not chosen him but he has chosen them. God chose them in Christ Jesus, whom he, himself, makes unto them wisdom, both righteousness, sanctification, and redemption.

Yet for all this glorious doctrine and experience, the flesh, and worldly wisdom, had come back again at Corinth. How could this be? By false teachers, with erroneous doctrines. Just as at the first the power of God had come in by the preaching of the cross, so now the working of Satan came in by false doctrine. Thus by fair words and flattering speeches pleasing to the flesh, the cross had been made 'of none effect' in those who embraced the error. 'For if he that cometh preacheth another Jesus, whom we have not preached, or if ye receive another spirit, which ye have not received, or another gospel, which ye have not accepted', why be surprised at the schisms? the heresies? the divisions? 'For such are false apostles, deceitful workers.'

'But', says the Apostle Paul, 'though we, or an angel from heaven, preach any other gospel unto you than that which we have preached unto you, let him be accursed.' Accursed? Yes, because it is by believing the gospel, in the true preaching of it, and believing the gospel alone, that men are saved, just as it is by rejecting the gospel that they shall be lost. The preaching of the cross therefore stands as the only hope of a fallen world. Accursed indeed let him be who perverts it, denies it, or corrupts it by worldly wisdom or human sentiment.

What will Paul do, now that the carnal mind, and worldly wisdom, had come in at Corinth? The cross is Paul's answer. The preaching of the cross is his antidote. It was that by which the Spirit had come in, and that by which the flesh had gone out, in the beginning. At the cross the body of the flesh had been hung up, accursed and execrated. Withal it was the body of sin, Rom. 6:6, and was made sin, II Cor. 5:21. The cross was the judgment of God upon sin in the flesh, in the body. It was not a question of the body in terms of out-ward appearances, the skin that appeared to the eye. It was what appeared to God, inward realities, what lay beneath the skin in the sight of God. That was what was seen in the substitutionary sacrifice on the cross.

It was the whole man, the old man, the body of sin, that had been mysteriously transferred to the Substitute by the work of God. Then, if the whole man, the head also. And if the head, the fleshly mind. And if the fleshly mind, then carnal wisdom. Or ever men could be saved, that must be condemned. And it was condemned, in the Saviour on the tree. How then could brethren at Corinth return to that which God had condemned, to save them? How was it that the carnal mind, and fleshly wisdom, had come in? How did it happen that there were contentions in the flesh, a party spirit?

And if these things were so, what had they to say of the cross? Well, they speculated about the cross, they had their own views, it was a question of opinion, of ideas. 'I am of Paul; and I of Apollos; and I of Cephas; and I of Christ.' In tears, afar off, Paul took up his pen, once again to apply the cross. 'Is Christ divided? was Paul crucified for you?' Paul had come, and now wrote, preaching the gospel. Not with the wisdom of words, lest the cross of Christ should be made of none effect. Paul did not come, or write, speculating, propos-ing, pleading or intellectually discussing. He came preaching, and preaching dogmatically.

Paul preached doctrinally, according to the revelation of the mystery which he had both received and experienced from Jesus Christ. 'How shall they hear without a preacher?'

That is, a preacher of this order. 'How shall one preach except he be sent?' But Paul was sent, and came preaching the word of the cross, a savour of life unto life to the saved, and of death unto death to the lost. The Lord had much people in the city of Corinth, and under the preaching of the gospel, as a savour of life unto life, God revealed the truth to them, calling them and saving them by the washing of regeneration and renewing of the Holy Ghost.

To the rest of the city, it was a savour of death unto death, this preaching: foolishness. Men mocked at it, or it saved them. It quickened them, or it slew them. 'Go into all the world and preach the gospel: he that believeth and is baptised shall be saved, and he that believeth not shall be damned.' Life unto life, or death unto death. Saved or lost, the gospel determined the issue. But it did not ask for man's opinion. It condemned it on the tree.

The preaching of the cross, of the gospel, is not therefore intellectual, or for intellectuals to debate. But that was what had come in at Corinth: as though the church of God, the pillar and ground of the truth, were a debating forum for intellectuals, pulling down the truth from heaven to earth, God to man, in order to pronounce upon it. They sought wisdom, they were following the academics, debating the cross, airing opinions, discussing the various views. Paul's view and Cephas', the Jesus of the Synoptics and the Johannine Jesus, this historical aspect and that, one tradition and another. But this whole carnal mind, how much more all that came from it, stunk in the nostrils of God.

It was a putrid reek that rose up from Corinth, a stinking offence. But God's goodness and everlasting mercy viewed not the departure but the Saviour. Not the apostacy but the Substitute. Not their debating but his crucifixion. Not carnal wisdom but a crucified Head. Not the offensive reek but the sweet-smelling savour of Christ. And he freely forgave them all.

Paul preached the cross, and he wrote of the cross, and this brought them back, who had erred and strayed like lost sheep at Corinth. By the word of the cross they were deeply convicted of their having shamed Christ and his gospel by their departure from the truth. The Holy Ghost came in again in power, and convinced them of the wickedness of the natural mind, its utter offensiveness to God, of the obnoxious nature of high thoughts to the Almighty. Oh, every thought was brought into captivity to the obedience of Christ, when the Holy Ghost brought in by the word of the cross the alarming, awakening, convicting, slaying, humbling work that marks out those whom God will bring to repentance.

The saints at Corinth were renewed in the spirit of their minds, transformed by the renewing of their minds, every imagination being cast down, every high thought, as the Holy Ghost subdued and mortified the flesh, bringing in the mind that was in Christ Jesus. What mind was this? The mind that the Spirit of God had begun to form in them, and would yet bring to completion in the new man. 'Let this mind be in you, which was also in Christ Jesus: who, being in the form of God, thought it not robbery to be equal with God: but made himself of no reputation, and took upon him the form of a servant, and was made in the likeness of men: and being found in fashion as a man, he humbled himself, and became obedient unto death, even the death of the cross.'

This is preaching the cross, and applying the preaching, with a witness. But with what effect? What real result came from all this doctrinal preaching? All this taking the doctrine of the cross concerning the crucifixion of the old man, and applying it particularly to the carnal mind, the fleshly mentality, that had come in at Corinth, what did it achieve?

What effect? What result? What did it achieve? 'Now', writes the apostle, having sent the first epistle, and having received the report of their response to that letter, 'Now I rejoice, not that ye were made sorry, but that ye sorrowed to repentance: for ye were made sorry after a godly manner, that ye might receive damage by us in nothing. For godly sorrow worketh repentance to salvation not to be repented of: but the sorrow of the world worketh death. For behold this selfsame thing, that ye sorrowed after a godly sort, what carefulness it wrought in you, yea, what clearing of yourselves, yea, what indignation, yea, what fear, yea, what vehement desire, yea, what zeal, yea, what revenge! In all things ye have approved yourselves to be clear in this matter.' II Cor. 7:9-11.

And this is called, Preaching the gospel effectually. 'For Christ sent me not to baptise, but to preach the gospel: not with wisdom of words, lest the cross of Christ should be made of none effect. For the preaching of the cross is to them that perish foolishness; but unto us which are saved it is the power of God. For it is written, I will destroy the wisdom of the wise, and will bring to nothing the understanding of the prudent.'

XIII

The Cross and the Law

IN the Epistle to the Romans the Apostle Paul systematically expounds the truth of the cross, duly opening up the deliverance of the people of God from the law. This is his teaching. It is objective: he sets forth the doctrine, not because the saints at Rome stood in greater need of it than others, or particularly required its application, but because he is preaching and teaching the gospel in due order. Therefore the apostle sets forth the position of the saints, and of the church, in relation to the law. Brethren are not under the law, they are delivered from the law, they are dead to the law by the body of Christ. It is essential that this doctrine be taught, and Paul teaches it forcefully, if objectively.

When the apostle comes to write the Epistle to the Galatians, however, an entirely different situation confronts him. It is no longer a question of objective teaching to a people in need of the doctrine in order that they might know the truth, but of a people entangled under the yoke of bondage. False teachers had come in to the churches of Galatia, and had perverted the gospel, they had enticed the saints from the truth. They had reintroduced the law. This did not call for objective doctrinal teaching, but for indignant subjective application, and that is exactly what the epistle conveys.

It is not surprising therefore to discover that though these particular epistles—Romans and Galatians—teach more about deliverance from the law than any other New Testament

200

epistles, Galatians, the smaller of the two, devotes more space to the matter. This is easily demonstrated. Deliverance from the law is by the cross. Galatians, although one of the shorter of the Pauline epistles, has the greatest number of references to the cross of all the books of the New Testament—including Romans—no matter what the length. Why is this? Because the apostle vehemently defends the gospel truth that the cross sets the saints free from the law. Then, deliverance is by the cross. Hence the highest number of references to the cross in one of the more brief of the New Testament books.

Eight times in seven texts the cross is mentioned within the small compass of the six short chapters of Galatians. And yet the blood of Christ is not mentioned once. Why is this? The truth of the blood of Christ reveals that God, in the substitutionary death of Christ, brought an entire people nigh to himself. The blood declares the mystery of what happened in the body on the tree. But the truth of the crucified body reveals that God, in the substitutionary death of Christ, took the entire body of sin far away in condemnatory judgment.

The cross declares the mystery of what happened to the body on the tree. It is not to the blood that deliverance from the law relates—save that, of course, the blood witnesses to everything that was accomplished and to all the price that was paid in death—but to the cross, to the doctrine of the cross as such. Hence the concentration of passages on the cross in Galatians, and the absence of any reference to the blood. It was not a question of a people being made nigh to God in Galatians, but of their going back past the cross, that is, of returning to the law.

It is striking to note that the absence of any reference to the blood of Christ is not confined to the Galatian epistle. There are no such references in II Corinthians, Philippians, I Thessalonians, II Thessalonians, I Timothy, II Timothy, Titus, Philemon, James, II Peter, II John, III John, and Jude.

That is, the blood of Christ is not mentioned in over half of the total number of books in the New Testament. Particularly remarkable is the fact that no reference to the blood of Christ appears in the pastoral epistles.

What are we to deduce from this? We are to deduce that there is a very great difference between modern evangelicalism and the doctrine of the apostles; a vast discrepancy between what passes for the gospel at the end of the age, and the gospel itself at the beginning of it; an immense divide separating the superficial preaching of every flippant, empty and uncalled pretender of today, and the mighty Spirit-filled preaching of the cross by the sound ministers of the gospel in the times of the New Testament.

We are to deduce that present day evangelicalism 'is fallen, is fallen', being reduced to the repetition of a limited number of well-worn texts—nowadays from some fashionably modern 'version'—wrenched out of context, at the expense of the whole truth, and, indeed, at the expense of the cross itself. We are to deduce that there is a deliberate evasion of vast and massive truth, a wilful ignorance indicated by the sparse smattering of texts to which loose and insecure evangelicalism clings, as to a talisman. Yet this biased and limited selection of theirs is very far from the full number of scriptures making up that part of the truth to which they confine themselves. How much further is it from the sum of all the parts in their fulness, which in proper proportion and balance comprises the gospel of God?

The early church held, and the early ministers preached, the whole of the truth of the gospel of God concerning his Son. They preached the doctrine of Christ, and held both the Father and the Son, declaring the vastness of that divinity encompassed in him who said, I am the truth. They taught his deity, humanity, birth, life, death, burial, resurrection, ascension, glory, and his coming again. The doctrine of

Christ, setting forth the Person and work of the Son, revealed the Father also, likewise declaring his Person and work, besides that of the Holy Ghost. The faith itself was the revelation of the deity, one God in three Persons, three Persons in one God: this was of the essence of the revelation of Jesus Christ, and was established upon the one foundation of his death. Nothing limited about this.

There is a vast range of truth in scripture, never discovered by superficial Christendom. There is a massive awesomeness to the gospel diminished and degraded by shallow evangelicalism. There is a dignity and glory to the church corrupted and prostituted by worldly and sectarian denominationalism. There is a soaring majesty to the doctrine humiliated and debased by the imposition of human systems and traditions of learning.

But the early church, under the primitive ministry, did not suffer from the insecurity inherent in that flimsy religion evidenced by wilful evasion of the whole truth on the one hand, and by blind, constant repetition of a few limited texts on the other. The early church had no need of false assurance. They possessed the full assurance of faith, and the reason was, that God himself, in Father, Son and Holy Ghost, had brought home the evangel inwardly and with power to their hearts.

The vast range of the gospel, and the apostolic liberty in teaching and admonishing from that whole body of doctrine, according to the leading and direction of the Holy Ghost, are illustrated further by the incidence of textual references to the cross. This is notable in that, like the blood of Christ, the cross is foundational to the faith. And yet—again like the blood—in many cases references are conspicuous by their absence.

The fact is that there are no references of any kind to the cross in I Thessalonians, II Thessalonians, I Timothy,

II Timothy, Titus, Philemon, James, II Peter, I John, II John, III John or Jude. Twelve books out of twenty-seven. Once more, the remarkable thing is that neither the crucifixion nor the cross are mentioned in any of the pastoral epistles, upon which hang the apostolic word to the future Christian ministry.

What a vast range of truth this indicates, and what calm confidence in presenting it! The heart of the truth is the knowledge of God, his nature, character, mind, attributes, ways, counsel, will, purpose and work. 'This is life eternal, that they might know thee the only true God, and Jesus Christ, whom thou hast sent.' And the essence of the knowledge of God is to know the Father through the Son, and the Son by the Spirit. This is the revelation of the gospel: the knowledge of God in Father, Son and Holy Ghost. This revelation is based upon the foundation of Jesus Christ and him crucified. And this in turn is revealed by the blood and manifest by the cross. Silence, in any given book of the New Testament on any one point of truth is indicative of the balance of the doctrine. Comparative silence indicates proportion: not prohibition. It would have been well had the lessons of proportion and balance inherent in scriptural usage both moulded the doctrine and tempered the mind of the professing church in times past.

Galatians is a unique epistle. It is silent on the blood of Christ. But it iterates and reiterates the truth of the cross, till it surpasses the number of references in any other two epistles, no matter that either one or both may be vastly larger than the Galatian letter. Eight times in seven texts the cross, the tree, or the being crucified, appear in the six short chapters that go to make up this smaller of Paul's many writings.

In the Epistle to the Romans the cross is seen in relation to the body of sin, the 'old man'. In that to the Corinthians the doctrine is applied to the carnal mind, the mentality of the old man. The Epistle to the Galatians however is different: it is not a question of the crucifixion of the old man, in part or the whole, but of the relationship of the law to those whose old man has been crucified, whose body of sin is reckoned to have been destroyed.

What has the law to say to those who are dead, those who have been crucified with Christ? What has that law which required righteousness from the 'old man', to say to those whose 'old man is crucified with him'? What has the rule that required works from the flesh, to demand of those who are not in the flesh? What obligation can the law place upon those accounted 'dead to the law by the body of Christ'? The epistle to the churches of Galatia gives the answers to these questions with immense clarity and forcefulness.

Paul the Apostle marvelled that the brethren who had so recently received the apostolic doctrine of the gospel, should have turned from it to receive another gospel at the mouth of those who took advantage of his absence, and were constant troublers of the work of God. 'I marvel that ye are so soon removed from him that called you into the grace of Christ unto another gospel: which is not another; but there be some that trouble you, and would pervert the gospel of Christ.' Gal. 1:6-7.

At this the apostle waxes bold, saying, 'But though we, or an angel from heaven, preach any other gospel unto you than that which we have preached unto you, let him be accursed. As we said before, so say I now again, If any man preach any other gospel unto you than that ye have received, let him be accursed. For do I now persuade men, or God? or do I seek to please men? for if I yet pleased men, I should not be the servant of Christ.'

Paul goes on to assert the verity of his gospel: 'But I certify you, brethren, that the gospel which was preached of me is not after man. For I neither received it of man, neither was I taught it, but by the revelation of Jesus Christ.' Which was what his traducers could never say.

If Paul was so vehement, what was this great error into which the brethren at Galatia had been drawn? What was so bad, that it evoked such strong language from the apostle? It was no more than what is taken for granted in certain so-called 'reformed' theological circles today. No more than what the schools, sectarian movements, and other vested interests, pass down to this generation as the word of God, when it is nothing other than the traditions of men. 'Howbeit in vain do they worship me, teaching for doctrines the commandments of men.' That is, they do, who never received the experience of the gospel in the whole of their lives, much less had it communicated by revelation that they might preach it to others. 'And he said unto them, Full well ye reject the commandment of God, that ye may keep your own tradition.'

What then was the error at Galatia? The mixing of the law with the gospel of Christ. What was the apostle's antidote? 'I through the law am dead to the law.' How was this? Through the cross: 'I am crucified with Christ.' And if crucified, then dead to the law. But by what rule should he live? 'Nevertheless I live; yet not I, but Christ liveth in me: and the life which I now live in the flesh I live by the faith of the Son of God, who loved me, and gave himself for me.' Gal. 2:19-20.

Paul was dead to the law, but the Galatian brethren were going back to the law, which, whether anyone else called it a rule of conduct, or moral advice, or Judaising, or whatever name, Paul insists is nothing but a rule of justification. For in its very nature the law can be nothing other than a rule of justification, no matter what it may be called, or rather miscalled, by those who put believers under its yoke.

Although the Galatians had been seduced, Paul still addressed them as 'The churches of Galatia', and as 'Brethren'. The apostle yet regarded them as the saints. Indeed, they still held a form of the gospel. But it was not the purity of the gospel which they had received from Paul at the beginning. False teachers had polluted that purity, they had added the law. This is what the Galatians had embraced. They had not given up the gospel, they had accepted its perversion. It was this mixture that Paul calls 'Another gospel'.

The law that had been added by the false teachers must have appeared to be compatible with the gospel, it was a question of subtlety, of seduction. Then, it was hardly the law in terms of the sacrifices or ceremonies. Neither yet in terms of most of the judicial law, given for the time 'when ye be come into the land which the LORD your God shall give you.' To mingle, to be capable of mixture with the gospel, to sound plausible, it must be the law in its moral content, the 'moral law' as they say, the law considered in a moral or spiritual light. It was this that the Galatians had accepted as fundamental to the outworking, and necessary to the doctrine, of the gospel. The truth was that it was neither. But the scheme pleased the flesh.

It is inconceivable that the brethren at Galatia had turned to Judaism as such. To the law of Moses in its entirety. Equally incredible is the notion that they had turned from the crucified Saviour set forth in the gospel as their justification before God, to the law of works as an alternative means of justification. Inconceivable and incredible because in no such case could Paul call it 'Another gospel'. He would have called it 'the law instead of the gospel.' The use of the description, 'perverting the gospel'—whilst correcting the error by preaching deliverance from the law through the cross—shows a mixture of law and gospel together. 'Another gospel.'

Had the Galatians turned from the gospel to the law in its entirety, it is very doubtful that Paul would have called them

'The church'. They would then have become the synagogue. Just as the description 'Brethren' would have been inappropriate. 'Proselytes' would have become the correct term. It would no longer have been a matter of seduction, but wilful apostasy. Not an error, but the great transgression. They would have left and attacked the Christian religion at its very foundation. Rather, they, through the labours of these circumcising false teachers, had reconciled law and gospel together, as that by which one could and should live consistently in Christ before God.

But with telling insistence, Paul labours and enforces the simple and yet vital truth that destroys this heresy, and leaves the false teachers without excuse. The simple truth is this: no matter what they said, the law is in fact a rule of justification. It is nothing else, and it never can be anything else, either in part or the whole. They had been 'bewitched', or were 'fools', if they thought otherwise. If they supposed that they could be justified by the gospel, but sanctified by the law, or saved by the gospel in order to walk by the law, then they had been blinded, and were in darkness. In such a case, no matter what was told them by whom, quoting whichever authority, they were actually giving up the gospel in favour of the law for justification. It is that and that alone of which circumcision was the sign, and, whether the sign were adopted or not, the thing signified was the reality.

Boldly Paul cries out, 'I'—whatever you may be—'I through the law'—which cursed Christ to death for me, in that substitutionary death—'am dead to the law.' With what effect? 'That I might'—not live unto sin under the law, as all legalists do, but, as dead to it—'live unto God.'

The apostle continues, 'I am crucified with Christ.' Crucified with Christ to what? Context determines irrefutably, Crucified with Christ to the law. To the law as such, not the ceremonial or judicial law only, cutting the law with the

theological penknife of man's manufactory, artfully preten-
ding rightly to divide the word of truth. Dead to the law as
such, not dead to two parts of the law! Dead to the law. But
these 'theological' hacks would cut out the 'ceremonial' and
'judicial' law, and have us dead to that, and leave the root,
the 'moral' law, as they call it, so as to align themselves with
the false teachers of the Galatians, and put brethren under
the—moral—law as a 'rule of life'.

This is contrary to Paul. 'Let them be accursed.' It is
contrary to Luther. It is contrary to the spiritual heritage of
the Reformation. It is contrary to the true faith and its ministers. Why? Because they, the false teachers, make the texts
which speak of our deliverance from the law apply only to
that which is irrelevant and inapplicable, and not to what is
pertinent and essential, namely, the—so-called—'moral' law.
The essence of that to which we are dead is the 'moral' law,
which by definition and in its very nature can be nothing
other than the law of justification. But 'I through the law am
dead to the law.' The law as such. The cross saw to that.
Otherwise we should be lost again and that without remedy.

The saints, the churches, are dead to the law. Does any
believe otherwise? They are fallen from grace. 'O foolish
Galatians, who hath bewitched you, that ye should not obey
the truth, before whose eyes Jesus Christ hath been evidently
set forth, crucified among you?' No legalist can say it, none of
them ever preached it, only free grace says and preaches this
pure doctrine, 'Before whose eyes Jesus Christ hath been
evidently set forth, crucified among you.' Gal. 3:1.

And if crucified, then dead to the law. That is, doubtless,
to the commandments, the 'moral' law. Set the law before the
people, under the guise of preventing sin, and sin they will.
Let the haters of the gospel shrill 'Antinomian'—which is
what they are—as much as they like, the truth is, the law
works wrath, genders pride, brings in enmity, and sentences

to death. Set Jesus Christ and him crucified before the people, and the gospel declares peace, brings forth humility, fills with love, and justifies freely by grace.

The ground of deliverance from sin, according to the scripture, is not the putting of believers under the law, but the taking of them out from under it, because that is precisely what answers to the work that God wrought in Christ at the cross. 'For sin shall not have dominion over you: for ye are not under the law'—when, evidently, sin did have dominion over you—'but under grace.'

It is abundantly clear that law and grace, works and faith, are utterly incompatible. What the false teachers preached, and what the foolish Galatians received from them, was wholly inconsistent, in any conceivable permutation: because the law and the gospel cannot subsist together. 'And if by grace, then it is no more of works: otherwise grace is no more grace. But if it be of works, then it is no more grace: otherwise work is no more work.' The truth is, none can preach Christ, and preach the law, joining the two together in any form, without a lie in his right hand and falsehood in his heart. It is another gospel. It is to darken counsel without knowledge. It is to overturn the cross.

He that believes on Christ has ceased from his works: but the law requires works. He has been justified by faith: but the law does not require faith. He has righteousness of God accounted to him: but the law requires righteousness of man from him. He has entered into rest upon mount Zion this side Jordan: but the law requires rest to be earned at mount Sinai the far side Jordan. He has been perfected for ever by one offering: but the law makes nothing perfect, requires legal perfection, and condemns all shortcoming. And what have those made perfect by the blood and body of Jesus to do with that legal system? Nothing at all. Thanks be to God, nothing is required of them, they have ceased from their own works, they are justified by grace and through faith, they have the righteousness of God imputed to them, they have entered into everlasting rest, and they are perfected for ever by the offering up of the body of Jesus once for all.

Where then is Moses? When they can find his missing body we will attend to their perverted gospel. But since their master has been about the business of looking for Moses' body for several millennia without making the discovery, we need not expect any success from these late arrivals in the search. Besides, the apostles having seen both Moses and Elias with Jesus in the mount, and having heard the Father himself preach the gospel, upon which both Moses and Elias disappeared from the view of the evangelists for ever, under apostolic direction we are not likely to hear anyone other than the Son, or see any man save Jesus only.

To confound Moses and Christ, the Old Covenant and the New, the law and the gospel, the Old Testament and the New Testament, faith and works, is to stumble upon the dark mountains, to grope for the wall like the blind, and to enter into that gloomy and howling wilderness in which no pathway ever appears. To confound together what God has separated is to fight against the Almighty, and these contenders need not be surprised at the consequences of such an issue. They have set themselves an impossible task, and, if they escape not, their desperation shall end in the mountain falling upon them and grinding them to powder.

This confounding together of law and gospel, this going back to the commandments after 'Jesus Christ hath been evidently set forth, crucified among you', lies at the heart of the Galatian error. No matter how specious the deception, irrespective of all the Jesuitical casuistry used by the perpetrators of this perversity, if the gospel be joined to the moral law, in whatever form or under whatever names, then 'Christ is become of no effect unto you, whosoever of you are justified by the law; ye are fallen from grace.' The deceivers of the brethren, conjuring up all manner of venerated rabbinical names, traditions, institutions and times of great quietness enjoyed under their providence, will cry out that the law they would put us under is not for justification, no, it is only for a guide or standard, but this is false. The law is a rule of justification, and it is nothing else.

The apostle refuses all sophistry about the law. He would have none of the subtlety of changing its name to 'a rule of life', or its nature to a series of parts, relieving believers of some parts—judicial and ceremonial—whilst leaving them under its very essence, called 'moral' law. Much less would Paul endure the notion that the penalty of the law was removed by the cross, but its rule, without either penalty or sanctions, was to be brought in for the believers' sanctification. Here is the law entering not by the door into the sheepfold, but climbing up some other way, with a witness. Law without sanctions? There is no such thing. A rule without sanctions is advice, not law. And, if advice, then purely optional. Thus, both law and gospel are ridiculed.

Is this the Schoolmen? Is it the Jesuits? No, it is supposed to be 'reformed theology'! No wonder they take refuge in name-dropping. Name-dropping? Hear Paul on this pathetic subterfuge: 'Whatsoever they were, it maketh no matter to me: God accepteth no man's person.' To Paul it is a question of the truth, as such, in and of itself. How foolish they make themselves, who profess to uphold law, yet do so illegally, not to mention unevangelically, and, moreover, reduce the law to toothless advice. And these call others 'Antinomians'?

To bring in the law to the believer, to reduce it to advice by denying its sanctions, is to make void the law indeed, and worse, to make the gospel of none effect. How is this? Because the cross is overturned. Paul calls this folly, the consequence of being bewitched. 'O foolish Galatians, who hath bewitched you?'

Whatever the legalists may say, to turn back to the law after, or together with, the gospel is to be 'foolish', 'not to obey', to be 'bewitched', to deny what was 'before' one's 'eyes', and to reject what was 'evidently set forth', Gal. 3:1. It is, Gal. 3:2, to deny the Spirit, to embrace unbelief, to stifle one's memory of first love, and to spurn the apostle. Moreover, it is to be 'so foolish', as to hold 'fleshly perfection', and to be totally inconsistent, 3:3. It is to have 'suffered so many things in vain', to be 'in vain' oneself, to be empty, subject to lightness and vanity, 3:4. Finally, Gal. 3:5, it is to turn to the killing letter, to embrace the ministry of death, to deny the mighty apostolic and early church miracles in their purpose and meaning, and to reject the ministry by which they came.

Thus the Galatians, without the Jewish temple, ceremonial or judicial law, without the synagogue, were going back to the—moral—law of works set before them as a rule of life and form of righteousness, instead of the cross. But the gospel had already shown them that they had been crucified to a rule of life and a form of righteousness that brought nothing but condemnation, a killing letter, a crushing burden, an unbearable yoke, a bitter enmity, self-delusion, self-righteousness, self-justification, wrath, death, a curse, and a certain fearful looking for of judgment beyond the grave.

But a sight of Christ crucified, freeing from the law which required works from the flesh, brought deliverance from witchcraft, light from darkness, liberty from guilt, peace from turmoil, and freedom from bondage. Believing the gospel, receiving the word of the cross, brought in the ministration of the Spirit, the ministry of righteousness, and the administration of glory. The gospel brought in faith, made the soul to hang upon hearing, and set the thankful heart to wait upon the coming of Christ and the bringing in of the world to come.

The gospel brought in a holiness, a righteousness, a sanctification the law could never give, and it did this without works or strife, by the beholding of 'Jesus Christ evidently set forth, crucified among you', without a sight or sound of the law in any degree whatsoever. Indeed, as long as the law was set before the people, both holiness and righteousness were unattainable, and sin and unrighteousness were inevitable. And, in truth, so long as the flesh strove for perfection according to the just demands of a holy law, the Spirit departed, wrath descended, Satan prosecuted and conscience tormented, causing rebellion to rise up and the curse to come down.

But Jesus Christ 'evidently set forth, crucified among you', solely, perpetually, set before the eye of faith, brought in, Gal. 3:1, 'the truth', that is, the truth that the law, moral or otherwise, had neither dominion over nor place with those who were crucified with Christ and therefore dead to its legal rule. It brought, Gal. 3:2, the supply of the Spirit, which never came from tables of stone, but which flowed out of the smitten rock, and, I Cor. 10:4, 'That Rock was Christ.' The Spirit came neither from a sight of nor from a striving for moral duty, but, 'Forthwith came there out of his side blood and water', Jn. 19:34. This flowing stream delivered the believer from dying of thirst under the works of the law, and gave him sweet peace in believing the gospel. It brought him a glimpse of the King in his beauty, a soul-refreshing sight of the celestial city, a glorious vision of the land that is very far off.

The seeing of Christ crucified, Gal. 3:3, conveyed the salvation of God to the foolish of this world, leading the just that live by faith on to the path that shineth more and more unto the perfect day. Thus Christ crucified became a light to the feet, and a lamp to the path, of the good man whose steps are ordered by the Lord. Such a view of the cross gave a deep satisfaction in lawfully having done with the law, and evangelically being taken up by the Spirit, putting away all striving for legal perfection.

Yes, Christ crucified alone led the willing feet of the saints on to a path of suffering and persecuted separation, Gal. 3:4, but not in vain, for they were kept by the power of God through faith unto salvation, ready to be revealed in the last time. Finally, such a revelation of the cross was accompanied by the witness of the Spirit, the heavenly testimony of God to the gospel of Christ crucified on mount Zion, utterly apart from mount Sinai, delivering from the law for ever, lawfully and evangelically, and that not in word only, but in power also, to the glory of God by Jesus Christ our Lord, world without end, Amen.

XIV

The Offence of the Cross

IN the crucifixion the body of the condemned was hung up to die. The shedding of blood was not necessitated by the crucifixion. Sin was condemned in the flesh. This was substitutionary. The man, the body, the flesh was vicariously condemned. The Epistle to the Romans shows that the 'old man', the body of sin, was crucified. The Corinthian epistle applies this to the carnal mind. Of necessity in the crucifixion the fleshly mind was condemned; the carnal mentality was judged when the Substitute was hung up on the tree.

The Epistle to the Galatians, however, does not enlarge upon the substitutionary crucifixion. That crucifixion being given, Galatians teaches the effect of it upon the law. The effect is, Gal. 2:19-20, that those who died with Christ died to the law.

This is the doctrine of the epistle generally. In Gal. 2:19-20 the saints are dead to the law. In Galatians 3:1-5 they are dead to the works of the law. And in Galatians 3:13 they are dead to the curse of the law. This is the position of the believer, and of the church. It is that into which the Holy Ghost, sent to glorify Christ, experimentally leads the gathered saints, as, indwelling, he takes of Christ's things and shows them to the assembly. 'As many as are led by the Spirit of God, they are the sons of God.'

In Galatians 5:11 the apostle opens up a further truth in relation to the cross. It brings offence. It creates a scandal.

216

This is particularly true with regard to the religious, called, in Paul's day, 'The circumcision'. 'And I, brethren, if I yet preach circumcision, why do I yet suffer persecution? then is the offence of the cross ceased', Gal. 5:11. Here observe that the cross definitely gives offence, that it makes one to suffer, and that the cause of this suffering is persecution. Further note that the persons initiating and maintaining this persecution are the 'circumcised'. That is, not atheists, agnostics, idolators, sinners or profligates, but moralists, legalists, and self-righteous, in a word, the religious.

This persecution rages because those who would be justified by works of the law are offended at those who are justified by faith. It rages because the ground of justification by faith is the cross, which condemns all human merit and ability as offensive to the righteousness of God. So offensive, that it must be crucified in Another, if sinners are to be saved. This is infuriating doctrine to the legalist, as to all Arminians, and Pelagians, who cannot bear to hear of the bondage of the will, or of total depravity. Hence, they avoid the cross, perverting its doctrine, and, if these things fail, and despite all their efforts the truth still prevails, they rage against it.

Another reason for this persecution is that the cross puts a difference as far as the east is from the west, as high as heaven is above the earth, as distant as God is from man, between the salvation of God and the self-help of the legalist. That is, between the flesh and the Spirit, between faith and works, between the law and the gospel, and between Moses and Christ. This was set forth from the beginning of the world in Cain and Abel, reiterated in Isaac and Ishmael, and confirmed in Jacob and Esau. It is the difference between the will of God and the will of man, the faith of the believer and the striving of the unbeliever, and between the church and the world. But the world hates this holy discrimination, it detests such separation. This is the offence of the cross.

217

'If the world hate you', saith Jesus, 'ye know that it hated me before it hated you. If ye were of the world, the world would love his own: but because ye are not of the world, but I have chosen you out of the world, therefore the world hateth you.' This is the offence of the cross.

But if soft-spoken, flattering, men-pleasing, self-seeking, college-bred preachers with their paper qualifications will please the world, especially the religious world, so that all are sweetly joined together, world and church, protestant and catholic, brethren and charismatic, then, lo, 'Then is the offence of the cross ceased.' All is harmony and light. the only persecution is that of which one reads in books from a former age. Now, however, a combination of education, community responsibility, church unity, love, equality and universal conformity, guided by both church and state, have put paid to such anti-social elements. And if not, there is always the psychiatric hospital for remedial treatment. 'Then is the offence of the cross ceased', Gal. 5:11.

The sign of those who went about to establish their own righteousness, who sought to be justified by the works of the law, was circumcision. By that outward mark one declared oneself for the moral law. In truth, however, that of which circumcision was the real sign was nothing whatsoever to do with the moral law. Circumcision was required of Abraham four hundred and thirty years before the law was given by Moses. And it was required as a seal of the righteousness of the faith which Abraham had, yet being uncircumcised.

How was circumcision a seal of the righteousness of faith? Because it was a sign of the removal of the flesh. It was a figure, a token, the removal of a small part of the flesh, signifying that nothing at all of the flesh, or of that which was born of the flesh, would have either part or lot in the salvation of God. Christ's birth was not after the flesh, nor was his death. It was all of God, the circumcision made without hands by the putting off of the body of the flesh. The sign of circumcision showed that in the true seed of Abraham, which was Christ, born not after the flesh but by promise, God would crucify the entire old man, and take away not merely the foreskin, but, vicariously, the whole body of sin, judging it in the promised Saviour, that it might not be judged in his people. Circumcision signified that. It sealed, by what it signified, the kind of righteousness on account of which Abraham was justified.

Thus circumcision was in reality a sign of justification by faith in Christ. It never was a sign of those who would justify themselves by the works of the law. How could it be, when that law did not appear in the world until more than four hundred years afterwards? After what? After circumcision first sealed the righteousness of faith freely bestowed upon Abraham when he was still uncircumcised.

How then can these legalists steal this sign of justification by faith, and make it the sign of the self-righteous? How? Easily. They are religious, and it is well known that such preachers of the law by no means oblige themselves to keep the least jot or tittle of what they impose on others. Neither, on the ground of their religion, do they feel bound to the laws of common decency or humanity. Like the Gentiles, but in another way, they are a law unto themselves.

It may be objected that circumcision is irrelevant today. So it is. But then, that was true of Paul's time also. How was this? Because circumcision was abused, and was not in fact the sign that the Jews made it out to be, rather the very opposite. For another thing, no sign has any signification in itself. Its whole importance is derived from the thing signified. It follows that, whatever may be true of circumcision, the thing signified could be—and, in fact, is—just as relevant today as it was then. It may be that in modern times signs other than circumcision signify self-righteous religion. But what difference does that make? The thing signified—whatever the sign—is the same, and the Jewish signification is human merit, a religion of the deeds of the flesh in order to earn the favour of God.

The legalist made circumcision the sign of one pledged to the works of the law, to keep it as the essential expression of God's will for the religious. This presupposed human strength, ability and liberty, together with the capacity to merit reward from God. The moralist may pretend, with his tongue-in-the-cheek humility, that he can do nothing without the Holy Spirit, but this is all cant. The Holy Spirit was never given under the law, and never came to aid men to keep the law. 'Received ye the Spirit by the works of the law, or by the hearing of faith?' If by the works of the law, then to help men keep the law. But if by the hearing of faith, then to glorify Christ, form a heavenly union with him, and establish everlasting communion with the Father.

To the legalist, the law, the moral law, is God's will and all God's will, and the full expression of God's will. It is the revelation of the whole of religion, and, to him, nothing else can be. The legalist really deifies the law, calling it 'The transcript of the divine nature.' But the honour of this description belongs to Christ alone. It is Christ that is 'The brightness of his glory, and the express image of his person.'

The law is accompanied by darkness and a tempest, it cannot bring brightness and glory. The law is the transcription of the rule of righteousness for man, being ordained by angels in the hand of a mediator. Before Moses gave the law upon mount Sinai, it was said neither to have been in the world, nor in existence, see Rom. 5:13. Long after creation, the fall, the flood, the fathers, the captivity in Egypt, says Paul, 'The law entered', Rom. 5:20. The law being 'given by Moses' stands in clear contrast to grace and truth coming by the very Son of God, whose being alone transcribes the divine nature.

What, a law given at a point in time, before which 'It was not', a transcription of the everlasting God? What, 'Thou shalt not covet thy neighbour's ox', a transcript of the divine nature? What, 'Thou shalt not kill' a transcription of the Eternal? Who ever can kill whom, in eternity? The law transcribe the nature of divine being? How can negative prohibitions transcribe even the nature of human being? Law cannot properly transcribe character, much less nature. Legal prohibitions, 'your law' as Jesus called it, apply to human relationships, whether towards God or man, and human relationships alone.

How could a law, given by Moses under blackness and darkness, with the way into the Holiest not yet made manifest, and the veil shutting out the knowledge of God from man, where distance and obscurity are the rule, how could such a law, I say, be said to transcribe the divine nature? How could a law, the essence of the promulgation of which was its limitation, the veiling of the knowledge of God, in which God was known as one Jehovah, one Person, one God, how could such a law, save to the most blindly prejudiced, transcribe Father, Son, and Holy Ghost, one God in three Persons, three Persons in one God?

Such a transcription required a rent veil, and a revelation through incarnation. But the rent veil was not under law, it was the end of the law, it was under the gospel. The truth is, it must be, and it was, a divine Person, the Person of the Son in human nature, who 'transcribed the divine nature'. He revealed the Father, and through him came the Spirit. 'He that hath seen me'—not Moses, much less tables of stone—'seen me, hath seen the Father.' But how can they have seen anything at all, who make more of blocks of stone than of the eternal Son, who glorify the temporal law at the expense of the everlasting gospel, and who magnify Old Testament obscurity above divine New Testament light?

The giving of the commandments on mount Sinai commenced with the words, 'I am the LORD thy God, which have brought thee out of the land of Egypt', Exodus 20:2. The law a 'transcription of the divine nature'? Let them think what they are saying. I put no words in their mouths. By what they are saying, their 'transcribed nature', in self-expression, must bring himself eternally from a non-existant land in an un-created world, must have no other gods before himself, take not his own name in vain from everlasting, and, moreover, before all worlds make no images, or before all time keep all sabbaths. What fools and blind are these hypocritical legal-ists! Whosoever they are: it maketh no difference to me.

They are the blind guides. They are the blind that lead the blind, and they are the persecutors that take such offence at such plain preaching of the cross. And no wonder, for it brings their rotten religion tumbling down, and washes the sand clean away from beneath the foundations on which these builders build. How shall we discern such builders? By the sign of circumcision? No longer. The sign today might be baptism, either of water, or else of what they call the spirit, or, it may be, some other token: it matters not.

It is not the sign itself, but the thing signified by it, that will show up these builders for what they are. How? By their attitude to the Seed of Promise. 'And Jesus saith unto them, Did ye never read in the scriptures, The stone which the builders rejected, the same is become the head of the corner: this is the Lord's doing, and it is marvellous in our eyes?' And 'they sought to lay hands on him.'

The cross of Christ brings the offence. It is this that causes the persecution. 'And I, brethren', says Paul, Galatians 5:11, 'if I yet preach circumcision, why do I yet suffer persecution? then is the offence of the cross ceased.'

In Galatians 5:11 the apostle poses a hypothetical question. If he yet preached circumcision, why is he yet persecuted? This cryptic question was designed in turn to evoke the query, What was the cause of his being persecuted? for it is evident that he was persecuted, and that his persecutors were those of the circumcision. The answer is that his preaching the cross rather than circumcision was the cause of his suffering.

By framing the question hypothetically, the apostle Paul shames the brethren who permitted themselves to be circumcised by these troublers, who were contrary both to himself and to the gospel. If he had done what they practised, in order to please man and conform to the religious world, he would not have been persecuted.

By such a question he shames them in their departure from the truth that he had preached. He preached the cross, not circumcision, and was persecuted. They had embraced circumcision, in consequence of which they no longer suffered affliction. For it was certain that they who submitted to circumcision, rather than suffer the offence of the cross, would never be persecuted.

Observe that the hypothetical question of Galatians 5:11 in fact assumes the cause of persecution suffered by the saints in the beginning. It was the preaching, and the receiving of the preaching, of the cross of Christ. Whence it must follow of necessity that the cross rightly taught and received shall always be accompanied by persecution.

At any time or place throughout the age, if any man comes preaching without this mark, he cannot be preaching the cross. He may be mentioning it, he may be paying it lip-service, he may be quoting the relevant texts, but he cannot be preaching the cross. In reality such a man must be avoiding it, he must be evading the spirit of it, he cannot be holding forth the truth and doctrine of it: else, he would suffer persecution for the cross of Christ. For at what time, and in what place, these things should cease to be, 'Then is the offence of the cross ceased.'

It is inevitable that whosoever preaches the doctrine of the cross must suffer persecution. Likewise those that embrace this preaching must suffer the same. It is equally certain that this persecution must come from the religious, the 'circumcision', not from the irreligious, save as they are stirred up by the blind guides. What the apostle speaks of is a persecution that is religious in its origin.

Another inevitability is that if 'preaching circumcision' be added to 'preaching the cross'—that is to say, that the cross be falsified to accommodate the persecutors—no suffering will follow. But if the cross be truly preached, if the preacher no more 'preaches circumcision', if 'another gospel' be repudiated, then the fury of the persecutors shall and must rage even to this very day, just as it did in Paul's day.

The bondchildren, Cain's seed, Ishmael's offspring, Esau's progeny, the carnal Jews, false brethren and a fallen church will 'charitably' stand for their law of self-righteousness and self-justification being added to the gospel, as a reality to a theory, as the substance to a shadow, but they will never stand for its subtraction. They will tolerate a change of sign, but will never tolerate a change of the thing signified. But Paul 'yet suffered persecution', because his gospel excluded sign and signification entirely, and that by total subtraction, through the crucified old man, the condemned body of sin, and a full and final death to the law, certified by the cross of Christ in the gospel.

When the word of the truth of the gospel is sent forth by Jesus Christ, when the preachers of that word are uncompromising, when the word of the cross alone is preached, persecutions must and shall arise. Once the religious, of whatever hue, Pharisee or Sadducee, papist or protestant, churchman or dissenter, charismatic or brother, once the religious understand that the cross rules out the will, strength, ability and place of man, and his works, in the church, fury will follow. Let the legalist see that the law is ruled out by the cross, and at once he is stripped of all his armour wherein he trusted. Then his countenance will fall, his arm will rise, and he will smite with the fist of wickedness as did his father Cain.

If Paul had paid court to the form of legality, if he had preached law, or flattered the flesh, or pleased man, or complimented the world, well might he say, 'Why do I yet suffer persecution?' If Paul had diminished the cross to an intellectual thesis or rabbinical paper, to be published abroad by the handiwork of the pigmy scribes whose name is legion, if he had degraded the cross to human sentiment, perverting it to an 'old rugged cross' to please entertainers and delight audiences, well might he say, 'Why do I yet suffer persecution?' If Paul had confounded the doctrine of the cross to overturn justification by placing it on a legal principle, or had he revived the old man to go back to the world behind the cross, or brought the law from the world past the cross, well might he say, 'Why do I yet suffer persecution?'

But Paul did none of these things. He was sent of God, he was not disobedient to the heavenly vision. He received his gospel by revelation, experimentally, not by education, academically. Paul was filled in his heart with the Holy Ghost, not in his head by so-called reformed theology. The word of God, the word of the truth of the gospel, the word of the cross, the word of Christ alone, inspired this uncompromising and faithful preacher.

With what result? He suffered persecution. He suffered persecution for a cross that utterly obliterated law and its signs to those who believed the gospel. He suffered persecution for a cross that took away the pride of the flesh, the intellectual vanity of the scribe, the haughtiness of the priest, in a word, the boasting and glory of man. He suffered persecution for a cross that opened the ground beneath the feet of every legalist, brought down the high thoughts of every will-worker, and shut the mouth of every self-justifier.

'And I brethren, if I yet preach circumcision, why am I yet persecuted? then is the offence of the cross ceased.' But it had not ceased, and it cannot cease, so long as God by the Lord Jesus Christ has one faithful witness left in the earth to the word of the cross.

Another assumption that lies behind the hypothetical question of the apostle in Galatians 5:11, is that the cross exposes the lie of every legalist. Otherwise, why do they become so furious? Why do they persecute? The answer is, because their rotten religion is exposed, because the hail has swept away their refuge of lies, and the waters have overflowed their hiding place. Therefore their covenant with death shall be disannulled, and their agreement with hell shall not stand, because they made lies their refuge, and under falsehood they hid themselves. Whence is the hail, and what is the water, that thus exposes the legalist? The word of the cross. Therefore they hate it, and persecute the faithful apostle.

But what is the falsehood of the legalist, and wherein lies his deception? The deceitfulness of the legal system is discovered in the presumption that every legalist makes in practice, and in which he glories. This presumption is that self-justification, self-righteousness, formalism, a fair show in the flesh, learning, clericalism, scorning, boasting, ambition, pompousness, pride, sanctimony and self-esteem are what the law really justifies. This is a lie. The law does not require or justify these things at all. Nevertheless, it is the cross that exposes them.

All these things, the whole deceitful fabric, the whole careful system of delusion, all are dashed down by the preaching of the cross. For the cross shows up all that the law ever could, or ever would, bring forth from man in experience, revealing its entire condemnation in the Saviour. For the law brought forth from the flesh not what the lawyers claim, but, Gal. 5:1, helpless entanglement, a snare, and a heavy yoke of bondage.

It brought forth hard labour under interminable outward forms, ceremonies, dead performances, and an empty, unprofitable round of religious duties, Gal. 5:2.

The law brought man into debt, bankruptcy, and perpetual insolvency, binding men under numerous obligations continuously, not only to the moral but equally to the entire and indivisible law, in all its parts: the whole law, Gal. 5:3. It resulted, through the weakness of the flesh, in ineffectualness, frustration, misery and hopelessness, Gal. 5:4. What chains of desperation, what cords of despair, what bonds of darkness, trap the tormented unbeliever upon mount Sinai. He cannot believe. His barrenness stares him in the face. The thunderbolts and the lightnings of God's wrath flash through the clouds of thick darkness, to light up and echo within the emptiness of his soul, letting fly a thousand piercing darts to strike into his accusing conscience.

And if there should be any exterior sight of the Saviour in the scripture, or any outward sound of Jesus' voice in the preaching of a minister of grace, at once, on seeing and hearing, he rejoices. But soon Satan claims the captive, and his cold legal heart quickly damps down every exterior encouragement. He then begins to cry, 'Master, we know thou art a teacher come from God: for no man can do these miracles that thou doest ...' and there he gives himself away. No man can 'do' that thou 'doest'. His carnal mentality sees and can see nothing but works: do, doing, doest. His native unbelief asserts itself over exterior gracious influences, and soon it is, 'Master, we would see a sign from thee.'

He cannot believe. He cannot trust. 'But ye believe not, because ye are not of my sheep, as I said unto you', Jn. 10:26. He starts to believe, but doubts the work, then the Spirit, then the preacher, last the message. Soon there is nothing on earth, nothing in heaven. First no man, then no God. Only blackness and darkness and a tempest.

Once full of appearances of sincerity, of seeking, when he first found the work of God, he rejoiced. But then he doubted. He cannot believe, his goatish, brutish heart must doubt. He questions, then probes. He envies, then judges. He sneers, then destroys. He cannot believe. 'Beware of the concision.' Mark the signs thereof.

The cross is the true measure of man's unavailing strength, and futile efforts, his empty works and useless religion, his fruitless ministry and unanswered prayers, his barren unbelief and hypocritical testimony. The cross shows the true measure, not only because that curse which must fall on all the works of the flesh under the law, is seen to fall vicariously upon the Accursed on the tree, Gal. 3:13, but also because it is at the cross that poor sinners discern 'He loved me, and gave himself for me', as within their inner man, faith is made to work by love, Gal. 5:6.

But in this way of grace, through faith that works by love, no faithless, unbelieving legalist can walk. He can neither run, walk nor stand. He sits in the scorner's chair immovable. He really is a hindrance to the work of God, with all his mixing of gospel texts. The fact is that his legal, unchanged heart and mind greatly hinder gospel obedience, being devoid of truth in the inward parts, if imitative of its sounds in the outward mouth. See Gal. 5:7.

Thus by the gospel the lie of the legalist concerning the use of the law is exposed. It is dashed to the ground by the word of the cross. All the pretension, hypocrisy, and false hope of the lawyers is utterly destroyed by one clear view of the substitutionary death of Christ. Why? Because the death of the cross exhibits the utter sinfulness of fallen man, the absolutely obnoxious nature of the flesh, just as it manifests the awful wrath of God revealed against such total depravity.

On the other hand, in the substitutionary Sufferer upon the tree, by the word of the cross is seen the poor sinner's only hope and refuge, the end of the law for righteousness to every one that believeth. Here is the preaching of the cross, stumblingblock to the Jew, foolishness to the Greek, presumptuousness to them that perish, but the power of God to every one that believeth.

This same cross is to them that put their trust in the law a downright scandal, and the cause of their persecuting them that preach it. 'And I, brethren, if I yet preach circumcision, why do I yet suffer persecution?' A hypothetical question, yes, but one which showed that Paul came preaching neither circumcision nor law, neither sign nor morality, neither duty nor charity. Then what did he come preaching? Let him answer for himself. 'And I, brethren, when I came to you, came not with excellency of speech or of wisdom, declaring unto you the testimony of God. For I determined not to know anything among you, save Jesus Christ, and him crucified.'

'And I was with you in weakness, and in fear, and in much trembling. And my speech and my preaching was not with enticing words of man's wisdom, but in demonstration of the Spirit and of power: that your faith should not stand in the wisdom of men, but in the power of God.'

The cost of this ministry was the most intense and consistent persecution, from the beginning of his course to the end of it, and that from the hand of those who appeared to be the most religious men in the world. And if ever it should come to pass that this no longer holds good, there can be but one explanation: 'Then is the offence of the cross ceased.'

Offence? The word is σκάνδαλον, *skandalon*, occurring fifteen times as a noun, and thirty times in the verb form. It is of course the origin of the English word, 'scandal'. Paul therefore speaks of 'The scandal' of the cross. By it the world is scandalized. Is not this the carpenter? And they were 'scandalized' at him. Jesus' disciples murmured at his saying that 'He that eateth my flesh, and drinketh my blood, dwelleth in me, and I in him.' Doth this 'scandalize' you? he enquired, Jn. 6:61. In Romans 9:33, Christ ascended, by the gospel, is 'A stumblingstone and rock of offence.' A scandal.

How can Christ ascended be a scandal by the gospel? Because the preaching of the cross excludes the moral law. To the world, the religious world, the absence of moral law after the cross is a scandal. The religious world rages and fumes at this. The advocates of the illegal, unevangelical, and irrational 'other gospel' cannot tolerate the idea of moral rectitude without the moral law. The truth is, there never was any with that law. Knowing this, how can they uphold what fails, and deny what succeeds? Because they are what Jesus called them, Fools and blind.

With such mongrel, cross-bred, and hybrid doctrine, it is not surprising to find these legalists double minded, two-faced, and fork-tongued. They make the law void, but call them that honour the law 'Antinomians'. They cannot believe that God can bring in a morality which the old tables of stone never did and never will produce, yet they still cling obstinately to what they know is futile and ineffective.

Legalists are scandalized at the idea of no moral law in the church. Antinomianism! Looseness! Lawlessness! Immorality! Licenciousness! But the truth is the very opposite, for when the gospel of free grace is proclaimed by the word of the cross then faith works by love, Christ is formed in the heart, and virtue is the fruit of divine union. The sins that the legalist claims will occur under the true gospel, he should look for under the rocks of his own system: they will soon crawl out, once the stones are lifted.

And must Paul preach circumcision? 'And I, brethren, if I yet preach circumcision', asks Paul: then what? Then Paul would by the sign of circumcision admit the thing signified into the gospel and within the church. Paul would then set Moses as a lawgiver before the believer. He would then enshrine the moral law within the doctrine of the gospel, and he would, moreover, establish the commandments as the standard in the church. He would, as did the perverters of the gospel in Galatia, mix law and gospel, faith and works, the cross and circumcision. But if he did that, he would no longer be persecuted. 'And I, brethren, if I yet preach circumcision, why do I yet suffer persecution?' Gal. 5:11.

If Paul 'yet preached circumcision', it would be a denial of all his doctrine. It would take Christ out of the grave as if he had never died, fill in the tomb, thrust down the substitutionary body from the tree, overturn the cross, and undermine the foundations of the gospel. But 'If the foundations be destroyed, what can the righteous do?' If Paul still preached circumcision, he would no longer be dead to the law, or crucified with Christ. He would be a wretched man all over again. Sin would have dominion over him, for he would not be under grace but under the law. He through the law would be alive to the law. He would build again the things which he had destroyed, and make himself a transgressor. He would be alive to the law without the body of Christ, now being delivered from the gospel, that being alive wherein he is held. But, then, he would not suffer persecution.

Now if this were the gospel which Paul had received by revelation of Jesus Christ from heaven, that he should preach circumcision, and bring in the law, then why was he persecuted? Not for ruling out the law by the cross, for such a gospel assumes it not to be ruled out. It proposes its retention in the church, not its exclusion from it. Suppose that Paul preached such a gospel, with its accommodating cross, it is certain that this would not be the cause for which he was persecuted.

Then, hypothetically, for some other cause. But whatever that other cause, it is no matter, the cause would not be the cross. Not that cross. Hence—allowing the hypothetical 'if' of Paul's preaching circumcision—if the cause of persecution be not the cross, 'Then is the offence of the cross ceased'! Gal. 5:11.

But the offence of the cross is perpetual. The 'if' of Paul's preaching circumcision is purely hypothetical. That gospel, their gospel, the Galatian 'other gospel', the gospel that reintroduced law in any shape or form past the cross into the church—deceitfully changing the cross into what it is not— would remove at a stroke the perpetual offence.

Thus by the irony of the hypothetical question in Gal. 5:11, and its conclusion 'Then is the offence of the cross ceased', the Apostle Paul illuminates with precision wherein the offence—the scandal—lies in its very nature. It lies in this: the cross is offensive—scandalous—to the self-righteous, the self-justifier, the moralist, the dead letter worker in religion. Why? Because the crucifixion of Christ for ever removes the law as such, and removes it as a rule of righteousness or life in any shape or form, from the sight of the believer, from the realm of the church, and from the body of doctrine that is called, The faith of the gospel of Christ. Amen.

XV

The Cross of Our Lord Jesus Christ

ALMOST at the end of the Epistle to the Galatians, after so much anguished soul-travail over the state into which the brethren had fallen, the Apostle Paul gives vent to an undefeated and vehement affirmation of victory. Having been bowed down with hard labour, burdened to bring forth the churches from bondage, he seems to look up, to see heaven open, and at once a great cry of triumph bursts forth from his lips, to be captured for posterity by the writing of his pen.

Paul had wept, prayed, fasted, laboured, written, sent brethren, kept vigil, and now, arising, the glory lighting his countenance, he mounts up with wings as an eagle, and the opening of his lips, the showing forth of the praise of his mouth, gives personal testimony to the unalterable witness of heaven. 'But God forbid that I should glory, save in the cross of our Lord Jesus Christ, by whom the world is crucified unto me, and I unto the world', Galatians 6:14.

This great and undaunted affirmation of the New Testament is prefixed, however, by the word 'But'. A word used to contrast one thing with another. That is, Paul contrasts his glorying with that of others, resolutely calling upon God to forbid his, Paul's, following their example. This introduces a negative. Many would rather avoid negatives, but this cannot be done. Desirable as it may appear, nevertheless it is not expedient.

Amidst enemies spiritual and temporal, in an alien world the god of which blinds the minds of them that believe not, in a divided and fallen church wherein Satan masquerades as an angel of light and his ministers as ministers of righteousness, in a body of sin and corruption, negatives from the pen of the apostle and the lips of God's servants are essential. Whilst there is spiritual wickedness in the heavenlies, persecuting wrath in the depths, and too much of a superfluity of naughtiness in our hearts, rebukes, checks, warnings and disciplines are what we need and must have. Without them, without negatives, we will not survive.

'But God forbid that I should glory, save in the cross of our Lord Jesus Christ.' As if to say, Their glorying is one thing, but my glorying is another. Their glory was of man, but Paul's was of Christ. Their glory was the world, but the apostle's glory was the cross. Their glorying was in the flesh, but Paul's was in the Spirit. A contrast indicated by the word 'But'.

Now, of whose glorying does the apostle thus speak? With whom is this contrast made? All false teachers, perverters of the gospel, all legalists, formalists and ceremonialists. All those sent by the high priests, elders, scribes, Pharisees and false brethren, that they might bring into subjection to themselves the work that had been raised up of God by the gospel. For Paul contrasts his glorying with that of those whose religion stood in what they could do, or what their religious system could do for them: the superstitious, to whom the meat and drink of religion stood in outward performances according to the tradition of the elders.

The sign of this, at the time at which Paul wrote, was circumcision. But that matters little. What matters is the thing signified by circumcision. For a sign may change, yet the thing signified remain. And, in truth, the legality and works of the flesh signified at that time by one thing, remain with us actively to this day, signified, however, by other signs altogether.

234

There are those who to this day would bring the brethren under the law of works. Not openly, for they mingle Old and New Testament, they confound the doctrine of Moses and Christ, merging indistinguishably law and grace, works and faith, the priesthood and the ministry, Israel and the church, the flesh and the Spirit. They marry together Abraham and Hagar, mix up the bondchildren and the freeborn, and rob the rightful heirs of their proper inheritance. They take the children's bread and give it to the dogs, leaving the crumbs for the children. These are the offspring of the legalists that troubled Paul, and their works will they do, bringing the old yoke on to the neck of those for whom it was never intended, taking away the believer's liberty of the Spirit and the gospel. That achievement was their glory. But not Paul's!

On the contrary, Paul contrasts their glorying with his own, no mistake about that. Negatives he will have, and we certainly need. Paul contrasts himself with those whom he has no hesitation in calling, by the Holy Ghost, by the word of truth, by the necessity of our salvation, Dogs, evil workers, the concision, Phil. 3:2. These he shows up in several ways. Firstly, Gal. 6:12, by exposing their motive. Their motive was not to glorify God, to save sinners, or edify the church. Their design was neither to honour the Lord, nor help the saints. It was 'To make a fair show in the flesh.' To be approved by the show which they made before the eyes of men. To so flatter the opinion of the religious world, that they would appear as some great ones. To have the name of being those whom the Lord used.

That was their motive, the whole of their motive, and nothing but their motive. That was why they professed religion, maintained a show of religion, and made a profession out of religion. And this prolific breed has so swarmed in our day, that an honest man will be hard put to find any other. 'But God forbid that I should glory, save in the cross of our Lord Jesus Christ.'

Secondly, Paul exposes their fear. The preachers whose religion was based on their own works were full of apprehension. They dreaded persecution. One eye was fixed on the danger to their well-being and good name in the world, all the time. Whatever they did, whatever else they did, it was qualified by the constant exercise of avoiding what they feared: 'Only lest they should suffer persecution for the cross of Christ.' Gal. 6:12, the last part. Then they are clearly manifest, in that persecution is what never happens to them.

Oh, they knew the gospel, they heard the apostolic preaching, understood all about the cross, and said as much, and preached as much of these things as would puzzle and captivate the faithful. But they could not bear the thought of being scorned, mocked, derided or persecuted. So, because of their love of the praise of the crowd and of the nod of the influential in religion, because of their fear of giving offence, though they knew the gospel, though they secretly knew what was the truth, they never actually stood by the cross. Had they done this they would have been persecuted. But their fear of losing man's approval was too great for that.

The dishonesty of those that gloried in the flesh is taken by Paul as the third mark by which they may be distinguished, who oppose the apostolic gospel. Though they compelled the Galatians, by a show of authority and antiquity from Jerusalem, into subjection to the law, they themselves did not keep it. They brought the Galatians into the bondage of that wherein they themselves were held captive. The law did not deliver them from guilt. It did not deliver them from sin. It gave them no power to do what it required, neither did it oblige God to assist them in the doing of it by any means whatever: only to judge their works. The law made matters infinitely worse, and relieved nothing at all. Knowing this, why were they so dishonest as to entice others into the net that had entrapped them?

The false teachers, who mixed the law with the gospel, came with fair speeches, flattering words, and shining promises of the blessing that would attend the Galatians, of how pleasing to God they would be, how rewarded, by heeding their doctrine. But this was false to their own experience, how could it become true of the Galatians? The law made the case desperate, it gave no amelioration. The law brought a curse, not a blessing. It was the gospel that brought the blessing. Upon them that tried to keep it the law had the opposite effect to that promised by its advocates. And all the while those same advocates dishonestly went on with their own laziness, covetousness, secret sin and worldliness, clean contrary to the very law which they themselves preached to others. See Gal. 6:13, the first part.

The fourth distinguishing feature which exposes the false teachers appears in the second part of Galatians 6:13. It is their hypocrisy: 'That they may glory in your flesh.' How pious was their appearance when they professed to give all the glory to God, but Paul assures us that this is all hypocrisy, they took all the glory to themselves in fact, who gave it all to God in lip. 'That they may glory' exposes their hypocrisy.

Their glory was in the flesh, that is, in the outward appearance of religion. Their glory was in forms imposed on the exterior man, outward reformations, making clean the outside of the cup and platter whilst all was filthy within. Tending the whited sepulchres, mowing the close-cropped grass, watering the abundant flowers that grew on the graves of rotting corpses and dead men's bones. Their glory was in loud prayers before men, alms-giving for all to see, a trumpeting of what they claimed to do for God, to the ears of all the world. Their glorying was in a religion which 'loved the praise of men more than the praise of God.'

Again, their glorying was in the flesh, that is, in the effect and appearance of numbers of converts. They gloried in numbers, in the crowds of 'converts' or proselytes which they made. Said Jesus, 'Ye compass sea and land to make one proselyte, and when he is made, ye make him twofold more the child of hell than yourselves.' And so confirms Paul, 'That they may glory in your flesh.' These numbers that they gain, and in which they boast, by perverting the gospel, enable them to make extravagant and boastful claims before men, and gain the approval of those moneyed people who buy themselves places on the most prestigious religious committees and boards. This is all-important to the showmen whose whole religion is before the eye of the world, to gain admiration, whose every work is done 'to be seen of men'.

'For he is not a Jew, which is one outwardly; neither is that circumcision, which is outward in the flesh: but he is a Jew, which is one inwardly; and circumcision is that of the heart, in the spirit, and not in the letter; whose praise is not of men, but of God', Rom. 2:28-29. Then these were neither Jews, nor did they respect the law they professed, much less the gospel they perverted, who gloried in the flesh 'For to be seen of men'. Their desire was that it should be thought what great preachers they were, how wonderfully the Lord had chosen and used them. But they were not great preachers, the Lord had not chosen them, neither had he used them. It was the man they despised and hated, Paul, of whom all these things were true, not them. The Lord had not chosen them, the Lord had chosen Paul, to their chagrin and bitter envy. Still, they went on in their hypocrisy. But 'that which is highly esteemed among men is abomination in the sight of God.'

Paul therefore puts himself in contrast with the legalists and all their works. Whatever was their glorying, it was not Paul's. He gloried in the very opposite, and not only so, he called upon God to forbid that he should glory in anything but the opposite. And what is the opposite to glorying in the flesh? The opposite to the works of the law, to the ability of men, of outward show in religion? The cross, glorying in the cross is the opposite. 'God forbid that I should glory, save in the cross of our Lord Jesus Christ.'

Why is glorying in the cross the opposite to glorying in the flesh? Because the cross, far from being the work of man, is the work of God. Far from demanding merit from man, righteousness is accounted to men. Far from requiring works from the flesh, justification is bestowed by faith. Far from obliging men to earn favour, grace is freely lavished upon debtors. Far from expecting anything from sinners, everything is accomplished by Jesus Christ. Far from the curse falling upon transgressors, the curse fell upon the Substitute. Far from setting the law before believers, believers are dead to the law by the body of Christ. Far from shutting up men to a lost eternity, the cross brings the redeemed into everlasting glory. Then no wonder Paul gloried in the cross!

Paul glories in the cross because by it the world was crucified to him. 'By which the world is crucified unto me.' Between Paul and the world, the cross stood, so that he could not see it for the cross. The cross stretched right across Paul's horizon, it filled his vision, whatever he saw, the cross was superimposed upon it. All visible, physical, temporal things, all that could be conceived by the senses, all that in which man glorified himself, the worldly honour for which he strove, was crucified to Paul. The cross lay over it all.

Between Paul and the flesh, stood the cross. That is, between Paul and all that was carnal, the entire natural realm, together with its religion. Paul saw that the flesh was crucified. He saw the carnal mind crucified. He knew that 'They that are Christ's have crucified the flesh with the affections and lusts', that is, they have accounted it crucified, because it was crucified in Another. Paul saw this, and he lived by it. The carnal man, in fleshly religion, lives as though his days in the flesh are the whole of his existence. Not so Paul. He was crucified to that existence. He lived in the Spirit.

Between Paul and men, stood the cross. The natural man lives in the world as though man were the only being. In religion too, appearance before men, man's applause, the traditions of the elders, the doctrine and custom of the sect or party, rule the natural man. Man lives for his own things, family, interests. He is taken up, absorbed with the things that pertain to man, in religion or out of it. So soon, he shall be called to account. Paul had already come to account. Between him, and men, stood the cross.

Between Paul and time, stood the cross. The worldly man lives as though he were here in perpetuity, as though time would go on for ever. In his youth he disregards or pays scant attention to time. The man of the world regards not his own advancing years, save to say to his soul, 'Soul, thou hast much goods laid up for many years; take thine ease, eat, drink, and be merry.' And yet his years advance not merely in age, which he ought to regard in and of itself, but into eternity. Paul lived for eternity. He lived for the world to come, for Christ Jesus, and for the Spirit of God. All was crucified to him. He lived on the other side of the cross from time and this present world.

Not only was the world crucified to Paul, but he was crucified to the world. Here is a dual crucifixion in a crucified Saviour. Three crosses. Upon the cross in question, Paul is crucified to the world. 'And I unto the world.' If crucifixion was true of the world to Paul, it was certainly true of Paul to the world.

All that the world saw of Paul was the crucifixion. Let the world try to find Paul, save through the cross: they could not. The cross was superimposed upon him. 'I bear in my body the marks of the Lord Jesus.' This was no fake franciscan stigmata, but the real spiritual verity. Awake, asleep, at home, abroad, no one could establish a relationship with Paul, save through the cross.

Whenever, wherever, however the world looked for Paul, he was always behind the cross. One could never separate Paul and the crucifixion. He cried, 'I am crucified with Christ.' The first man Adam, the flesh, the world, time, the age itself, Paul was crucified with Christ to it all. Christ had been crucified out of this world, had risen above it, and now reigned over all through the cross. All that he had left below was the wood upon which he had hung, and Paul gloried in it. This was all Paul's glory, all that he acknowledged, owned, and confessed in the world, this cross was that by which he was crucified to the world, 'And I unto the world.'

Here Paul shames the whole professing church, past and present, and challenges every professing Christian, then and now. How does he do this? Observe the pronouns, Galatians 6:14. God forbid that 'I'. Others claimed the Lord's name, but disclaimed the cross. This cannot be done. Others claimed to be Christians, and met with the church, but, practising legal works, overturned faith and perverted the gospel. God forbid, whatever others, however many others, even all others did, God forbid that Paul—'I'—should glory save in the cross of our Lord Jesus Christ.

This was said by the man who was reduced more and more to just this position. 'At my first answer no man stood with me.' But the Lord stood by his faithful servant, and that faithful servant stood by the Lord. He needed no help from man, no comfort from others. He could bear the isolation of no others at all. His heart was fixed. He loved the Lord, and that with a deep, intense, inward, untouchable love that needed no exterior support, a love which many waters could not quench, neither could the floods drown it, a love as strong as death itself.

Yet Paul did not regard himself as unique in this love. He regarded himself as an example. The love which Paul had for the Lord was a spontaneous response of the whole heart to the knowledge that 'He loved me and gave himself for me.' How could there be a lesser response? There could not. The whole heart must be his, who first 'gave himself for us.' This is what every Christian is saying by virtue of his making a profession, it is of necessity. It goes with the name. Hence Paul says to those who were dishonouring the cross and the name, 'The cross of our'—not my, our—'Lord Jesus Christ.' It was that cross by which Paul was crucified to the world, and the world to Paul. But what of the brethren, what of the churches? Whatever might be true of them, 'I'—I—'unto the world.' Paul could say so, yes, but the ground of this was no more than the necessity laid upon all who name the Lord's name, because the cross is that of 'our' Lord Jesus Christ, not at all a cross unique to the apostle.

Then what is this cross, what is entailed by it? What does Paul mean by the cross of 'our' Lord Jesus Christ, that is, of all who name the name of the Lord? The apostle explains this clearly, bringing forth divers proofs, comparing spiritual things with spiritual, and opening up many places in scripture to comfort us with this holy doctrine of the faith.

First observe that the apostle specifically says 'cross', not 'blood', a distinction largely lost, to the immense detriment of the truth and of experimental religion, upon those who boldly claim to be evangelicals. There is in fact no mention of the blood of Christ in Galatians, although the crucifixion is referred to eight times, a point of very great significance. The cross is that stake of wood on which the crucifixion took place. It is also that on which the blood was shed, but in and of itself the cross is the instrument of crucifixion.

These things must be distinguished if we are to observe the apostolic doctrine, and be led by the Spirit into all truth. It is useless to follow the traditions of men, the deadening 'theology' endorsed by the institutes of worldly and philosophical learning, or the limitations inherent in the writings

of those who recovered some particular truth out of the
darkness of their age, short of the whole body of the truth
itself. To fail to separate what was really revealed to them,
from that which was not, is fatal. We are to observe all that
the Lord himself gave by revelation, and separate that, and
honour it, and honour those through whom it was given. For
the rest, we must do what they did who went thus to the Lord,
and his word, alone, whether they were Reformers, Puritans,
Non-conformists, Brethren, or whatever. Divinely taught
humility will be our safeguard, because, for all its gentle
meekness, it will never permit us to sacrifice truth on the
altar of preference for some person, age or party.

The cross is not the same as the blood, in the apostles'
doctrine. One may say it is the same, but it is not, nor is it
treated as such in the scripture. Crucifixion may take place
without blood shedding as such. The cross was the instrument
of crucifixion, and the spear was the instrument of blood
shedding.

The cross set forth the condemnation of the flesh. Not its
forgiveness but its condemnation. It is not forgiven, and it
cannot be forgiven. It is incorrigible. Flesh and blood cannot
inherit the kingdom of God. That is what the cross teaches.
It has to do with the destruction of the body of sin.

The blood however does speak pardon. It speaks of the forgiveness of sinners, of God being propitiated in his wrath
against the sinner. Blood expiates sin, sins are covered by the
blood of Christ, and the guilty are freely pardoned. The
blood remits sins, redeems sinners, speaks peace and brings
nigh. But, doctrinally, one thing is seen by the blood, and
another by the crucifixion of the body. Both spring from, and
the doctrine pertaining to each opens fully, the death of the
Lord.

This is clearly seen in the Lord's supper, where that which
represents the body of Jesus, and that which represents his

blood, are carefully distinguished. Even the elements are completely different. One is solid, another is liquid. One is from grain, the other from grape. One is blessed, another received with gratitude. One is treated in one way, the other in another way. One is broken, another is poured. One they are to eat, the other they are to drink. 'This is my body' is said of one, 'This is my blood' is said of the other. Tell me, what could be more different? And, again, Tell me, is it to be supposed that this has no spiritual or doctrinal significance? If it has significance, what is it? Clearly the significance is that something is to be taught from scripture and inwardly received by the Holy Ghost from heaven about the body of Jesus, and, equally, that something else is to be understood and taken within by the revelation of the Spirit concerning the blood of Jesus. What is that? It is, in essence, what has been opened up in the preceding chapters of this book according to the word of truth.

The same thing is seen in the sin offering, the blood of which was poured out at the bottom of the altar, some being taken in to the sanctuary, to be sprinkled before the veil. The slain body however was taken outside the camp to be wholly burned up with fire. It was totally consumed. It follows of course that the blood represented what was accepted before God on the sinner's behalf, but the flesh, the body, showed what could never be accepted, what must be taken out of the presence of God and destroyed in place of that which it represented in the sinner. Could anything be clearer?

In the Epistle to the Romans, in which the apostle expounds the gospel of Christ in order, he deals first with sins, and the guiltworthy sinner brought to account before God. Here he sets the eye of faith upon Christ and his blood. 'Whom God hath set forth a propitiation through faith in his blood.' Sinners are thus 'justified freely by his grace.' How? Through 'the righteousness of God which is by faith of Jesus Christ, unto all and upon all them that believe.' This justification, or

being reckoned righteous before God, is freely bestowed upon the ungodly, as it is said, 'Being now justified by his blood.' This shows not only the forgiveness, but the acceptance of the ungodly and sinners through righteousness of God being put to their account because of the blood of Jesus Christ. Thus far, Romans 1:18 to 5:11.

At this point in the epistle, and not before it, the apostle introduces the question of sin, not a matter of the sinner's volition and action, but of his condition and birth. Not the guilt of the transgressors, but the standing of mankind as a race. Not what the individual has done, but what Adam did on his behalf. This is another thing altogether than that which preceded. In Rom. 5:12-21 the apostle teaches the effect of the judgment of God upon the transgression of Adam, and the consequence of this to his, Adam's, posterity. The consequence of this transgression, and the judgment of God upon it, is that sin and death pass upon the whole human race.

The gospel reveals that the Saviour, Jesus Christ, is raised up as the head of a new order of mankind. He acted on behalf of his posterity also, an act of unparalleled love, in giving himself as the Substitute of his people. This was not despite the wrath of God, it was because of the love of God. God gave him in grace that he might yield himself in sacrifice. This is called the obedience of faith. The obedience of Jesus Christ was judged, just as the transgression of Adam was judged. How much more shall God's judgment of such obedience abound in righteousness and life upon all the posterity of that second man, the last Adam?

From Ch. 5:12-21 blood is not mentioned in Romans. It is all, Cross, crucify, crucified. Why? Because it is a question not of our forgiveness, but of our deliverance from the old man. Therefore of condemnation. The judgment of that man is in our Substitute. 'Our old man is crucified with him, that the body of sin might be destroyed.' For us, Christ took upon

245

himself the terrible state of fallen man, that is, the state of sin. 'He was made sin for us.' It was condemned in him on our behalf. In that way we are judicially clear of it, of its body, and of its head, of the old man. We are 'crucified with Christ.' In that he died, 'he died unto sin once', and that death is ours. Now we are under another head, alive in a new man, and belong to a new creation of humanity called 'The sons of God'.

'It doth not yet appear what we shall be: but we know that, when he shall appear, we shall be like him; for we shall see him as he is.' It must follow. As is the head, so must be the posterity. If it was true of Adam, much more shall it be true of Christ. The crucifixion of the old man, the destruction of the body of sin, is the foundation upon which this wonderful work of God rests. That, the body of Jesus upon the tree teaches in and of itself.

Romans 8:3 expounds this further. 'What the law could not do, in that it was weak through the flesh, God sending his own Son in the likeness of sinful flesh, and for sin, condemned sin in the flesh.' Here it is a question of the Son of God being sent in the likeness of sinful flesh. That was the incarnation. Without sin, nevertheless made in the likeness of men who were full of sin. Why then in such a likeness? 'For sin.' That is, made, though sinless, in the likeness of sinful flesh, 'for' the purpose of the condemnation of 'sin', at the place of substitutionary sacrifice, namely, the cross. There sin was condemned in the flesh, his flesh, once without sin, now made sin, once in the likeness of sinful flesh, now in the place of sinful flesh, that, vicariously, it might be destroyed by judgment, condemned in his body on the tree.

This is the meaning of John 12:31. Sin being proper to the whole human race, the entire posterity of Adam, the 'flesh'— for that which is born of the flesh is flesh—it follows that the condemnation of the flesh in the Substitute is the condemnation of the entire race. 'Now is the judgment of this world.'

Hence, Jesus is the Lamb of God which taketh away the sin of the world. Sin, as such, was condemned in his body on the tree. It has been judged, once and for all, in the vicarious sacrifice. As the antitype of the sin offering, in him the body of sin has been reduced to ashes in the sight of God, as in the view of everlasting justice. Now, this has been done on behalf of all believers, so that they are dead, crucified. Sin is not imputed to them, sin has been condemned in the flesh on their behalf, they are not in the flesh, and no condemnation pertains to them.

Just so in Galatians 5:24, 'They that are Christ's have crucified the flesh.' Here virtually all the commentators are patently ridiculous, implying that 'they that are Christ's' have crucified their own flesh. As if they have crucified themselves. Pray, let the commentators try it. Perhaps they will tell me, having driven the first nail through the one hand, how they will suspend the other nail in thin air, whilst driving this remarkable peace of metal through the hand that is holding the hammer? Nonsensical rubbish. Calvin and his servile train should know better. They that are Christ's have the flesh, with the affections and lusts, crucified in the substitutionary sacrifice at Golgotha. That is the standing and position which the Spirit freely and inwardly supports for faith. Consistent with all the doctrine of the cross, the apostle teaches that in Christ, the flesh, the fleshly affections and lusts, have been crucified. They that are Christ's have the flesh crucified because of what is reckoned to them in him who died for them in the place of condemnation.

Ephesians 2:15 confirms this. There Christ has 'abolished in his flesh the enmity.' Abolished it. Not forgiven it. Abolished it. The body of sin is 'put off' at the cross, Col. 2:11, never to be seen again. Indeed, in the counsels of God, it is put off to be reduced to ashes by the fires of eternal wrath. Thus believers are reconciled, through that thorough exchange of places, in the body of his flesh through death. Col. 1:22.

This doctrine is taught with great clarity in Hebrews 9:26-28. 'But now once in the end of the world hath he appeared.' Observe that Christ hath appeared 'now' and that 'once'. This appearance is 'in the end of the world', that is, the end of the world judicially before God, at the cross. 'Now is the judgment of this world.' Christ having 'appeared once in the end of the world', the purpose is clear: to put away, not forgive, not pardon, not remit, to put away sin. That is, put it away in judgment. Put it away in condemnation. Put it away out of God's sight for evermore. How? By the sacrifice of himself, made sin, in the place of sin, to bear its condemnation and bear it away for his people, by the sacrificial offering up of himself. 'But now once in the end of the world hath he appeared to put away sin by the sacrifice of himself.' Heb. 9:26.

Hebrews 9:28, 'So Christ was once offered to bear'—not now to put away, but to bear: not to condemn, but to remit—'to bear the sins'—the sins, not the sin—'of many'—not of all, but of many. 'And to them'—that is, all them that believe in this true and apostolic doctrine of the crucifixion, the blood, and the cross—'to them that look for him shall he appear without sin'—not sins, but sin, who was made sin, who put sin away, in whom the old man was crucified, the body of sin destroyed—'without sin unto salvation.' Here the distinction of doctrine between sins and sin, blood and cross, is made to a nicety.

This holy doctrine of the cross is reiterated in Heb. 13:11. 'The bodies of those beasts'—that is the body, not the blood—'whose blood is brought into the sanctuary'—that is the blood, not the body—'are burned without the camp.' That is, the bodies are burned without the camp, outside of God's presence and that of his people. On the contrary, the blood shed at the altar is taken into God's presence on behalf of that people. The death is one, but the doctrine of it is expounded, in the nature of the body and blood of the sacrifice, distinctively. Thus was foreshadowed the work of God in the sacrificial death of Christ, in which his body and blood respectively set forth salvation from the sin of mankind in Adam, and the sins of God's people in themselves. He that hath ears to hear, let him hear.

The Apostle Paul concludes the great affirmation of Galatians 6:14 by applying the cross. It is the cross 'Of our Lord Jesus Christ.' In this place he does not call it the cross of Jesus. Nor does he say, the cross of Christ. Neither is it the cross of Jesus Christ, Christ Jesus, the Lord Jesus, the Lord Christ, or the Lord. It is 'the cross of our'—mark that, our: it is not 'the'—'our Lord Jesus Christ.' Here is Christ's full ascended title. It is his name, now, from the ascension. The name by which the Holy Ghost glorifies and honours him, and delights to glorify and honour him, according to the will of God and the Father. He is both Lord and Christ. God hath highly exalted him, and hath given him a name that is above every name, the name of the Lord Jesus Christ. Wherefore let all the people know assuredly that this same Jesus, even Jesus Christ, is Lord, to the glory of God the Father. Amen.

He who is thus ascended and glorified, is so glorified not apart from but in his manhood. Sonship is seen in glorified manhood. If so, the scars of that manhood are glorified. He received those marks in the lowest place of humiliation. Four marks were made at one time, in the palms of his hands and the soles of his feet. Those marks preceded his vicarious sufferings, the depths of his agony. When all was concluded, the last mark was made. This was in his side, after he was dead. Hence the marks in the body of Jesus bracket the hours of substitutionary atonement.

During these hours he hung there, determined upon the redemption of his people as their sole head and Surety, determined to remove all sin, sins, condemnation and wrath, for time and eternity, from their heads to his head, from their bodies to his body, from their souls to his soul, from their account to his account. And he did so. Come the fifth mark, the account was cleared.

The first four scars marked the beginning. The last scar punctuated the end. Between them he had finished the transgression, made an end of sins, made reconciliation for iniquity, and brought in everlasting righteousness. During the interval separating the four scars from the fifth, every one of the people of God from the beginning of the world to the end of it—the patriarchs, all Israel, the church—had been brought from the foulest depths of sinful iniquity to the purest heights of sinless perfection, from the most fearful torment of perpetual burning to the most wondrous bliss of everlasting glory. After the four marks, just before the fifth, the countless myriads of the entire election had been justified, and had been glorified. Jesus did this, even Jesus, which delivered us from the wrath to come.

This is he who, raised from the dead, exalted on high, has been crowned both Lord and Christ. But not without the scars. With the scars. He sits at the right hand of the Majesty on high, made higher than the heavens, in the heaven of heavens, in the excellent glory. He sits, at rest, in the presence of God, in divine righteousness, in the light unapproachable which no man hath seen nor can see. And he sits with five glorified scars.

In the time between the wounds being inflicted upon him on earth, by three nails and one spear, in the Spirit he was no longer seen as himself alone. He was all his people, and all his people were him. All their birth in Adam, all their sinfulness in themselves: he was them and they were him. But it had all gone, and gone in the sight of God's own righteousness, before the last scar was made in his side. It had all gone, and as before what had been theirs became his, so afterwards what was his became theirs.

His perfection was theirs. The righteousness of God was theirs, 'The righteousness of God in him.' And his glory was theirs. He carried them up in himself. 'I ascend to my Father and your Father, my God and your God.' The Father, viewing the seated Son, beholds for ever the scars that show forth an interval of some six hours. And in those six hours the Father sees the justification, the glorification, the everlasting perfection of every believer. This is called, Being accepted in the beloved. As near as he is, they are: the Son's place in glory, on the throne of glory, is their place. 'Seated in heavenly places in Christ.'

Yes, but the scars are glorified. Then, he has carried what marked out the six hours on the cross, and the marks of the cross itself, up into glory. All that he did for his people, for ever before the face of God and the Father. Then, it is not the cross of Jesus, or of Christ, neither of Jesus Christ, nor Christ Jesus. It is not here the name of the Lord Jesus, neither of the Lord Christ, nor yet the Lord. It is the Lord Jesus Christ. It is the cross of our 'Lord Jesus Christ.'

Our short and uncertain pilgrimage passes through the scene of his rejection, the valley of Baca below where men inflicted upon him the scars of his humiliation. Now exalted to the heights of heavenly glory, with a name above every name, seated in righteousness upon the right hand of the Majesty on high, he displays those same glorified scars before the face of the Father. Thus from the glory he is not ashamed to confess his crucifixion on earth below. It is the cross of our 'Lord Jesus Christ.' The cross which he bore below, the cross whose doctrine is preached on earth, is the cross that he owns and proclaims from heaven.

The cross was the beginning of everything, and, from the glory, it is the continuation of everything. Nothing continues on earth, everything continues from glory. All reformation, all revival, all recovery, all is from the glory in the present ministry of the Lord from heaven.

The cross was the beginning of the ministry, as it was the foundation of the church. But from the glory. It is the cross of 'our Lord Jesus Christ'. The ministry and the church are from the glory. That side, the glory side, of the cross there is no room for the flesh, the world, time, decay, or the apostasy. All is from the glory. The Spirit is from the glory. And the church is in the realm of the Spirit. And where the Spirit of the Lord is, there is liberty. This liberty is called 'Glorious liberty'.

Now this gospel of the glory is what has been forgotten: it is that from which the departure is to be measured. It is the foundation. Nothing can be built other than upon 'Jesus Christ and him crucified'. Other foundation can no man lay than that which is laid. No basis other than this glorious basis can take the weight of spiritual things. Everything else is sand, which must and shall give way. Save the cross of our Lord Jesus Christ. Though all should depart, Paul is crying, though all should depart, my heart is fixed, my heart is fixed: 'God forbid that I should glory, save in the cross of our Lord Jesus Christ, by whom the world is crucified unto me, and I unto the world.' Amen and Amen.

INDEX

TO OTHER PUBLICATIONS

PSALMS, HYMNS AND SPIRITUAL SONGS

THE PSALMS

OF THE

OLD TESTAMENT

The Psalms of the Old Testament, the result of years of painstaking labour, is an original translation into verse from the Authorised Version, which seeks to present the Psalms in the purest scriptural form possible for singing. Here, for the first time, divine names are rendered as and when they occur in the scripture, the distinction between LORD and Lord has been preserved, and every essential point of doctrine and experience appears with unique perception and fidelity.

The Psalms of the Old Testament is the first part of a trilogy written by John Metcalfe, the second part of which is entitled *Spiritual Songs from the Gospels,* and the last, *The Hymns of the New Testament.* These titles provide unique and accurate metrical versions of passages from the psalms, the gospels and the new testament epistles respectively, and are intended to be used together in the worship of God.

Price £2.50 *(postage extra)*
(hard-case binding, dust-jacket)
ISBN 0 9506366 7 3

SPIRITUAL SONGS

FROM

THE GOSPELS

The *Spiritual Songs from the Gospels*, the result of years of painstaking labour, is an original translation into verse from the Authorised Version, which seeks to present essential parts of the gospels in the purest scriptural form possible for singing. The careful selection from Matthew, Mark, Luke and John, set forth in metrical verse of the highest integrity, enables the singer to sing 'the word of Christ' as if from the scripture itself, 'richly and in all wisdom'; and, above all, in a way that facilitates worship in song of unprecedented fidelity.

The *Spiritual Songs from the Gospels* is the central part of a trilogy written by John Metcalfe, the first part of which is entitled *The Psalms of the Old Testament*, and the last, *The Hymns of the New Testament*. These titles provide unique and accurate metrical versions of passages from the psalms, the gospels and the new testament epistles respectively, and are intended to be used together in the worship of God.

Price £2.50 (*postage extra*)
(hard-case binding, dust-jacket)
ISBN 0 9506366 8 1

THE HYMNS

OF THE

NEW TESTAMENT

The *Hymns of the New Testament*,. the result of years of painstaking labour, is an original translation into verse from the Authorised Version, which presents essential parts of the new testament epistles in the purest scriptural form possible for singing. The careful selection from the book of Acts to that of Revelation, set forth in metrical verse of the highest integrity, enables the singer to sing 'the word of Christ' as if from the scripture itself, 'richly and in all wisdom'; and, above all, in a way that facilitates worship in song of unprecedented fidelity.

The *Hymns of the New Testament* is the last part of a trilogy written by John Metcalfe, the first part of which is entitled *The Psalms of the Old Testament*, and the next, *Spiritual Songs from the Gospels*. These titles provide unique and accurate metrical versions of passages from the psalms, the gospels and the new testament epistles respectively, and are intended to be used together in the worship of God.

Price £2.50 *(postage extra)*
(hard-case binding, dust-jacket)
ISBN 0 9506366 9 X

'THE APOSTOLIC FOUNDATION
OF THE
CHRISTIAN CHURCH' SERIES

FOUNDATIONS UNCOVERED

THE APOSTOLIC FOUNDATION
OF THE
CHRISTIAN CHURCH

Volume I

Foundations Uncovered is a small book of some 37 pages. This is the introduction to the major series: 'The Apostolic Foundation of the Christian Church'.

Rich in truth, the Introduction deals comprehensively with the foundation of the apostolic faith under the descriptive titles: The Word, The Doctrine, The Truth, The Gospel, The Faith, The New Testament, and The Foundation.

The contents of the book reveal: The Fact of the Foundation; The Foundation Uncovered; What the Foundation is not; How the Foundation is Described; and, Being Built upon the Foundation.

'This book comes with the freshness of a new Reformation.'

Price 30p *(postage extra)*
(Laminated cover)
ISBN 0 9506366 5 7

THE BIRTH OF JESUS CHRIST

THE APOSTOLIC FOUNDATION
OF THE
CHRISTIAN CHURCH

Volume II

'The very spirit of adoration and worship rings through the pages of *The Birth of Jesus Christ*.

'The author expresses with great clarity the truths revealed to him in his study of holy scriptures at depth. We are presented here with a totally lofty view of the Incarnation.

'John Metcalfe is to be classed amongst the foremost expositors of our age; and his writings have about them that quality of timelessness that makes me sure they will one day take their place among the heritage of truly great Christian works.'

From a review by Rev. David Catterson.

'Uncompromisingly faithful to scripture ... has much to offer which is worth serious consideration ... deeply moving.'

The Expository Times.

Price 95p *(postage extra)*
(Laminated Cover)
ISBN 0 9502515 5 0

THE MESSIAH

THE APOSTOLIC FOUNDATION
OF THE
CHRISTIAN CHURCH

Volume III

The Messiah is a spiritually penetrating and entirely original exposition of Matthew chapter one to chapter seven from the trenchant pen of John Metcalfe.

Matthew Chapters One to Seven

GENEALOGY · BIRTH · STAR OF BETHLEHEM
HEROD · FLIGHT TO EGYPT · NAZARETH
JOHN THE BAPTIST · THE BAPTIST'S MINISTRY
JESUS' BAPTISM · ALL RIGHTEOUSNESS FULFILLED
HEAVEN OPENED · THE SPIRIT'S DESCENT
THE TEMPTATION OF JESUS IN THE WILDERNESS
JESUS' MANIFESTATION · THE CALLING · THE TRUE DISCIPLES
THE BEATITUDES · THE SERMON ON THE MOUNT

'Something of the fire of the ancient Hebrew prophet ....
Metcalfe has spiritual and expository potentials of a high order.'

The Life of Faith.

Price £2.45 *(postage extra)*
(425 pages, Laminated Cover)
ISBN 0 9502515 8 5

THE SON OF GOD AND SEED OF DAVID

THE APOSTOLIC FOUNDATION
OF THE
CHRISTIAN CHURCH

Volume IV

The Son of God and Seed of David is the fourth volume in the major work entitled 'The Apostolic Foundation of the Christian Church.'

The book refers to the irreducible summary of the apostolic gospel in Romans 1:3-4, attention being drawn to truths which the modern 'gospel' never mentions, much less considers foundational.

'The author proceeds to open and allege that Jesus Christ is and ever was *The Son of God*. This greatest of subjects, this most profound of all mysteries, is handled with reverence and with outstanding perception.

'The second part considers *The Seed of David*. What is meant precisely by 'the seed'? And why 'of David'? With prophetic insight the author expounds these crucial verities.'

Price £1.10 *(postage extra)*
(250 pages, Laminated Cover)
ISBN 0 9506366 1 4

OTHER TITLES

DIVINE FOOTSTEPS

Divine Footsteps traces the pathway of the feet of the Lord the Son of man from the very beginning in the prophetic figures of the true in the Old Testament through the reality in the New; doing so in a way of experimental spirituality. At the last a glimpse of the coming glory is beheld as his feet are viewed as standing at the latter day upon the earth.

Price 40p *(postage extra)*
(Laminated Cover)
ISBN 0 9502515 1 8

THE RED HEIFER

The Red Heifer was the name given to a sacrifice used by the children of Israel in the Old Testament—as recorded in Numbers 19—in which a heifer was slain and burned. Cedar wood, hyssop and scarlet were cast into the burning, and the ashes were mingled with running water and put in a vessel. It was kept for the children of Israel for a water of separation: it was a purification for sin.

In this unusual book the sacrifice is brought up to date and its relevance to the church today is shown.

Price 75p *(postage extra)*
ISBN 0 9502515 4 2

THE WELLS OF SALVATION

The Wells of Salvation is written from a series of seven powerful addresses preached at Tylers Green. It is a forthright and experimental exposition of Isaiah 12:3, 'Therefore with joy shall ye draw water out of the wells of salvation.'

Price £1.50 *(postage extra)*
(Laminated Cover)
ISBN 0 9502515 6 9

NOAH AND THE FLOOD

Noah and the Flood expounds with vital urgency the man and the message that heralded the end of the old world. The description of the flood itself is vividly realistic. The whole work has an unmistakable ring of authority, and speaks as 'Thus saith the Lord'.

'Mr. Metcalfe makes a skilful use of persuasive eloquence as he challenges the reality of one's profession of faith ... he gives a rousing call to a searching self-examination and evaluation of one's spiritual experience.'

The Monthly Record of the Free Church of Scotland.

Price £1.20 *(postage extra)*
ISBN 0 9502515 7 7

OF GOD OR MAN?

LIGHT FROM GALATIANS

The Epistle to the Galatians contends for deliverance from the law and from carnal ministry.

The Apostle opens his matter in two ways:

Firstly, Paul vindicates himself and his ministry against those that came not from God above, but from Jerusalem below.

Secondly, he defends the Gospel and evangelical liberty against legal perversions and bondage to the flesh.

Price £1.45 *(postage extra)*
(Laminated Cover)
ISBN 0 9506366 3 0

A QUESTION FOR POPE JOHN PAUL II

As a consequence of his many years spent apart in prayer, lonely vigil, and painstaking study of the scripture, John Metcalfe asks a question and looks for an answer from Pope John Paul II.

Price £1.25. *(postage extra)*
(Laminated Cover)
ISBN 0 9506366 4 9

'TRACT FOR THE TIMES' SERIES

THE GOSPEL OF GOD

'TRACT FOR THE TIMES' SERIES

The Gospel of God. Beautifully designed, this tract positively describes the gospel under the following headings: The Gospel is of God; The Gospel is Entirely of God; The Gospel is Entire in Itself; The Gospel is Preached; The Gospel Imparts Christ; and, Nothing But the Gospel Imparts Christ.

Price 25p *(postage extra)*
(Laminated Cover)
No. 1 in the Series

THE STRAIT GATE

'TRACT FOR THE TIMES' SERIES

The Strait Gate. Exceptionally well made, this booklet consists of extracts from 'The Messiah', compiled in such a way as to challenge the shallowness of much of today's 'easy-believism', whilst positively pointing to the strait gate.

Price 25p *(postage extra)*
(Laminated Cover)
No. 2 in the Series

ETERNAL SONSHIP
AND TAYLOR BRETHREN

'TRACT FOR THE TIMES' SERIES

Eternal Sonship and Taylor Brethren. This booklet is highly recommended, particularly for those perplexed by James Taylor's teaching against the eternal sonship of Christ.

Price 25p *(postage extra)*
(Laminated Cover)
No. 3 in the Series

MARKS OF THE
NEW TESTAMENT CHURCH
'TRACT FOR THE TIMES' SERIES

Marks of the New Testament Church. This exposition from Acts 2:42 declares what were, and what were not, the abiding marks of the church. The apostles' doctrine, fellowship and ordinances are lucidly explained.

Price 25p *(postage extra)*
(Laminated Cover)
No. 4 in the Series

THE CHARISMATIC DELUSION
'TRACT FOR THE TIMES' SERIES

The Charismatic Delusion. A prophetic message revealing the fundamental error of this movement which has swept away so many in the tide of its popularity. Here the delusion is dispelled.

Price 25p *(postage extra)*
(Laminated Cover)
No. 5 in the Series

PREMILLENNIALISM EXPOSED
'TRACT FOR THE TIMES' SERIES

Premillennialism Exposed. Well received evangelically, particularly through the influence of J.N. Darby, the Schofield bible, and the Plymouth Brethren, Premillennialism has assumed the cloak of orthodoxy. In this tract the cloak is removed, and the unorthodoxy of this system is exposed. A remarkable revelation.

Price 25p *(postage extra)*
(Laminated Cover)
No. 6 in the Series

JUSTIFICATION AND PEACE

'TRACT FOR THE TIMES' SERIES

Justification and Peace. This tract is taken from a message preached in December 1984 at Penang Hill, Malaysia. In this well-known address, peace with God is seen to be based upon nothing save justification by faith. No one should miss this tract.

Price 25p *(postage extra)*
(Laminated Cover)
No. 7 in the Series

FAITH OR PRESUMPTION?

'TRACT FOR THE TIMES' SERIES

Faith or presumption? The eighth tract in this vital series exposes the difference between faith and presumption, showing that faith is not of the law, neither is is apart from the work of God, nor is it of man. The work of God in man that precedes saving faith is opened generally and particularly, and the tract goes on to reveal positively the nature of saving faith. Belief and 'easy-believism' are contrasted, making clear the difference between the two, as the system of presumption—called easy-believism—is clearly shown, and the way of true belief pointed out with lucid clarity.

Price 25p *(postage extra)*
(Laminated Cover)
No. 8 in the Series

EVANGELICAL TRACTS

EVANGELICAL TRACTS

1. *The Two Prayers of Elijah.* This tract, first printed in 1972, was reprinted in 1982. It shows the spiritual significance of the drought, the cloudburst, and the two prayers of Elijah. Green card cover, price 10p.

2. *Wounded for our Transgressions.* An evangelical message taken from Isaiah 53. Declaring the salvation of God, this is a tract intended to help those seeking the Saviour and his work.
Gold card cover, price 10p.

3. *The Blood of Sprinkling.* Taken from Hebrews 12:24 this booklet expounds the things to which the people of God are not come, besides those to which they are come. Obvious from the context, this is striking in the exposition. The saving grace of God is clearly preached in this evangelical tract.
Red card cover, price 10p.

4. *The Grace of God that brings Salvation.* An evangelical message preached in South East Asia in 1985, this tract brings home to the heart the work of God in the salvation of the sinner.
Blue card cover, price 10p.

These tracts may be ordered directly from the Trust, or through Bookshops. If money is sent with order, please add letter post allowance.

MINISTRY BY JOHN METCALFE

TAPE MINISTRY BY JOHN METCALFE
FROM ENGLAND AND THE FAR EAST
IS AVAILABLE.

For Tapelist please contact the John Metcalfe Publishing Trust, Church Road, Tylers Green, Penn, Buckinghamshire, HP10 8LN.

Owing to the increased demand for the tape ministry, we are unable to supply more than two tapes per order, except in the case of meetings for the hearing of tapes, where a special arrangement can be made.

THE MINISTRY OF THE NEW TESTAMENT

The purpose of this 32 page A4 gloss paper magazine is to provide spiritual and experimental ministry with sound doctrine which rightly and prophetically divides the Word of Truth.

Readers of our books will already know the high standards of our publications. They can be confident that these pages will maintain that quality, by giving access to enduring ministry from the past, much of which is derived from sources that are virtually unobtainable today, and publishing a living ministry from the present. Selected articles from the following writers have already been included:

ELI ASHDOWN · JOHN BUNYAN · JOHN CALVIN · JOHN CENNICK
J.N. DARBY · JOHN FOXE · WILLIAM GADSBY · WILLIAM HUNTINGTON
HANSERD KNOLLYS · JAMES LEWIS · MARTIN LUTHER · JOHN METCALFE
ROBERT MURRAY MCCHEYNE · ALEXANDER—SANDY—PEDEN
J.C. PHILPOT · J.B. STONEY · JOHN VINALL · GEORGE WHITEFIELD

Price £1.75 *(postage included)*
Issued Spring, Summer, Autumn, Winter.

NEWLY PUBLISHED

The Elect
undeceived

TRACT FOR THE TIMES 9

The Elect undeceived, the ninth Tract for the Times, earnestly contends for 'the faith once delivered to the saints' in a way that is spiritually edifying, positive, and subject to the Lord Jesus Christ according to the scriptures.

The Tract is a response to the pamphlet 'Salvation and the Church' published jointly by the Catholic Truth Society and Church House Publishing, in which the Anglican and Roman Catholic Commissioners agree together about JUSTIFICATION. The pamphlet shows how they have agreed.

The Elect undeceived responds by revealing that not only have the R.C.-C. of E. Commissioners struck at the heart of Article XI of the Church of England, 'JUSTIFICATION BY FAITH ONLY', but, in so seeking to overthrow the massive bulwarks of the Reformation, they have also threatened the very foundations upon which our fathers built for our future. 'If the foundations be destroyed, what shall the righteous do?'

The Tract is subsidised to a fraction of its real cost because of the love and concern of godly men and women. Please do help us to distribute THIS VITAL RESPONSE.

Tract for the Times No. 9. Special laminated gloss finish stiff cover, price 25p.

Price 25p *(postage extra)*
(Laminated Cover)
No. 9 in the Series

Order Form

Please send to the address below:-

		Price	Quantity
A Question for Pope John Paul II		£1.25	......
Of God or Man?		£1.45	......
Noah and the Flood		£1.20	......
Divine Footsteps		£0.40	......
The Red Heifer		£0.75	......
The Wells of Salvation		£1.50	......

Psalms, Hymns & Spiritual Songs (Hardback edition)

		Price	Quantity
The Psalms of the Old Testament		£2.50	......
Spiritual Songs from the Gospels		£2.50	......
The Hymns of the New Testament		£2.50	......

'Apostolic Foundation of the Christian Church' series

		Price	Quantity
Foundations Uncovered	Vol.I	£0.30	......
The Birth of Jesus Christ	Vol.II	£0.95	......
The Messiah	Vol.III	£2.45	......
The Son of God and Seed of David	Vol.IV	£1.10	......
Christ Crucified (Hardback edition)	Vol.V	£6.95	......

Tracts

		Price	Quantity
The Two Prayers of Elijah		£0.10	......
Wounded for our Transgressions		£0.10	......
The Blood of Sprinkling		£0.10	......
The Grace of God that Brings Salvation		£0.10	......

'Tract for the Times' series

		Price	Quantity
The Gospel of God	No.1	£0.25	......
The Strait Gate	No.2	£0.25	......
Eternal Sonship and Taylor Brethren	No.3	£0.25	......
Marks of the New Testament Church	No.4	£0.25	......
The Charismatic Delusion	No.5	£0.25	......
Premillennialism Exposed	No.6	£0.25	......
Justification and Peace	No.7	£0.25	......
Faith or presumption?	No.8	£0.25	......
The Elect undeceived	No.9	£0.25	......

Name and Address (in block capitals)

. . . .

. . . .

. . . .

If money is sent with order please allow for postage. Please address to:- The
John Metcalfe Publishing Trust, Church Road, Tylers Green, Penn, Bucks, HP10 8LN.